GORBACHEV AT THE HELM:
A New Era in Soviet Politics?

GORBACHEV AT THE HELM

A NEW ERA IN SOVIET POLITICS?

R.F.Miller, J.H.Miller and T.H.Rigby

CROOM HELM
London • New York • Sydney

© 1987 R. F. Miller, J. H. Miller and T. H. Rigby
Croom Helm Ltd, Provident House,
Burrell Row, Beckenham, Kent BR3 1AT

Croom Helm Australia, 44–50 Waterloo Road,
North Ryde, 2113, New South Wales

Published in the USA by
Croom Helm
in association with Methuen, Inc.
29 West 35th Street
New York, NY 10001

British Library Cataloguing in Publication Data

Gorbachev at the helm: a new era in
Soviet Politics?
    1. Gorbachev, M. S.   2. Soviet Union —
Politics and government — 1953–
I. Miller, Robert F.   II. Miller, J. H.
III. Rigby, T. H.
320.9'47'0924   JN6511
ISBN 0-7099-5506-5

Library of Congress Cataloging-in-Publication Data

Gorbachev at the helm.

    Includes index.
    1. Kommunisticheskaia partiia Sovetskogo Soiuza —
S'ézd — (27th: 1986: Moscow, R.S.F.S.R.) 2. Soviet
Union — Politics and government — 1982– . 3. Soviet
Union — Economic policy — 1981– . I. Miller, Robert F.,
1932– . II. Miller, J.H. (John H.) III. Rigby,
T.H. (Thomas Henry), 1925–
JN6598.K5 1986z   947.085'4   87-14094
ISBN 0-7099-5506-5

Phototypeset in English Times by
Pat and Anne Murphy, Dorset.
Printed and bound in Great Britain by
Biddles Ltd, Guildford and King's Lynn

Contents

List of Tables

Introduction
R. F. Miller   1

1. Old Style Congress — New Style Leadership?
   T. H. Rigby   6

2. The Programmatic Documents of the 27th Congress
   G. Gill   40

3. How Much of a New Elite?
   J. H. Miller   61

4. The Mass Party Membership: Steady as She Goes
   J. H. Miller   90

5. The Soviet Economy: Problems and Solutions in
   the Gorbachev View
   R. F. Miller   109

6. Soviet Reforms in the 1980s: Current Debate
   V. Zaslavsky   136

7. Agricultural Reform, the Food Program and the
   27th Party Congress
   S. G. Wheatcroft   161

8. Foreign Policy and Defence
   G. Jukes   189

9. The Soviet Union and Eastern Europe: Genuine
   Integration at Last?
   R. F. Miller   214

Conclusion: The Gorbachev Era Launched
T. H. Rigby   235

Index   247

List of Tables

1.1 CPSU delegates, 1961–86: age structure   18
1.2 CPSU congress delegates, 1961–86: period of
     admission to party   18
1.3 CPSU congress delegates, 1961–86: current
     occupational affiliation   20
1.4 Changes in voting membership of Politburo
     between 26th and 27th Congresses   22
1.5 Renewal of central party and government
     leadership since Brezhnev   23
1.6 Membership of key executive bodies after 27th
     Congress   24

3.1 Central Committee department heads   65
3.2 Composition and turnover of leading CPSU organs   70
3.3 CPSU leading organs: age and party seniority   72
3.4 CPSU leading organs: some newly co-opted
     members in 1986   73
3.5 Female membership of leading CPSU organs   74
3.6 CPSU leading organs: nationality   76
3.7 Central Committee membership, 1981 and 1986,
     distributed by occupational base   77

4.1 CPSU: size, growth, admissions and losses,
     1971–86   91
4.2 Party membership in the major regions 1981–86   94
4.3 Men and women in the CPSU 1976–86   95
4.4 Age distribution of communists 1977–86   97
4.5 Original class background of communists   98
4.6 Party membership and levels of education   100
4.7 Employment of communists in branches of the
     economy   102
4.8 Ethnic composition of the party   104

5.1 Selected indicators of Soviet economic
     performance, 1971–85   115
5.2 Tempos of growth of national income by Five-Year
     Plans   115

7.1 The rising levels of net grain imports, agricultural subsidies and the imbalance between agriculture's share in national income and total capital investment   162
7.2 Growth in agricultural production, 1961–65 to 1976–80   165
7.3 Average annual agricultural growth rates   166
7.4 Consumption of basic foodstuffs   168
7.5 Sown and fallow area in the USSR   171
7.6 Livestock productivity indices   172
7.7 Retail overhang indicators   173
7.8 The share of capital investment allocated to agriculture, agricultural complexes and agro-industrial complexes   174

Appendix 1: Grain production and net imports   185

Appendix 2: Per capita food consumption in the USSR   186

Appendix 3: Gross agricultural production   187

Appendix 4: Capital investment in agriculture, agricultural complexes and agro-industrial complexes   188

8.1 CPSU Congresses, number of paragraphs in each report   190

9.1 Growth of produced national income in Eastern Europe and the USSR, 1971–83   218
9.2 Annual rates of growth of GNP in Eastern Europe, 1970–84   218

Introduction

Robert F. Miller

Following the lead of General Secretary Mikhail S. Gorbachev, the Soviet media have been seeking to portray the policy decisions taken at the 27th Congress of the CPSU in February–March 1986 as a major 'turning point' in Soviet history. Such an impression is undoubtedly desired by Gorbachev and his colleagues, and it is probably true that a significant proportion of the Soviet is ready for major changes. Whether or not the policies actually announced or introduced during and after the congress represent a real turning point, however, remains to be seen. The essays assembled in the present volume, some of which were presented at a workshop on the 27th Party Congress at the Australian National University in April 1986, consider this question for a number of policy areas and from a variety of perspectives. The authors seek to examine the degree to which the policy initiatives and associated personnel changes brought forth by Gorbachev and his lieutenants in certain key areas — domestic politics, general economic policy and administration, agriculture, ideology and foreign policy — constitute substantial innovations. Proceeding from their analyses, the authors also attempt to evaluate the potential of Gorbachev's proposals for achieving the intended transformational impact.

As Gorbachev himself suggested at the time, the rather vague principles and decisions enunciated at the congress were merely the beginning of the major 'reconstruction' (*perestroika*) he had in mind for the revitalisation of Soviet society and its performance at home and abroad. Gorbachev has travelled incessantly throughout the country to build support for the concrete policy changes that have issued forth continuously since the congress. The disaster at Chernobyl' proved to be no more than a temporary interruption in this process of directed 'acceleration'. Nor have predictions that the USSR under Gorbachev would be so immersed in domestic problems as to have little time or energy for foreign adventures proven accurate. Like N. S.

1

Khrushchev, with whom he is often compared, Gorbachev evidently considers aggressive policy initiatives and tactical flexibility to be a more effective strategy for the attainment of Soviet international objectives than a defensive, ideologically rigid approach, such as has often been practised in the past during periods of enforced internal socio-economic change and stress.

Gorbachev's heavy reliance on mobilisation and the centrality of the 'human factor' for the implementation of his policies mean that early evidence of success will be vital for his particular mode of leadership. So far the record has been mixed in a number of the areas examined by the authors. The central focus of the individual chapters is on the congress itself and the period leading up to it. By the time most of the contributions were completed for the present volume, however, enough evidence of early performance had accumulated to permit some informed preliminary judgements on the direction and likely outcomes of policies in certain key areas.

The organisation of the book is broadly thematic. The first four chapters deal with the crucial political and ideological aspects of policy-making in the new Gorbachev era. The following three chapters are concerned with major elements of economic policy and the continuing debates for and against structural reform. The final two chapters examine the regime's early orientations in international relations with respect to both the communist and non-communist worlds. Here, perhaps even more than in domestic policy-making, the situation since the 27th Party Congress has been marked by exceptional fluidity, although here, too, the basic directions are already apparent. The aim of the book is to set forth and examine these basic directions, rather than seek to encompass all of the latest developments in each area.

In Chapter 1, T. H. Rigby considers the symbolic functions of communist party congresses in the Soviet political system and the ways in which the 27th Party Congress differed from past congresses in both form and substance. He also analyses changes in the personnel composition of the leading party and government bodies since the end of the Brezhnev era and emerging from the 27th Congress. Rigby concludes that the congress bore Gorbachev's personal stamp and reflected a degree of consolidation of personal power that is unusual so early in the career of a General Secretary.

Graeme Gill's analysis of the new party Program and party

Rules in Chapter 2 underlines the substantial difference in the level of generality of the new Program as compared with the Khrushchevian edition of some 25 years earlier. The Gorbachev version is characterised by a more pedestrian concern for general principles, rather than specific goals, and a recognition of the unpredictability of the contingencies involved in 'communist construction'. The new edition of the party Rules contains few substantive changes. As in the party Program, the major empha- sis of the amendments adopted concerning the role of the party is on the principle of collectivity of party leadership and the personal responsibility of individual communists for the imple- mentation of new initiatives — both important Gorbachevian themes.

In Chapter 3, John H. Miller examines the 'top fifty' politi- cians at the apex of the party-state machine and the 'top five hundred' middle-level executives represented in the Central Committee and the Central Auditing Committee to establish just where Gorbachev's widely publicised personnel changes have actually taken place. His analysis shows that although the new corps of policy-makers and executives differs substantially from its predecessors in such characteristics as generational cohort and the variety and locale of their experience, the basic patterns of their recruitment and promotion have remained remarkably unchanged. If Gorbachev is indeed committed to a fundamental transformation of the socio-economic system, this fact does not augur well for his ultimate success.

Continuing his analysis in Chapter 4, John Miller examines the changes in the basic membership of the CPSU since the last party congress in 1981, as recorded in the official data published four months after the 27th Party Congress. Against the general slowdown in party recruitment during the five-year period, he finds evidence of greater selectivity in terms of region, profes- sion and gender. Miller advances several hypotheses to explain these patterns and link them with Gorbachev's express concern for quality of leadership and the 'human factor'.

In Chapter 5 Robert F. Miller considers the problems of the Soviet economy on the eve of the Gorbachev era and the solutions currently being proposed to address them. In general the problems can be categorised as of either a resource allocation and utilisation or an organisational and managerial nature. In the real world, of course, the two categories are deeply inter- twined, whereas the Soviet approach — under Gorbachev, as under his predecessors — is to try to treat them as quite separate. Without attacking the basic political and organisational problems of the Soviet system as it has evolved over the past half-century, the author argues, it is doubtful whether the radical shifts in resource-allocation strategy being promoted by Gorbachev will have the intended effect.

Victor Zaslavsky examines in Chapter 6 the unusually vigorous debates on economic reforms that have been taking place in the Soviet Union since the end of the Brezhnev era. If proposals for radical, market-type reforms are not yet quite legitimate, it is already clear that demands for a return to rigid centralisation are no longer welcome to the new leaders. Most of the proposals with a chance for adoption in the short run are what Zaslavsky calls 'within-the-system' changes, which do not threaten the basic political structures of the system, but he does not exclude the possibility of a more radical reconstruction in future if the present changes do not produce the desired results.

In Chapter 7 Stephen G. Wheatcroft compares the current administration of the USSR Food Program favourably with that under Brezhnev. Although agricultural investment projections announced at the 27th Congress represented a slight decline over recent years, Wheatcroft is relatively optimistic on the prospects for improvement in certain key sectors because of what he sees as a commitment to a more rational use of existing agricultural resources, such as the expanded acreage under clean fallow. The dramatic increase in the grain harvest of 1986 would appear to lend support to this evaluation.

Geoffrey Jukes examines in Chapter 8 some of the foreign policy and military aspects of the changes announced by the new leadership. He notes some important shifts in the official perception and ideological interpretation of current world events, particularly with respect to the main capitalist opponents, who, although characterised as moribund and riven with internal contradictions, are fated to survive in coexistence with the socialist world for a long time to come. The military implications of this assessment, he points out, may not be to the liking of the Soviet defence establishment, and Gorbachev will have to attend carefully to the maintenance of discipline and efficiency in a context of a relatively stagnant military budget. Jukes presents evidence of just such an emphasis in current party-military relations.

In Chapter 9 Robert F. Miller discusses the impact of the Gorbachev team on Soviet relations with the East European bloc countries. From the outset Gorbachev let it be known that he considered the recent deterioration of economic performance to be a bloc-wide phenomenon, requiring a transnational solution within the COMECON framework. As in the Soviet economy he has sought to break institutional and psychological barriers to closer co-ordination and integration, in this case across international frontiers. There is evidence of continuing resistance to Soviet pressures for integration, but Gorbachev shows no signs of weakening his resolve to bring it about.

From these brief summaries it will be apparent that the authors do, indeed, diverge somewhat in their assessments of the Gorbachev era and the likely success of the new leader's reform efforts. All agree that he is trying to introduce major changes in a broad range of Soviet policies and in the efficiency and effectiveness of their implementation. What is less clear and more debatable is whether Gorbachev will be willing and able, for reasons of domestic politics and ideology, to make the revolutionary political and structural changes that most of the contributors agree will be necessary for the kind of systematic performance breakthrough he correctly regards as essential to maintain the USSR's status as a genuine superpower.

1

Old Style Congress — New Style Leadership?

T. H. Rigby

At 10 am on Tuesday 25 February 1986 over 5,000 men and women thunderously applauded General Secretary Mikhail Gorbachev as he strode briskly to the podium in the great marble and glass Hall of Congresses within the ancient walls of the Kremlin to declare the 27th Congress of the CPSU open. And there, right up to the morning of 6 March, this great assembly, which included the leading figures in all walks of life both in the Soviet capital and in every constituent republic and province, was to sit for many hours each day (with the exception of the Sunday, when they rested from their creative labours) listening to scores of speeches, before finally endorsing the resolutions of the congress and the new composition of the party's Central Committee. What was there about this gathering that required all the top-echelon officials of a mighty but troubled super-power to devote to it over a week of their busy time? Surely Soviet party congresses cannot be the empty formality they are sometimes imagined.

CPSU CONGRESSES — RITUAL AND POLICY

About their *formal* importance there can be no doubt. Article 31 of the revised party rules defines the congress as the 'supreme organ of the CPSU', while the CPSU itself is described in the preamble as 'the highest form of socio-political organisation, the nucleus [*iadro*] of the political system, the leading and directing force of Soviet society' — formulas which are echoed in the state constitution of the USSR. CPSU congresses are thus empowered to make decisions binding not only upon all subordinate bodies, officials and ordinary members of the party itself, but on every governmental and non-governmental organisation in the country, on all organised social groups with a legal right to exist.

Is this, then, why the elite of Soviet society sat for over a week at the 27th Congress — because they were weighing and deciding great issues in every major sphere of national life? This, indeed, is how the Soviet media and party spokesmen represent the matter. But even a cursory reading of the congress proceedings makes it plain that 'weighing and deciding' was not what was going on there. One must go back six decades, to the 1920s, to find congresses which did 'weigh and decide', which debated and voted on alternative approaches to great policy issues, and at which the incumbent leaders were subjected to sharp criticism and obliged vigorously to defend their records and their programs. This ended with the establishment of Stalin's dictatorship, and although Stalin's successors revived the practice of holding regular congresses, which had lapsed in his later years, they have never, despite their protestations, conducted these meetings according to those 'Leninist norms' which had permitted criticism of top leaders and open policy debate.

The simple explanation why all those powerful and busy people were gathered in the Hall of Congresses from 25 February to 6 March 1986 lies in the unparalleled symbolic importance of party congresses in the political life of the Soviet Union. Does this mean, then, that they have no *practical* importance? Not at all, and to assume this would be to ignore the enormous potency of symbol and ritual in reinforcing and perpetuating any established system of power and authority, and in legitimating its current leaders and their policies.

Let us consider policies. Congresses, as we have seen, are not occasions for deciding policy, but they *are* occasions for periodically stating in the most authoritative and solemn setting just what policy actually is in major areas of domestic and foreign affairs, occasions for national stocktaking and for setting national goals. The recent practice of synchronising CPSU congresses with the adoption of the five-year economic plans has reinforced this stocktaking and goal-setting function. But its main vehicle remains the so-called accountability report (*otchetnyi doklad*) of the Central Committee, presented by the General Secretary. Furthermore, the particular formulas used by the latter in referring to various long-standing problems and pressing issues have great practical force, as they indicate to subordinate officials the current assessments and priorities of the leadership, the boundaries of admissible action and opinion, and the directions in which the highest rewards and severest punishments are likely to be forthcoming. Thus the *ukazaniia*, *otsenki*, *soobrazheniia* (indications, assessments, evaluations) voiced by the General Secretary will largely set the parameters for the behaviour and public utterances of party and government officials for some time ahead. At the congress itself, other speakers will no doubt trim the texts of their speeches, and in particular the wishes and criticisms they express, to harmonise with them.

The 27th Congress, then, like other congresses before it, was of major practical importance in providing the policy definitions, targets, priorities and behavioural guidelines in terms of which those entrusted with managing the manifold affairs of society were to exercise their responsibilities in the ensuing period. The actual content of these policy definitions, targets, priorities and guidelines will be the object of analysis in subsequent chapters. Their force derives, as noted above, precisely from the symbolic centrality of party congresses in Soviet political life. In this respect a CPSU congress is somewhat analogous to the speech from the throne at the opening session of a British parliament.

But this symbolic function also operates on a more fundamental level of political life than that of current policy and administration; for CPSU congresses have a ritual, ceremonial aspect through which they proclaim and celebrate the achievements and might of the USSR, the unity of the party and the nation and the loyalty of the various divisions of the Soviet elite and the population at large to the party, the state, and the current leadership. Congresses display and solemnise the existing distribution of authority within the latter and particularly the primacy of the incumbent General Secretary, they seek social catharsis by articulating grievances and heaping them on scapegoats, and while identifying the chief evils and enemies to be combated, they rededicate the party and the nation to the struggle. In short, the party congress is the Soviet regimes' supreme legitimacy ritual.[1] A Soviet party congress, then, is a carefully contrived political event serving primarily those two symbolic functions outlined above: that of giving force and authority to the leadership's current policy orientations, and that of a legitimacy ritual.

Of course the essence of a political symbol or ritual is that it displays or acts out a familiar pattern. It derives its force by repetition. But by the same token any departure from the familiar will make a special impact, sometimes out of all proportion to its intrinsic significance. Important signals may be given at a CPSU congress, as in the celebration of a church liturgy, through the contrived interplay between established patterns and selective innovations. Let us now consider Gorbachev's first congress with these points in mind.

THE 27th CONGRESS — TRADITION AND INNOVATION

In most respects the 27th Congress followed very closely the patterns inherited and subtly adapted by the Brezhnev regime. Here are the most important of them.

Size

CPSU congresses had become substantial gatherings even in Lenin's time, and their growth thereafter went hand in hand with the withering away of their deliberative functions. The number of delegates remained limited, however, to a little over 2,000 by the seating available in the largest suitable hall in the Kremlin, until Khrushchev, who had a liking for mass audiences, commanded the new Palace of Congresses to be built, with its capacity of over 5,000. Since the 22nd Congress in 1961 the norms of representation at the congress have been progressively adjusted neatly to fill this venue, and the 27th was no exception.

Duration

About a week has been standard for post-Stalin congresses. The slight increase (from seven and a half to eight and a half days) between the 26th and 27th Congresses served to accommodate the extended 'debates' discussed below.

Seating arrangements

As in all important political assemblies in the USSR, the top leadership (in this case the full and candidate members of the

Politburo) sit up front, immediately behind the rostrum, facing the mass of the delegates, and backed by a 'Presidium' of several score members, who comprise the cream of the central and provincial political elites and a scattering of lesser mortals 'representing' major social and occupational groups; and towering above the latter, also facing the ordinary delegates, stands a great effigy of Lenin, in heroic pose, with a vast Soviet flag as backcloth. Whoever speaks from the rostrum, therefore, does so directly under the eye of the ruling oligarchy, and in the name, as it were, of a consensus claiming the unqualified authority of Lenin himself. It is an arrangement that blankets out differences, except those between the more and the less powerful.[2]

Effective agenda

Traditionally this consists of two main items, namely the General Secretary's 'accountability' report on behalf of the Central Committee and the Chairman of the Council of Ministers' report on the draft economic plan, the presentation and discussion of the former taking about twice the time given to the latter. The Chairman of the party's Central Auditing Commission also gives a brief report on mundane housekeeping matters which is supposed to be discussed along with the General Secretary's report, but which is virtually ignored. And then, of course, there is the election of the new Central Committee and Central Auditing Commission at the end of the congress. At the 27th Congress the formal agenda included two further items, namely the new version of the CPSU Program and changes in the Party Rules. However, 'a proposal was received' not to have separate reports on these but to 'set out their essentials' in the main Central Committee report.[3] In practice there was no substantial discussion of these items at all, and the traditional shape of the congress proceedings was thus preserved.

Pattern of speeches

The General Secretary's report, which takes some hours to deliver, is followed by relatively brief speeches by the party first secretaries of each of the constituent republics[4] and of the most important regional committees of the RSFSR, in approximate order of seniority, interspersed with those of delegates representing all major fields of activity and social groups — economic administrators, workers, collective-farmers, the Academy of Sciences, the Komsomol, the Armed Forces, and so on. The Chairman of the Council of Ministers' far shorter report is followed by a smaller number of speeches from a similar mix of delegates; and at each session there are a few short addresses by leaders of foreign communist parties and other friendly parties, most of them showering praise on the Soviet Union and its leaders. This pattern was also followed faithfully at the 27th Congress.

Content of delegates' speeches

Here again Gorbachev's first congress followed time-hallowed precedents. With minor variations speeches contain the following components, usually in the order listed here. First, there is a salute to the General Secretary, normally by reference either to the excellence of his report or to the fundamental importance and correctness of the decisions of the April (1985) CC Plenum, the first presided over by Gorbachev and currently used as his 'brand-name' (just as the October 1964 Plenum was once used as the 'brand-name' for the post-Khrushchev Brezhnev-Kosygin regime). It is noteworthy that this and the other components discussed below are generally found in the speeches ostensibly 'debating' the plan report and not only in those explicitly on the report of the General Secretary himself.

Second comes the declaration of unconditional support, in the form of a statement that the regional delegation or other organisational or social category represented by the speaker totally approves the main report and the other documents before the congress.

Third, the delegate moves to his *samootchet*, his outline of the achievements and shortcomings of his organisation, focusing on those task-areas for which the latter is primarily looked to by the party leadership, and usually including a passage of 'self-criticism' (which in cases where the speaker has recently taken over the leadership or the organisation — quite frequent at the 27th Congress — amounts to criticism of his predecessors).

And finally come the requests, complaints and suggestions; and this calls for a balancing act no less hazardous than that

11

between self-praise and self-criticism. For along with the opportunity to make a mark in the eyes of his superiors, his peers, or his 'constituency', the speaker may risk suspicion of 'immodesty' (asking for too much), 'localism', 'departmentalism' or other variants of sectional interest, or even, Lord forbid, of 'demagogy' (courting personal popularity by voicing justified popular grievances). The requests (described as 'demands' or 'claims' by those who believe that interest-group pressure is the engine of Soviet political life, though 'humble petitions' might better reflect the power realities of the situation) usually ask for the allocation of resources for some project of local importance or for the expediting of some decision of special concern to the region or group concerned. The complaints (or 'criticisms') never, of course, touch on the incumbent leadership or their policies, but only on the way intermediate-level officials carry out the leadership's policies. Often they have a self-exculpatory twist; *we* would have done better if only ministry X or region Y had done *their* job properly. In such cases (particularly if consumer goods or services are involved) it may be understood by all concerned that X or Y failed to meet their commitments simply because they lacked the resources to do so, and a pattern of scapegoating is discernible here. Suggestions are expected to be 'businesslike', to be confined, that is, to minor structural or procedural improvements aimed at carrying out the leadership's programs more efficiently.

As already indicated, political scientists differ in the significance they attach to what I have termed the requests, complaints and suggestions voiced in the course of congress delegates' speeches, and the questions at issue cannot be seriously explored in the present context. The concern of Soviet officials to protect and promote the reputations, resources, and 'turf' of their organisations is undoubtedly an important factor in Soviet bureaucratic politics. While its pursuit is mostly subterranean, it can overflow into public speeches or writings, which may even, conceivably, influence outcomes.[5] We should not, however, make the elementary error of underestimating the asymmetrically vertical structure of power in the USSR, which makes it the chief interest of every Soviet official to please his superiors. This and the political functions served by congresses, should be borne in mind when analysing the content of delegates' speeches. The chief point to be made here, however, is that the requests, complaints and suggestions voiced at the 27th Congress again conformed to the norms and constraints entrenched in recent decades.

The fealty rituals

These have a distinctly tribal aura, in sharp contrast with the generally 'businesslike' tone of most of the congress proceedings, and hence my name for them: the ceremony of youths and maidens, and the ceremony of the warriors. They likewise conformed closely to precedent. On the evening of the fourth day 'it was as if spring itself, bright and sunny, reigned in the Palace of Congresses',[6] for the hall was filled with the banners of the Komsomol and Young Pioneers, and Pioneers and tiny Young Octobrists presented flowers to every number of the congress Presidium. One after another four young men and one young woman representing worker and peasant, youth, budding scientists and creative artists, and technical trainees, made their declarations of gratitude and loyalty. Then the Pioneers and Octobrists chorused *their* declarations in ringing verses, the greatest applause being evoked by the lines 'And we shall strive to live/ in such a way to earn/ our Komsomol badge/ then a party card!' The hall burst into a further ovation as young men and women from every republic, and others with outstanding production records, approached the Presidium and solemnly handed General Secretary Gorbachev the Komsomol's duty report (*raport*) to the 27th Congress, against chants of 'Lenin! Party! Komsomol!' And finally the 'young successors' march out to the tune of 'And the Battle Continues Anew', which resounds both as a 'parting injunction' to them and 'youth's oath of fealty to the cause of the older generations — the cause of the party of Lenin'.

The second fealty ceremony came four days later. 'Under their battle banners clothed in glory', in march columns of troops representing all ranks and branches of the Armed Forces. 'The Congress participants stand and greet the Soviet warriors with prolonged applause.'[7] A fanfare of trumpets, then tank commander Major-General V. S. Mikhailov makes his solemn declaration 'to the Communist Party and to the whole Soviet people, that the warriors of the Armed Forces reliably defend the sacred borders of our Motherland'. Pointing out that the troops now standing in the Palace of Congresses include men

13

decorated for 'gallant deeds performed in our present days in the execution of their international and patriotic duty' (i.e. veterans of the Afghanistan war), he declared that 'warriors of the Armed Forces stand ever ready, along with soldiers of the fraternal armies of the socialist commonwealth to deliver a crushing blow to any aggressor'. Roars of 'Long lives' for the Motherland, the people, and the CPSU, chants of 'Glory! Glory! Glory!' and the warriors march out, banners aloft.

In all these ways, then, the liturgy of the 27th Congress conformed to time-hallowed precedent. There were, however, some novelties which stand out all the more against this background of overall conformity to tradition. Four of these deserve special comment.

Title of the main report

For the first time since the 16th Congress in 1930, it contained the word 'political', as it had in Lenin's day.[8] This probably reflects, in part, the evolving concept of party bodies as 'organs of political leadership', but was perhaps also intended to signal the high seriousness and historical significance of this particular congress, and the great issues of power and policy now confronting the Soviet regime.

More speakers

The number of speakers to the General Secretary's report was 61, compared with 40 at Brezhnev's last congress, while those speaking to the plan report increased from 14 to 25. As noted above, the core speakers in both cases consisted, as always, of regional party bosses and the heads of such bodies as the Trade Unions, the Komsomol, the Academy of Sciences, the Writers' Union, and so on. What is interesting is that their numbers did not significantly increase at the 27th Congress. On the other hand, the total number of manual workers and farmers speaking rose only from six to nine. Most of the increase was, in fact, made up of party, government and other leaders and administrators at various levels and in various fields. It would be misleading, therefore, to see this widening of the range of speakers outside of the ranks of central and provincial bosses as populist in intent. Its thrust was towards not so much a rallying of the masses around the new leadership as a rallying of the elites.

More top leaders speaking

In recent congresses the practice has been that, apart from the rapporteurs, Politburo members and candidates do not speak unless they are serving as first secretaries of a republican, provincial (Leningrad) or city (Moscow) committee, in which case they figure as the latter's spokesman (the spokesman for the RSFSR is the Chairman of its Council of Ministers). This tradition was broken at the 27th Congress, where, apart from the rapporteurs Gorbachev and Ryzhkov, and the 'local representatives' Vorotnikov (RSFSR), Shcherbitskii (Ukraine), Kunaev (Kazakhstan), El'tsin (Moscow), Solov'ev (Leningrad) and Sliun'kov (Belorussia),[9] five other full members and two candidate members also spoke in the 'debate' on the General Secretary's report. They comprised second-ranking CC Secretary Ligachev, Chairman of the Presidium of the Supreme Soviet Gromyko, KGB Chairman Chebrikov, Chairman of the Committee of Party Control Solomentsev, Foreign Minister Shevardnadze, Defence Minister Sokolov and Minister of Culture Demichev. Is this simply to be placed in the context of the 'rallying of elites' discussed above? Quite likely, but one should perhaps ask whether it does not also reflect, or is intended to suggest (perhaps misleadingly) a change in power relationships within the Politburo, a greater level of equality in the 'collective leadership'. Such an interpretation would be difficult to escape if *all* Politburo members, or at least all full members, spoke, but they did not. Two full members, namely First Deputy Premier Aliev and CC Secretary Zaikov, and two candidates, namely First Deputy Premier and Gosplan Chairman Talyzin and CC Secretary Dolgikh, failed to address the congress. If the intention were to stress collegiality, then one would expect either *all* members to speak or *no* members to speak unless they were rapporteurs or regional representatives (as in recent practice). Thus the evidence is ambiguous, but it seems possible that, in addition to giving a voice, as it were, to various elite groups, the inclusion of these additional Politburo members among the speakers was intended to display the new leadership as men of individual talent and ideas all firmly aligned behind their General

Secretary. As Ligachev put it, 'we have all been given a single mandate, namely to support, strengthen and develop the line of the April Plenum of the CC'.[10]

Tone and style

The three breaks with tradition so far discussed are demonstrable facts, however we interpret them, but the last is relative and impressionistic. While this is far from applying across the board, many of the speeches had a greater than usual freshness and individuality of style and, in particular, a greater boldness in their criticisms and suggestions. It should be stressed that not one of them transgressed the long-standing taboos on criticising, however indirectly, the incumbent leaders or their policies, and on engaging in polemics with other speakers. But they lent a touch of life and drama to the proceedings which has not been seen at a CPSU congress for a quarter of a century — since the 21st in 1961, with its attacks on Stalinism and the 'anti-party group' of Molotov, Malenkov and Co. This comparison immediately invites the question: are we not dealing here simply with the practice usual to incoming Soviet leaders of scapegoating their predecessors by attributing to their failings evils which are in fact inherent in the system? This practice is observable after the change of top leaders or the resolution of factional struggles not only in the Kremlin, but also at republican and local levels, as illustrated by the recent examples of the Rashidov regime in Uzbekistan and the Grishin machine in Moscow. It is always a time for relatively plain speaking and for 'frank' revelations about inefficiency and corruption in high places. Undoubtedly the touches of liveliness at Gorbachev's first congress compared with the blandness of Brezhnev's last three are largely explainable in these terms. There appears, however, to be an extra flavour, most evident in the speech of El'tsin on the second day, and compounded, perhaps, of a heightened awareness of the daunting problems facing the Soviet system and a realisation that the party will never be mobilised to tackle them simply by parroting stereotyped formulas.

THE DELEGATES

The extraordinarily low turnover in the Soviet elite throughout the 18 years of the Brezhnev era came to an end with his successor Andropov, who initiated extensive changes in the upper levels of the party, government and other bureaucracies, changes which have accelerated since Gorbachev's takeover as General Secretary. The turnover has been highest within the ruling oligarchy itself, a point we shall come back to later. At the next level down, that of officials enjoying full membership of the Central Committee, about two-fifths of those elected in 1981 failed to be re-elected in 1986, compared with one-fifth between 1976 and 1981. These changes will be examined in detail in John Miller's chapter. The turnover in the 5,000 or so delegates to successive CPSU congresses gives no more than the roughest indication of movements within wider circles of the Soviet elite, since only a minority of these delegates are chosen *ex officio*, most of them being there as worthy representatives of various occupational and other categories of the party membership. It has been customary to change the majority of these between congresses, presumably in order to spread the privilege and experience of attendance more widely. That said, it is worth noting that the turnover of delegates between the 1976 and 1981 congresses was 71 per cent, and between the 1981 and 1986 congresses it rose to 76 per cent. The question, however, is not so much whether new people were elected to the 27th Congress as whether they were new *sorts* of people, whether their characteristics differed substantially from those of their predecessors at other recent congresses.

One obvious change is their somewhat lower age profile. It is clear from Table 1.1,[11] despite the complications due to inconsistent cohort classification, that there was a substantial 'greying' of CPSU congress delegates in the 1960s and 1970s. Those aged over 50 made up 37.4 per cent at Brezhnev's last congress compared with 22.5 per cent at his first, 15 years earlier. At the 27th Congress there was a 2.6 per cent reduction in the over 50s. It is worth noting, however, that this was concentrated in the over 60s, while the percentage of delegates aged in their 50s — the Gorbachev generation — actually increased slightly. Meanwhile the generation aged 40 and under still had 10 per cent fewer representatives than at Brezhnev's first congress. On this evidence, the rejuvenation of cadres in the 1980s is so far scarcely comparable with that under Khrushchev in the 1950s, when thousands of young men (and a few women) aged in their thirties were brought into the middle ranks of

Table 1.1: CPSU delegates, 1961–86: age structure (percent of congress delegates)

Age	22nd 1961	23rd 1966	24th 1971	25th 1976	26th 1981	27th 1986
Up to 30	22.0	8.0	5.1	12.5	12.2	30.5
31–35			12.8			
36–40	16.6	32.2	13.9	58.0	50.4	
41–50	37.9	34.3	41.6			34.7
51–60	23.5	21.7	20.7	19.7	25.7	26.5
Over 60		3.8	5.9	9.8	11.7	8.3

Note: Percentages for the 22nd Congress available for voting delegates only. Inclusion of non-voting delegates would produce a slightly older age profile.

Table 1.2: CPSU congress delegates, 1961–1986: period of admission to party (percent of congress delegates who joined CPSU)

	22nd 1961	23rd 1966	24th 1971	25th 1976	26th 1981	27th 1986
Before World War II	31.9	20.7	13.5	7.6	5.4	1.7
During World War II	26.6	24.7	19.5	14.5	9.2	4.0
1946–55	23.1	24.2	25.0	55.3	52.7	75.4
1956–65	18.4	30.4	33.4			
1966–75			8.7	22.6	32.7	
1976–						19.0

Note: Percentages of 22nd Congress delegates apply to voting delegates only. Percentages for 22nd to 24th Congresses and also 27th include those admitted in the first half of 1941 with wartime admissions, while those for 25th–26th Congresses evidently do not: numbers involved are very small.

party, government and managerial officialdom.

A further aspect of generational change is apparent in Table 1.2. Delegates who joined the party before World War II have now been reduced to a tiny remnant, and even wartime recruits are down to one in twenty compared with a quarter of all delegates 20 years ago. When one also takes into account that recruitment to the party was very low in the period 1946–53 it appears that roughly nine-tenths of the delegates to the 27th

Congress had joined the party in the three decades since Stalin's death.[12]

The men of the Gorbachev generation who now dominate the Soviet political elite, and who began their official careers in the grim years of the 'Leningrad Case' and the 'Doctors' Plot', find themselves ruling through a mass of subordinate officials and activists who have known only the relatively benign climate of the Khrushchev and Brezhnev eras. One can only speculate on the likely consequences for political behaviour.[13] Will those, like Gorbachev, whose political initiation took place in Stalin's last poisonous years be more, or less, inhibited from using Stalinist measures than their predecessors of the Brezhnev generation, whose political initiation took place during the 'heroic' years of industrialisation and collectivisation and then lived through the Great Terror? Will the young officials and activists of today be less easily intimidated than their predecessors, and therefore present greater problems of control, or will they be looking forward with a less anxious eye than the latter to the prospect of a spell of strong and stern leadership?

When Khrushchev convened the first congress to be held in his new Palace of Congresses, the nearly threefold increase in the number of delegates brought a changed balance of representation in terms of fields and levels of employment. As we see in Table 1.3, the pattern then established was followed at all the congresses held under Brezhnev, with only minor changes in ratios of representation. The most significant trend was the increased proportion of delegates from industry (including construction, transport and communications), and some decline in the representation of the party apparatus (which has been continuous since the 1930s).[14]

The close conformity of the pattern of occupational representation at Gorbachev's first congress with that of Brezhnev's last is truly striking. No two successive congresses in the past have exhibited such uniformity of representation. What data we have on levels of employment within particular fields show the same picture. For example there were 589 city and district secretaries among the party officials at the 26th Congress and 570 at the 27th. In both cases only about one quarter of the delegates working in industry and related fields were managerial personnel and the rest were mostly blue-collar workers and shop-floor supervisors. When one considers the weakness of objective constraints on the pattern of representation and the big changes

19

Table 1.3: CPSU congress delegates, 1961–1986: current occupational affiliation

	22nd 1961	23rd 1966	24th 1971	25th 1976	26th 1981	27th 1986
Total delegates	4813	4943	4963	4998	5002	5000
Party apparatus	1158	1204	1205	1114	1077	1074
Trade Unions/ Komsomol	104	126	126	693	691	682
Government apparatus	465	539	556			
Industry[a]	1391	1577	1565 +	1703	1728 +	1730
Agriculture	784	874	870	887	887	872
Education, arts, 'culture'[b]	?	147	120	272	269	270
Science[b]	?	?	138			
Armed forces[c]	350	352	383 –	314	360 –	372 –

Notes: In no case were figures fully complete, the nearest complete being those for the 25th Congress, which accounted for all but 15 delegates.
a. Figures for 1971 and 1981 near-complete.
b. Borderlines between these two categories not strictly consistent.
c. Figures for 1971, 1981 and 1986 estimates from residuals.

made at times in the past (notably between the 20th and 22nd Congresses) the symbolic significance of this extraordinary level of continuity is apparent. If the leadership had wished to signal some change in the balance of influence among different bureaucracies, or in the social appeal or character of their regime, e.g. to represent it as more populist, more technocratic, more committed to law-and-order, or what have you, nothing would have stood in the way of their adapting the balance of representation at this first post-Brezhnev congress accordingly. The evidence, however, suggests that they leaned over backwards to avoid allowing the impression of any such signals. The effect was to give symbolic reassurance that, however radical the measures they might adopt to deal with particular problems, the inherited character of the socio-political order remained sacrosanct.

It is not possible to check the balance of change and continuity in the ethnic composition of 27th Congress delegates, as no relevant data were offered.[15] The gender balance, however, was another striking case of contrived continuity. The Chairman of the Credentials Commission evoked a round of applause when he announced that '1,352 women have been elected to the 27th Congress, which makes them 27 per cent of all delegates. This is the largest number in the whole history of the CPSU both in absolute and in percentage terms'. This is literally true, but what he did not add was that the percentage has been going up at *every* successive congress, and the scarcely perceptible 0.4 per cent increase at the 27th Congress was the *lowest* since 1934.[16] How could this have been allowed to happen at a time when the need to promote more women is receiving unusual emphasis in the rhetoric (if not the practice) of cadres policy? The clue is that for some time female representation at CPSU congresses has been virtually pegged to their percentage of the party membership as a whole. But this principle is not applied generally, e.g. with respect to the representation of certain occupational groups, and there was nothing to prevent its being discarded in the case of female representation as well; nothing, that is, except the concern to employ the pattern of representation at the 27th Congress to signal, above all, political continuity.

THE LEADERSHIP

The election of the new Central Committee and Central Auditing Commission took place not on the final day of the 27th Congress but, again in accordance with long-established precedent, at the end of the second-last day. Then on the morning of the final day proceedings were suspended while the Central Committee held its first plenary meeting in order to elect the new Politburo and Secretariat and approve the Chairman of the Committee of Party Control, and for the Auditing Commission to elect its Chairman. As usual, no information about the election proceedings either for the Central Committee or for its inner bodies was provided. The congress session resumed, to be informed of the CC's 'decisions', although no candidate would have been in doubt that the CC in its brief meeting had been required to do no more than unanimously endorse the lists presented to it by the 'outgoing' leadership. The re-elected General Secretary Gorbachev then made a brief and stirring closing speech, frequently interrupted by applause, and proceedings ended with the singing of the Internationale.

The CPSU leadership as it emerged from the 27th Congress

Table 1.4: Changes in voting membership of Politburo between 26th and 27th Congresses

Members March 1981 (26th Congress)	Departed since	Added since	Members March 1986 (27th Congress)
L. I. Brezhnev	Brezhnev D11/82		
V. V. Grishin	Grishin R2/86		
A. P. Kirilenko	Kirilenko R11/82		
D. A. Kunaev			Kunaev
A. Ia. Pel'she	Pel'she D5/83		
M. A. Suslov	Suslov D1/82		
V. V. Shcherbitskii			Shcherbitskii
Iu. V. Andropov	Andropov D2/84		
A. A. Gromyko			Gromyko
G. V. Romanov	Romanov R7/85		
D. F. Ustinov	Ustinov D12/84		
K. U. Chernenko	Chernenko D3/85		
N. A. Tikhonov	Tikhonov R10/85		
M. S. Gorbachev			Gorbachev
		G. A. Aliev 11/82	Aliev
		M. S. Solomentsev 12/83	Solomentsev
		V. I. Vorotnikov 12/83	Vorotnikov
		E. K. Ligachev 4/85	Ligachev
		N. I. Ryzhkov 4/85	Ryzhkov
		V. M. Chebrikov 4/85	Chebrikov
		E. A. Shevardnadze 7/85	Shevardnadze
		L. N. Zaikov 3/86	Zaikov

Note: Month and year of change indicated, e.g. thus: 3/83 = March 1983. R = resigned/removed. D = died in office.

Table 1.5: Renewal of central party and government leadership since Brezhnev

Numbers of members in March 1986 who were co-opted to membership under:

	Brezhnev	Andropov	Chernenko	Gorbachev	Total
Politburo: members	4	3	0	5	12
candidates	2	0	0	5	7
CC Secretariat	3	1	0	7	11
Government Presidium	4	2	1	5	12

looked radically different from that which surrounded Brezhnev at the end of his lengthy incumbency. As we see from Table 1.4, only three full members of Brezhnev's 1981 Politburo apart from Gorbachev himself were still there in 1986. It is, in fact, at the level of the supreme leadership that the turnover in the Soviet elite since the death of Brezhnev has been most rapid. As shown in Table 1.5, this applies not only to the leadership's innermost circle, the voting members of the Politburo, but also to the latter's non-voting (candidate) members, the members of the CC Secretariat, and the members of the Presidium of the Council of Ministers (i.e. its Chairman, First Deputy Chairmen and Deputy Chairmen who collectively run the Central Government machine).[17] This table also shows that the leadership changes were given a brisk start during Andropov's brief General Secretaryship, were virtually halted under Chernenko, and resumed at an accelerated pace under Gorbachev.

This wholesale renovation of the topmost levels of Soviet officialdom is attributable to the personnel policies pursued under Brezhnev, which entailed a relatively low turnover and stressed seniority when replacements were made. This meant that the majority of members of these leading bodies at the time of Brezhnev's death were already well past the official retiring age of 60. Of the ten full members of Brezhnev's 1981 Politburo who were no longer there in 1986, five had died in office and most of the others had retired at a very advanced age. The only clear exception was Romanov, whose early retirement allegedly on health grounds has been generally attributed to his rivalry with Gorbachev. Nevertheless, it would be misleading to explain the dynamics of leadership turnover since Brezhnev purely in 'biological' terms. The timing of leaders' deaths was not politically controllable, but the timing of retirements was, and so

Table 1.6: Membership of key executive bodies after 27th Congress

Name	Politburo	Secretariat	Presidium C of M	Post(s) held
M. S. Gorbachev	M	M		General Sec CC, Ch State Defence Council
G. A. Aliev	M		M	1st DCh CM
V. I. Vorotnikov	M			Ch CM RSFSR
A. A. Gromyko	M			Ch Presidium Sup Soviet
L. N. Zaikov	M	M		Sec CC
D. A. Kunaev	M			1st Sec CC Kazakhstan
E. K. Ligachev	M	M		Sec CC
N. I. Ryzhkov	M		M	Ch CM
M. S. Solomentsev	M			Ch Committee Party Control
V. M. Chebrikov	M			Ch KGB
E. A. Shevardnadze	M			Min Foreign Affairs
V. V. Shcherbitskii	M			1st Sec CC Ukraine
V. I. Dolgikh	C	M		Sec CC
B. N. El'tsin	C			1st Sec Moscow City Committee
N. N. Sliun'kov	C			1st Sec CC Belorussia
S. L. Sokolov	C			Min Defence
Iu. F. Solov'ev	C			1st Sec Leningrad Regional Committee
N. V. Talyzin	C		M	1st DCh CM, Ch Gosplan
P. N. Demichev	C		a	Min Culture
A. P. Biriukova		M		Sec CC
A. F. Dobrynin		M		Sec CC
M. V. Zimianin		M		Sec CC
V. A. Medvedev		M		Sec CC
V. P. Nikonov		M		Sec CC
G. P. Razumovskii		M		Sec CC
A. N. Iakovlev		M		Sec CC
I. V. Arkhipov			M	1st DCh CM
V. S. Murakhovskii			M	1st DCh CM
G. I. Marchuk			M	DCh CM
A. K. Antonov			M	DCh CM
B. E. Shcherbina			M	DCh CM
Ia. P. Riabov			M	DCh CM
I. S. Silaev			M	DCh CM
L. A. Voronin			M	DCh CM
Iu. D. Masliukov			M	DCh CM

Note: M = full member, C = candidate, Sec = secretary, Ch = chairman, Min = minister, DCh = deputy chairman, CM = Council of Ministers, CC = Central Committee.

a. See note 17.

was the appointment of new members to replace those deceased or retired. For example, there were clearly political reasons why Grishin lost his place on the Politburo at the 27th Congress, while the 74-year-old Kunaev did not.

Table 1.6 sets out the composition of the Soviet leadership as it stood after the 27th Congress. It lists all those forming the 'interlocking directorate' of Politburo, CC Secretariat and Government Presidium, the ruling oligarchy of the USSR, showing the posts they held. It is at the weekly meeting of these three bodies that the country's most important political and administrative decisions are taken, the Secretariat dealing with business channelled through the party machine and the Presidium dealing with business channelled through the government machine, both of them passing to the Politburo matters of particular importance, complexity, contention or sensitivity. The pattern of their overlapping memberships, their working relationships, and the effective powers of their key members has varied greatly over the history of the Soviet regime, and they constitute the chief variables defining the structure of supreme power at any particular time.[18]

The Gorbachev-led oligarchy of 1986 comprised 35 individuals, occupying all told 42 positions on these three top bodies. It is worth comparing it with the oligarchy as it stood after Brezhnev's last congress in 1981. To start with, it is somewhat more compact than the latter, which comprised 38 individuals occupying 46 positions, although not nearly as compact as at certain earlier periods, notably immediately after the death of Stalin.

Secondly — and this is its most significant structural change — the Government Presidium had substantially improved its position *vis-à-vis* the CC Secretariat as measured by the number of its members serving also on the Politburo. There have been times in the past when members of one or other of the lesser bodies have constituted a majority of the Politburo. Thus in Stalin's last years all but one full member of the Politburo were also on the Government Presidium, while immediately following Khrushchev's victory over the 'anti-party group' in 1957, members of the CC Secretariat jumped to two-thirds of the Politburo membership. In the early 1960s the 'representation' of each body in the Politburo was brought into approximate balance and each was well short of forming a majority in the latter. By 1981, however, after a decade and a half in which

Brezhnev's party machine was gradually gaining in authority over Kosygin's government machine, the new Chairman of the Council of Ministers Tikhonov was the only member of the latter's Presidium in the Politburo, whereas five CC secretaries were full members of the Politburo and two more were candidate members. The situation following the 27th Congress was radically different: the voting members of the Politburo now included three members of the Secretariat and two of the Government Presidium, and the non-voting members one of each. The implications of such changes for the way power is distributed and exercised are obviously too great for them to have occurred by accident. It suggests *either* that Gorbachev's primacy was still considerably weaker than Brezhnev's had been at the height of his power, *or* that his personal authority over all his Politburo colleagues, including those in the Government Presidium, was such that he did not need to rely so heavily on the institutional weight of the Secretariat. The final section of this chapter adduces some evidence bearing on this question.

A third change of interest is the appearance in the leadership of a woman: the first since the political demise of Khrushchev's protegee Ekaterina Furtseva in the 1960s. Aleksandra Biriukova was a 56-year-old trade union official who made her earlier career as an executive in the traditionally female domain of textile manufacturing. Her appointment to replace Kapitonov in the junior secretariat portfolio of consumer goods and welfare, while matching her qualifications and experience, must be regarded as the minimal gesture the leadership could have made towards observing its own injunctions to promote more women to senior posts.

Let us now focus on the core of the ruling oligarchy, the twelve voting members of the Politburo, and enquire how substantially and in what respects they differed from their predecessors at the end of the Brezhnev era.[19] There has been, most obviously, an influx of younger men, but the extent of rejuvenation was not as great as is sometimes imagined, the average age of Politburo members after the 27th Congress being 64, compared with 68 after the 26th. Gorbachev, at 55, was the youngest; Ryzhkov was 56 and Shevardnadze 58; six were in their 60s (Aliev, Vorotnikov, Zaikov, Ligachev, Chebrikov and Shcherbitskii) and three in their 70s (Gromyko, Solomentsev and Kunaev). It is sobering to note that in 1971, when the Brezhnev-Kosygin regime had already been in office for seven years, the average age of voting members of the Politburo was only 61. The great majority of the 1986 Politburo, like their predecessors of 1981, had joined the party under Stalin, the exceptions being Ryzhkov (1956) and Zaikov (1957), although only three dated their party membership to before World War II, compared with nearly all the 1981 Politburo.

The most noteworthy change in the ethnic composition of the Politburo is the further reduction in the number of Ukrainians. Under Khrushchev many Ukrainians had risen to top party and government positions, and in the early 1970s there were still four of them among the voting members of the Politburo. By the end of the Brezhnev era, however, these were down to two, and by 1986 only the First Secretary of the Ukrainian CC Shcherbitskii was left.[20] There was a slight reduction in the preponderance of Great Russians — from ten out of fourteen in 1981 to eight out of twelve in 1986 — but their share of Politburo places remained well above their share of the Soviet population and even of the party membership, where they were already substantially over-represented. Meanwhile, the number of non-Slavs had gone up from two to three, although one of these, Kunaev, was obviously close to retirement, and there was no reason to assume that he would be replaced in the Politburo by another non-Slav.

In the Brezhnev period the changes in the characteristics of Politburo members which presented the greatest political and sociological interest were those constituting their educational and career profile. In the 1960s and early 1970s there was a greater and greater preponderance of members with what might be called Brezhnev-type careers: a technological training to tertiary levels, some industrial experience, then many years as hard line party officials, including substantial periods as provincial or republican first secretaries. In Brezhnev's last years, however, the preponderance of men with this educational and career profile had declined. In 1971 there were only two full members of the Politburo whose appointment to top leadership positions in Moscow had not been preceded by lengthy service as regional party bosses; by 1981 there were five. Between 1971 and 1981 graduates in the social sciences and humanities increased from three to five, while the number whose post-secondary education had been limited to technological or agricultural fields was reduced from ten to seven.[21] This trend to greater diversity in educational and career experience carried over into the post-Brezhnev years, but it is important to stress that the essential components of the Brezhnev-type career still characterised the majority of Gorbachev's Politburo in 1986. Eight out of twelve of them had qualified as engineers and had managerial experience in industry, and eight out of twelve (admittedly not precisely the same eight) had served for at least five years as first secretary of a provincial or republican party committee.

At the same time we note two other career types, each represented by two members of the 1986 Politburo. The first is what Frederic J. Fleron has called 'co-opted' officials, that is to say, technically qualified personnel who, instead of being 'recruited' to full-time party work at an early stage of their working lives are 'co-opted' to it, and then at a high level, after many years in senior industrial administrative posts.[22] Two such men, namely Katushev and Dolgikh, were made Central Committee secretaries under Brezhnev, but contrary to expectations never achieved promotion to the Politburo. Now Ryzhkov and Zaikov have done so. The former climbed the managerial hierarchy from foreman to plant director to First Deputy Chairman of Gosplan, before being appointed at age 53 to his first party job, namely as CC Secretary on economic questions. In October 1985 he succeeded Tikhonov as Chairman of the Council of Ministers. Zaikov worked for 36 years in industry before his appointment in 1976 as Chairman of the Executive Committee of the Leningrad City Soviet; in 1983, he was catapulted to succeed Romanov as First Secretary of the Leningrad Regional Committee and in July 1985 was made CC Secretary responsible for the defence industries. The presence of two such 'co-opted' officials in the Politburo is significant, but it should be noted that there were no members in 1986 who had made their careers *exclusively* within the economic administrative apparatus, as did Saburov and Pervukhin (members in the mid-1950s) and Brezhnev's colleague Kosygin.[23] The second divergent career-type is represented by Politburo members Aliev and Shevardnadze, both of whom were history graduates who got their first party job as republic first secretaries (in Azerbaidzhan and Georgia, respectively) after several years in high-level police work (the former in the KGB, the latter in the MVD). Typologically Shevardnadze is the more interesting of the two. Since Stalin's day several officials have achieved high office after graduating in the humanities or social sciences, serving several years as high-level Komsomol officials, and then doing a stint in senior security, personnel management or media-control jobs. Shelepin was Shevardnadze's only predecessor in the Politburo who had followed this career line, and he and his pushy following of career look-alikes came to political grief in the mid-1960s. In East Germany under Honecker, however, education and career along these lines has become perhaps the commonest path to top-level office. Should leadership recruitment follow the same course in the USSR, this might have important effects on the outlook and priorities of the regime, but here we are in the realm of speculation.

To sum up, although there had been a two-thirds turnover in the Politburo's voting membership between Brezhnev's last congress and Gorbachev's first, it would be hard to argue on the evidence available that its character was yet greatly changed. The 1986 members were younger on average, but already older than their predecessors had been until well into the Brezhnev era, and like their predecessors, most of them had spent their formative years and embarked on their political careers under Stalin. All were still men and two-thirds of them were still ethnic Russians. In terms of their education and careers they were less stereotyped than the Politburo of Brezhnev's first decade, but two-thirds of them were still engineers by training and two-thirds had still been co-opted to top office in Moscow on the basis of their successful careers as provincial *apparatchiki*. Only a naive scientism would assume that such similarities of background and career experience exclude the possibility of radical differences of commitment and attitude. In the absence, however, of substantial evidence of such differences in their public statements, including those made at the 27th Congress, there seems little justification for positing them simply on the basis of the observed relatively minor changes in their objective characteristics. There might be a stronger case for examining in detail all available information about each individual member, studying him precisely as an individual rather than as a bundle of sociological traits, and attempting to estimate the political capacities and proclivities that each of them brings to the work of the Politburo. It would be beyond my scope to undertake such a detailed and necessarily still speculative analysis here. However, something more must be said about the General Secretary, for Gorbachev is surely a man of a very different stamp from Brezhnev, and experience shows that General Secretaries *are* capable of making a major impact on the character and policies of the Soviet regime.

THE GENERAL SECRETARY

Other chapters in this volume will be giving attention to Mikhail Gorbachev's style and approach in major areas of public policy. There seems to be general agreement that he showed himself in his first year in office as innovative, reformist but far from radical in his policy orientations, and relatively plain-spoken, low-key, down-to-earth yet dignified in presentation. But how strong was the new General Secretary as he emerged from his first congress? Was he, as Brezhnev appeared to be during *his* first congress two decades earlier, little more than spokesman for an oligarchy of near equals? Or was he already the clearly dominant figure in this ruling oligarchy, as Brezhnev was to become in the course of the 1970s and as Khrushchev had been from 1957 to 1964? I shall try to identify and evaluate the formal and informal sources of his power and authority, with the *caveat* that the evidence is inconclusive and other interpretations are possible.

The necessity of making analytical distinctions should not lead us to obscure the constant interplay between these formal and informal sources — and manifestations — of power and authority. This applies in political systems anywhere, but especially in the Soviet case, where the *powers* of the particular posts and particular bodies that make up the leadership subsystem are so weakly defined by rule or convention. Appointment as General Secretary automatically confers a certain primacy within the Politburo, but the character and extent of this primacy has to be built up by the new incumbent in interaction with his colleagues and subordinates. At the beginning it tends to be highly limited by the circumstances that few if any of his Politburo colleagues owe their positions to him, and until recently some, at least, will have enjoyed no less authority than he under the previous General Secretary. Since, however, he will normally chair Politburo and Secretariat meetings and thus exert a disproportionate influence over their agendas and proceedings, since he will enjoy at least a veto power over all major personnel appointments and organisational decisions, and since subordinates will have an interest in deferring first and foremost to his wishes and interests, his informal power will almost inevitably snowball, the speed of its growth depending on contingencies of personality and circumstance. Sooner or later it will find overt expression in such ways as the terms in which he is referred to at political meetings and in the media, the promotion to senior party and government posts and to the Politburo itself of officials clearly enjoying his patronage, and his acquisition of additional positions, titles and honours.

In Brezhnev's case the snowballing process was a very slow one, largely because of the reaction against Khrushchev's domineering style and his never-ending reorganisations, policy panaceas and personnel replacements. This found expression in the agreement (embodied in a CC Plenum resolution) that future General Secretaries should not hold the chairmanship of the Council of Ministers as well (as Stalin and Khrushchev had done) and in the consensus against structural innovations and in favour of security of tenure for high-level officials. This inhibited Brezhnev's opportunities for building his authority through extension of his formal powers, innovatory leadership, or stacking the oligarchy with his supporters. It is possible that these contextual factors were reinforced by aspects of Brezhnev's own character, for despite his manifest vanity he seems to have taken naturally to a consensual, conservative, 'chairman of the board' role. Nevertheless, imperceptibly at first and then gradually accelerating, the snowball grew, becoming all too obvious in the latter stages of his incumbency, by virtue of his assumption of the Chairmanship of the Presidium of the Supreme Soviet and the Chairmanship of the State Defence Council, his promotion to Marshal of the Soviet Union and investment with the (rarely awarded) Sword of Honour, the constant stream of public praise of his qualities and grotesque exaggeration of his achievements, and the advancement to the inner circles of power of old cronies from his days in Dnepropetrovsk, Zaporozh'e, Moldavia and Kazakhstan.

This by now familiar story is recalled here in order to bring out important differences in Gorbachev's position at the outset of his incumbency. After years of immobilism in the face of worsening economic and social problems the Soviet elite was aware that it could no longer settle for a quiet life, as it had after the overthrow of Khrushchev, and was looking instead for energetic and resolute leadership and was generally, it seems, ready to accept substantial within-system reform and policy innovation. Pressing practical need, and not just moral revulsion, made for a heightened intolerance of the slacking, inefficiency and corruption which had flourished in the live-and-let-live atmosphere of the Brezhnev years. The pathologies

31

of extreme job security and promotion by seniority were now as obvious as those of job insecurity and arbitrary sackings of personnel had been 20 years earlier. Ambitious and energetic middle-level officials were fretting at the meagre opportunities for advancement. All this generated an atmosphere congenial to accelerated personnel change at high levels which, as we have seen, was made inevitable by the demise of several aged officials. A new General Secretary would not have a free hand in senior appointments and in the co-optation of new members to the oligarchy's inner executive bodies, but his voice would carry the greatest weight, and his favour would be a prime resource, and arguably an essential one, for advancement to high party or government office.

A further relevant factor was what a number of writers have referred to as the 'three-stage succession'. By the time Gorbachev became General Secretary several of Brezhnev's most senior colleagues were no more, while others were weakened by age and sickness. The new voting members of the Politburo, Aliev, Solomentsev and Vorotnikov, were clearly junior to him in status. Moreover, both in the latter months of Andropov's brief incumbency and throughout Chernenko's he was clearly number two and may even have been *de facto* leader for some time before the latter's death. He thus began his incumbency with far greater personal authority within the leadership than had Brezhnev in 1964, let alone Khrushchev in 1953. Romanov was now the only party leader of comparable standing, and Gorbachev secured his retirement within four months.

Turning now to the overt manifestations of Gorbachev's power and authority, we note first that he quickly followed his three predecessors in becoming Chairman of the State Defence Council. He did not, however, assume the Chairmanship of the Presidium of the Supreme Soviet, although this post, too, had seemingly tended to become the prerogative of the General Secretaryship (Brezhnev acquired it after 13 years, Andropov after seven months and Chernenko after two months). With the many changes in the Politburo, Secretariat and Government Presidium the first obvious Gorbachev protégés began to appear in these bodies: Shevardnadze among the voting members of the Politburo, Murakhovskii (the new First Deputy Chairman responsible for the 'Agro-industrial Complex') in the government Presidium, and in the Secretariat the agriculture secretary Nikonov and the secretary responsible for personnel and organisational matters Razumovskii. Thus by the time of the 27th Congress Gorbachev supporters occupied the key positions in the strategically important fields of foreign affairs, agriculture and personnel, a situation which none of his predecessors had contrived in anything like such a short time (if at all). The pattern suggests a sharper concern for the substance of power than for the appearance of it. For example, his acquiescence in Gromyko's appointment as Chairman of the Presidium of the Supreme Soviet meant postponing perhaps for some time his own assumption of the dignities of this office, but by opening up the Ministry of Foreign Affairs for his junior ally, Shevardnadze, it allowed him quickly to assert an unequivocal primacy in the conduct of Soviet foreign relations.

Gorbachev also outdid his predecessors in the media 'visibility' he achieved during his first year, a product of his youthful energy combined with the clear primacy he already enjoyed over his most senior colleagues (Andropov and Chernenko lacking the former and Stalin, Khrushchev and Brezhnev the latter). As we observed earlier, the focal role he played in the 27th Congress by virtue of his office automatically confirmed and reinforced this primacy. The deference shown to him at this first congress over which he presided, however, went far beyond what was to be expected or what was shown to his predecessors at their first congresses. That most speakers should pay homage to him either directly by name or by reference to the April Plenum, his 'brand-name', was not surprising, but there were also references to his personal qualities and to his exceptional standing in the leadership which were quite unprecedented at such an early stage of a General Secretary's incumbency.

Thus Politburo member Vorotnikov, giving the opening speech in the 'debate' on Gorbachev's report, said that there was a constant awareness within the leadership of 'the political will and great organisational work of the General Secretary of the CC CPSU Mikhail Sergeevich Gorbachev'.[24] The following day Gorbachev's No. 2 in the CC secretariat Ligachev went further. 'As a member of the CC', he said, 'I should like to report to the Congress delegates that the ideas of the April Plenum have become the defining ones in the activity of the Party's Central Committee, the Politburo and the Secretariat *under the leadership of Mikhail Sergeevich Gorbachev*' (my emphasis).[25] This cue was then picked up by the Lithuanian and Bashkir party bosses, both of whom referred to 'the Politburo headed by'

(*Politbiuro vo glave s*) Gorbachev — a formula that has never before been used of a General Secretary until he has firmly established his dominance after many years in office.[26] Shevardnadze made his contribution, claiming that hope had been reborn in the ten months since the April Plenum, stemming from the 'new style and the strength of logic and conviction' which Gorbachev had brought to bear in his talks with the world's leaders.[27] And the Moldavian First Secretary Grossu declared that 'with special force and profound gratitude we note the superlative (*velichaishuiu*) wisdom and genuine courage manifested by the CC CPSU, the Politburo and by Mikhail Sergeevich Gorbachev personally in the struggle for peace and social progress'.[28]

Another striking signal that Gorbachev was boss was the tendency to direct remarks to him personally. Thus the Komsomol chief Mishin said that he wanted 'to assure the Congress delegates and you, Mikhail Sergeevich' that Soviet youth apply themselves to a particular task mentioned in the CC report.[29] A boarding school teacher declared to 'respected Mikhail Sergeevich' that he had been quite correct in stating that 'a strong family is one of the most important supports of our society'.[30] Foreign representatives joined in, and none more enthusiastically than Fidel Castro. Having referred to Gorbachev's 'brilliant and bold report' he went on to declare: 'we believe in the great motherland of Lenin, we believe in the Soviet people, its glorious party, its leadership, and in you, Comrade Gorbachev'.[31] Nor was Gorbachev himself beyond emphasising his special status by interrupting speakers with comments, in the manner of Khrushchev at the height of his power.[32] And he allowed the praise and flattery to go on for five days before interrupting one speaker with the words 'let's not run through all the grammatical forms of Mikhail Sergeevich' (*Davaite ne budem skloniat' Mikhaila Sergeevicha*).[33] One is reminded of Stalin's famous rebuke to his flatterers when the 'cult' was getting under way, and just as on that occasion Gorbachev's audience responded with prolonged applause, but did not mend their ways. For the very next day a retired mines inspector related how the miners and other workers had been inspired and redoubled their efforts when Gorbachev sent greetings to the mine where the Stakhanovite movement began.[34] And the Ulianovsk party leader Kolbin contrived to offer the most remarkable encomium of all while avoiding direct mention of the General Secretary. 'Today', he assured the delegates,

> the authority of the CC CPSU and its Politburo have grown
> immeasurably in the eyes of our whole people and progressive
> world opinion. In this each of us can see the manifestation of
> simple human wisdom: an acknowledged leader (*lider*) is he
> who evokes in people's hearts and minds unfeigned respect for
> his ability, with profound dignity and with historical insight
> into likely future developments (*istoricheskim videniem
> perspektivy*), to represent the interests of his people both
> within the country and in the international arena.[35]

Opinions among leading specialists differ, but my reading of
the evidence is that Gorbachev's clear primacy was firmly established by the time of the 27th Congress and that his power and
authority would continue to snowball. This is not the place for
elaborate Kremlinological speculation, but a couple of general
points should be noted. The voting members of the Politburo in
1986 included only one (Shevardnadze) who had long-standing
personal links with Gorbachev, but on the other hand, there was
now no one who was, or had been, in a relationship of rivalry
with him. Most of them were in some sense beholden to him,
either as younger officials who had earned promotion under him
or as tolerated leftovers from the Brezhnev regime. Some of the
former joined the central leadership by virtue of Andropov's
favour, which Gorbachev also enjoyed. A common patron does
not guarantee continued mutual loyalty, but it is hard to see any
of this group now turning against him. The 'second' secretary
Ligachev, whose public statements seem to mark him as relatively
conservative in outlook, is sometimes seen as an alternative focus
of authority who could come to challenge Gorbachev's dominance, but he is already 65, and it is hard to see him mounting such
a challenge so long as the latter retains his health and vigour and
avoids extravagantly gross errors.

Nor is it easy to see the lineaments of a faction within the
Politburo that might act in concert to limit the growth of his
authority, so divided are its members in terms of institutional
interest and regional affiliation. Ever since the 1930s common
service in particular bureaucracies and especially in particular
regional party organisations has been the chief basis of factional
alignment in the Politburo. In this connection it is worth recalling
an unusual passage in Ligachev's speech at the 27th Congress.

Insisting that no officials should enjoy an immunity from criticism, whatever their institutional or regional affiliation, he went on to list several of the latter specifically, in all cases regions in which members of the Politburo had served or were now serving: Moscow (El'tsin), Leningrad (Zaikov, Solov'ev), Ukraine (Shcherbitskii), Kazakhstan (Kunaev), Stavropol' (Gorbachev), Tomsk (himself) and Sverdlovsk (Ryzhkov).[36] This was clearly intended as an assurance to the party officialdom as a whole that Politburo members would not give special protection and preference to 'their' cadres. Incidentally, however, it acknowledged unequivocally the central importance of regionally based links in the informal structure of power in the USSR. Both Khrushchev and Brezhnev had exploited the different regional groupings among their own followers and colleagues in winning and maintaining power, and with such a diversity in Gorbachev's Politburo he should find it even easier to do so. Nor can one imagine him committing Khrushchev's error of behaving so high-handedly and so arbitrarily towards his Politburo juniors as to foment an incongruous cross-factional coalition into deposing him. Moreover, time is on his side: given the age-structure of the Politburo, there will be no shortage of opportunities to mould its membership increasingly to his liking, without his having to risk opposition by initiating dismissals.

Gorbachev's first congress, then, is unlikely to be his last. Instead, it brought to an auspicious close the first phase of what may prove to be a lengthy Gorbachev era.

NOTES

1. The political rituals, ceremonies and symbols of the USSR still await serious analysis. The considerable literature on political legitimation in Soviet-type systems has very little to say about them: cf. T. H. Rigby and Ferenc Feher (eds), *Political Legitimation in Communist States* (London: Macmillan, 1982) and Paul Lewis (ed.), *Eastern Europe: Political Crisis and Legitimation* (London: Croom Helm, 1984). On the other hand, Christel Lane's admirable *The Rites of Rulers. Rituals in Industrial Society — The Soviet Case* (Cambridge: Cambridge University Press, 1981) does not concern itself with the specifically political sphere. Nevertheless her theoretical analysis appears very pertinent to the matters discussed here. Soviet political rituals, including those embodied in CPSU congresses, may be seen (in Clifford Geertz's terms) as a 'model for' rather than a 'model of' social relations in the USSR, that is they help to impose perceptions of Soviet social and

political realities as the regime would have them perceived rather than as they really are. They serve, *inter alia*, as 'one important means of glossing over conflictual social relationships' (Lane, p. 33).

2. In addition to the Presidium, three other 'congress organs' are also designated, namely a Secretariat, an Editorial Commission, and a (Delegates') Credentials Commission. These are far too large to function as working committees, any meetings they may hold presumably being limited to formalities, and their chief significance lies in registering the superior authority of a further 130 delegates.

3. *Pravda*, 26 February 1986, p. 1.

4. The Chairman of the Council of Ministers in the case of the RSFSR, which has no separate republic level party executive.

5. Thane Gustafson has suggested that the arguments of two provincial party secretaries may have brought the Politburo to change its position on certain water-diversion projects. See his *Reform in Soviet Politics. Lessons of Recent Policies on Land and Water* (Cambridge: Cambridge University Press, 1981), pp. 77–8.

6. *Pravda*, 1 March 1986, p. 8.

7. *Pravda*, 5 March 1986, p. 1. The report continues on p. 7.

8. There were several changes in the nomenclature of reports from the early 1920s on. At the 10th and 11th Congress Lenin gave a 'Report on the Political Activity of the Central Committee' and there was also a 'Report on the Organisational Activity of the CC'. At the 12th the titles were the same, with Zinov'ev giving the political one, as he did at the 13th, but it was now called the 'Political Report (*otchet*) of the CC'. From the 14th to the 16th Stalin gave the 'Political Report' and a succession of his minors gave the 'Organisational Report'. Beginning with the 17th Congress the main report was called the 'Accountability Report' (*otchetnyi doklad*). There was still a 'Report on Organisational Questions' at the 17th Congress, but only as one of several lesser reports, and thereafter organisational matters were dealt with as part of the main report. At the 22nd Congress the latter was simply called 'Report of CC' (*otchet TsK*), at the 23rd and 24th it went back to 'Accountability Report' and at the 25th and 26th it was titled 'Report (*otchet*) of the CC CPSU and current tasks in domestic and foreign policy'. A separate report on the economic plan has been given regularly since the 20th Congress. The 21st Congress, however, was an 'extraordinary' one convened solely to deal with Khrushchev's new party program.

9. Solov'ev and Sliun'kov only became Politburo candidates at the 27th Congress.

10. *Pravda*, 28 February 1986, p. 4.

11. Tables 1.1 to 1.3 are based on figures given in the reports of the Credentials Commissions presented at the respective congresses. See *XXII s''ezd Kommunisticheskoi Partii Sovetskogo Soiuza. Stenograficheskii otchet* (Moscow: Politizdat, 1961), vol. 1, pp. 421–31; *XXIII s''ezd Kommunisticheskoi Partii Sovetskogo Soiuza. Stenograficheskii otchet* (Moscow: Politizdat, 1966), vol. 1, pp. 278–85; *XXIV s''ezd Kommunisticheskoi Partii Sovetskogo Soiuza. Stenograficheskii otchet* (Moscow: Politizdat, 1971), vol. 1, pp. 330–6; *XXV s''ezd*

Kommunisticheskoi Partii Sovetskogo Soiuza. Stenograficheskii otchet (Moscow: Politizdat, 1976), vol. 1, pp. 293–9; *XXVI s''ezd Kommunisticheskoi Partii Sovetskogo Soiuza. Stenograficheskii otchet* (Moscow: Politizdat, 1981), vol. 1, pp. 215–20; and *Pravda*, 28 February 1986, p. 5.

12. The latter estimate is borne out by the age figures in Table 1.1, which show that only 8.3 per cent of delegates were aged over 60 in 1986, i.e. were over 20 in 1946, when admissions to the party under the age of 21 were already somewhat unusual, though not yet exceptional.

13. For two valuable discussions of the relationship between age-related life experiences and likely political attitudes and behaviour, see Jerry F. Hough, *Soviet Leadership in Transition* (Washington: Brookings Institution, 1980), and Seweryn Bialer, *Stalin's Successors. Leadership, Stability and Change in the Soviet Union* (Cambridge: Cambridge University Press, 1980), Parts I and II.

14. Party officials formed 66 per cent of the delegates at the 15th Congress (1927), 42 per cent at the 18th (1939), 37 per cent at the 20th (1956) and 24 per cent at the 22nd (1961: the first enlarged congress in the Palace of Congresses).

15. It was merely stated that the delegates were drawn from 72 'nations and nationalities'. No ethnic breakdown of CPSU congress delegates has been offered since 1930. Figures were given for the size of delegations from the various union republics, but each of these was of course ethnically mixed and the totals simply reflected the number of party members of all nationalities in the respective republic.

16. The increase at Brezhnev's last congress was 1.5 per cent. The most striking advance in female representation was made under Khrushchev.

17. These comprise the *ex officio* members of the Government Presidium. The Constitution allows the appointment to it of additional members of the Council of Ministers but no official information on any such appointments is available. Soviet scholars have reported occasional such appointments in the past, from such diverse fields as finance, state control, culture and agriculture. Minister of Culture Demichev was the most likely candidate in the period studied here. It is unlikely that the ministers of Foreign Affairs and Defence or the KGB Chairman ever serve on the Government Presidium, as matters of any importance in their respective fields probably go straight to the Politburo.

18. See T. H. Rigby, 'The Soviet Political Executive, 1917–1986', in Archie Brown (ed.), *Political Leadership in the Soviet Union* (London: Macmillan, 1987).

19. More information on the 1981 Politburo will be found in R. F. Miller and T. H. Rigby (eds), *26th Congress of the CPSU in Current Political Perspective* (Canberra: Department of Political Science, RSSS, Australian National University Occasional Paper No. 16, 1982), pp. 80–6. For comparison with earlier periods see T. H. Rigby, 'The Soviet Politburo: A Comparative Profile 1951–1971', *Soviet Studies*, vol. xxiv, no. 1 (July 1972), pp. 3–23. The analysis of Politburo members offered in this section is based on official biographical data, mostly drawn from the Yearbooks (*Ezhegodniki*) of the *Bol'shaia*

sovetskaia entsiklopediia, 3rd edn., and successive volumes of collections of potted biographies of Supreme Soviet deputies entitled *Deputaty Verkhovnogo Soveta SSSR* ...

20. There is some ambiguity about Ryzhkov's registered nationality. Some earlier sources cite him as Ukrainian, but more recent ones as Russian.

21. In 1981 there were two members (Gromyko and Gorbachev) with tertiary qualifications in both the social sciences — economics and law, respectively — and agriculture, while Suslov also graduated in economics, Pel'she evidently in history, and Chernenko in education.

22. See Frederic J. Fleron, 'Representation of Career Types in the Soviet Political Leadership', in R. Barry Farrell (ed.), *Political Leadership in the USSR and Eastern Europe* (Chicago: Aldine, 1970).

23. Kosygin did spend a few months as a local party official in the purge period, but this was a mere hiccup in his career in industrial administration. Ustinov (died 1984) also spent most of his life in industrial management, but like Ryzhkov was 'co-opted' from the Council of Ministers to serve some years as CC Secretary.

24. *Pravda*, 27 February 1986, p. 2.

25. Ibid., 28 February 1986, p. 4.

26. See ibid., 1 March 1986, pp. 2, 3.

27. Ibid., 2 March 1986, p. 3.

28. Ibid., p. 2.

29. Ibid., 1 March 1986, p. 8.

30. Ibid., p. 3.

31. Ibid., 27 February 1986, p. 7.

32. See ibid., 27 February 1986, p. 5, speech of President of the Academy of Sciences Aleksandrov, and 1 March 1986, p. 7, speech of Omsk First Secretary Maniakin.

33. Ibid., 2 March 1986, p. 5. The speaker L. A. Kulidzhanov, First Secretary of the Cinema Workers' Union, had been saying how he suffered a pang of regret when Mikhail Sergeevich's report came to an end and he left the rostrum.

34. Ibid., 3 March 1986, p. 2.

35. Ibid., p. 3.

36. Ibid., 28 February 1986, p. 4.

2

The Programmatic Documents of the 27th Congress

Graeme Gill

The 27th Congress of the CPSU introduced revised versions of the party's two major programmatic documents, the Party Program and Rules. The documents replace those introduced at the 22nd Congress in 1961, and in the case of the Rules partially amended in 1966 and 1971, and therefore purely in terms of the effluxion of time were well overdue.

The new Program has been some five years in the coming. At the 26th Congress in 1981, Leonid Brezhnev declared that although the existing Program (adopted in 1961) 'correctly mirrors the laws of social development', it was now outdated in various respects and was in need of revision.[1] Nothing more was heard of this until the June 1983 Central Committee Plenum when Iurii Andropov repeated the phrase cited above and also declared that the Program was, in some respects, divorced from reality, ran ahead of developments and was too detailed. It needed to be in tune with the principles of developed socialism and would accordingly be revised at the forthcoming congress.[2] Andropov's successor, Konstantin Chernenko, reaffirmed this timetable and the thrust of Andropov's comments; in a meeting of the commission to draft the new Program in April 1984, he declared that the Program should provide an 'objective and realistic picture' of society under developed socialism and its 'gradual advance to communism'.[3] But despite the obvious interest that Chernenko showed in the Progam, the final drafting was completed under his successor, Mikhail Gorbachev.[4] The draft was published in *Pravda* on 26 October[5] and was subject to public discussion prior to adoption in its final form at the congress.[6]

It may be that there were significant differences over the draft among those taking a direct and immediate interest in its content. Although four and a half years from the announcement of the need for revisions until the appearance of the draft may appear to be a long time, such a document could only be ratified by a congress and so, unless an extraordinary congress was convened specifically for this purpose, the new document had to fit into the regular five yearly cycle. Moreover, given the close personal involvement and interest a General Secretary would have in the content of a new Program, the three changes of party leader during this period are likely to have had a significant effect on the drafting process. Nevertheless, the fact that the draft did not appear until the end of the report and election meetings for the primary party organisations that preceded the congress, thereby denying rank-and-file party members an obvious forum in which to discuss the new provisions, suggests that there may have been a delay caused by unforeseen circumstances.

Successive party leaders' discussions of the question of the party Program focused on the need for realism and an objective appraisal of the party's achievements and the future course of development. The over-optimistic expectations and rhetoric of the Khrushchev period, the presentation of excessive detail and the imposition of a timetable for the achievement of communism were all criticised.[7] The Program that has been adopted by the congress, for the most part, reflects these criticisms of the earlier document. The new Program is shorter and much less detailed than its predecessor.[8] In its tone it is sober and down-to-earth, with the confident outlook of its Khrushchevian predecessor much more subdued. This does not mean that the ideas which were such an important part of the earlier Program are lacking. The document still speaks of the advance into communism and the improvement in the human condition that this will bring; despite evident downgrading during the Brezhnev period, 'socialist self-administration' and the disappearance of the state as a separate political entity still find a place in the Program. But these are presented as coming about through 'the country's accelerated socio-economic development', through the perfection of the existing structure, through the improvement of what exists rather than through the creation of something completely new. The utopian hopes and soaring aspirations characteristic of the earlier Programs[9] have been displaced by the pedestrian chores of economic and social management. This is the program of the economic manager rather than the visonary, perhaps the careful reformer rather than the revolutionary, the pragmatist rather than the idealist. So, although the traditional communist ideals are present in the Program, it is not these which give it its tenor, but a modesty of outlook and expectation that jars sharply compared with the ethos of the Khrushchev Program of 1961.

The more modest outlook of this document is not surprising. The exaggerated hopes and impractical dreams of the Khrushchev era had long been recognised in both the policy and doctrinal spheres, with the whole tenor of Soviet development since 1964 reflecting a move away from the enthusiasm of that period. This was reflected in the ideological sphere by the generation of the concept 'developed socialism'. Khrushchev's Program had promised the achievement of communism by the 1980s, a development which presupposed the direct transition of Soviet society into the communist phase. The unreality of this timetable soon became clear to all, with the result that during the Brezhnev period, a new stage of development was ushered in, developed socialism. The introduction of this 'qualitatively new historic stage of development'[10] was significant in that it lengthened the timetable for the transition of Soviet society, which formally had achieved socialism in 1936, into communism. Subsequent leaders have been at pains to emphasise that this stage would not be short: Andropov declared that the Soviet Union was only at the beginning of this long historical stage,[11] Chernenko argued that developed socialism would 'comprise an entire historical epoch' and would 'have its own specific stages',[12] and Gorbachev referred to it as an 'historically protracted stage'.[13] While the new Program presents developed socialism as merely one part of the phase of socialism, which is itself seen as merely the preliminary phase of the single communist formation, simply by introducing this concept the Program rejects both the timetable and the theoretical conception of the nature of the transition espoused by Khrushchev. With the economic slowdown experienced by the Soviet Union in the late 1970s–early 1980s and with the economic factor of such importance in the process of transition, added to the political problems in meeting such a commitment, a postponement of the planned achievement of communism in this Program was inevitable.

However, this postponement created a problem. Given that

the Soviet Union had already achieved socialism, and given that, according to the Program, socialism and communism are 'two consecutive phases of one communist formation' with 'no distinct dividing line between them', how was this postponement to be handled ideologically? The answer had been suggested by Chernenko in terms of the generation of stages within developed socialism. The 1986 Program links earlier Programs with specific phases of Soviet development: the first with the overthrow of capitalism, the second with the building of socialism and the third with the building of communism and the entry of the society to the stage of developed socialism. The new Program is not presented as a fourth Program, but as an up-dated and revised version of the third. It is thus meant to relate not to a new phase of development of Soviet society, but to 'a qualitatively new stage of Soviet society', which appears to constitute a stage within developed socialism. In the draft Program this stage was called 'integral socialism', but in the adopted version this name was omitted, although discussion of the stage remained, perhaps reflecting the existence of some disagreement within ideological circles about the nature and status of this stage and its relationship with developed socialism.

If the new Program does not herald entry to a new phase in the society's historical development and if it is to be concerned with the perfection of a socialism which already exists in the Soviet Union, a proposition which implies tinkering rather than major renovation, it may be wondered why a new version of the Program was considered necessary. The force of this question is confirmed by the fact that the 1986 Program, in speaking of its predecessor, affirms 'the correctness of its main theoretical and political propositions'. The answer provided by the Program is that the 'accumulated experience and scientific understanding' of both internal and external developments has enabled the party 'to define more accurately and concretely the prospects for Soviet society's development, the ways and means of attaining the ultimate goal — communism, and the tasks of international policy in new historical conditions'. This is a thinly-veiled admission of the charges of impracticality and unreality levelled at the 1961 Program by the earlier leaders cited above and reflects the attempt to jettison the more extreme and embarrassing aspects of the Khrushchev document. Without denying the basic thrust of the earlier Program the current document, through omission and emphasis, rejects many of the earlier commitments and targets which have been found impossible to fulfil.

The transition to communism is now seen to be a much more complex and multi-faceted phenomenon. Although the Program still expresses confidence in the inevitability of humanity's advance to communism, this advance is characterised 'by unevenness, complexity and contradictoriness'. This is reflected in the disinclination of the new Program to follow the 1961 document in specifying a date at which full communism would be achieved in the Soviet Union. This does not, however, mean that the Program contains no target dates for the achievement of specific goals. The year 2000 is designated to be the date by which the following are to be achieved: the doubling and fundamental and qualitative renewal of the country's production potential, an increase in labour productivity of some 130–50 per cent, the doubling of resources channelled into meeting popular requirements, and the provision of their own living quarters for 'practically every Soviet family'. The achievement of these goals is highly unlikely unless there is substantial improvement in Soviet economic performance[14] and some restructuring of the Soviet economy. The Program recognises this.

Like its predecessor, the Program directs the blame for recent problems and inability to meet targets upon past leaderships. While the party is seen as having done much to eliminate the consequences of the 'personality cult' and, in an innovation in this Program (and in the Rules), 'errors of a subjectivist, voluntaristic nature', it has now to overcome the problems associated with the more recent past. According to the Program,

along with undeniable successes, the 1970s and early 1980s saw certain unfavourable trends and difficulties in the country's development. To a great extent these were due to failure to assess promptly and appropriately changes in the economic situation and the need for profound transformations in all spheres of life, and to a lack of persistence in carrying them out. This prevented fuller use of the potentialities and the advantages of the socialist system and impeding onward movement.

The use of the code words for Stalin ('personality cult') and Khrushchev ('subjectivist' and 'voluntaristic') enabled the

Program to distance the current leadership from the short-comings of these two leaders, while the pointed criticism of the 1970s and early 1980s signalled an attempt to make a radical break with the legacy of the Brezhnev administration. The means whereby this is to be brought about is the concept of acceleration (*uskorenie*).

Breaking out of the sense of drift and lethargy that are seen to have characterised the last years of the Brezhnev era through this process of acceleration of socio-economic development also constitutes a strengthening of the process of transition from socialism to communism. In this context, the Program provides an outline of the main features of socialist and communist societies. At the heart of a socialist society is the principle 'everything for the sake of man, everything for the benefit of man'. The society itself is characterised by the following ten features:

1. 'the means of production are in the hands of the people', and exploitation, social oppression, rule by a privileged minority and mass poverty and illiteracy are eliminated;
2. there is the widest scope for 'dynamic and planned development' of the productive forces, and scientific and technological progress contribute to popular well-being rather than unemployment;
3. the principle 'from each according to his ability, to each according to his work' is reflected in the existence of an equal right to work plus fair remuneration for it; in addition, all enjoy such social benefits as free medical service and education and housing at minimal rental;
4. the unshakeable alliance of the working class, collective farmers and intelligentsia prevails, there is real sexual equality, the future of the young generation is assured, and 'veterans of labour' have guaranteed social security;
5. there is real equality, friendship and brotherhood among all nationalities;
6. genuine democracy, which is power exercised for and by the people, exists and is developing further, and there is equal and increasingly broad citizen participation in the management of production and public and state affairs;
7. the ideas of freedom, human rights and individual dignity have real meaning, the unity of rights and duties is ensured, and uniform laws, moral norms and a single discipline apply

to all, creating favourable conditions for the all-round development of the personality;

8. truly humanist Marxist-Leninist ideology is dominant, the people have access to all sources of knowledge, and an advanced socialist culture exists which takes in all that is best in world culture;

9. at the basis of the socialist way of life are social justice, collectivism and comradely mutual assistance; this way of life 'gives working people confidence in the future, elevates them spiritually and morally as creators of new social relations and of their own destiny';

10. in the international sphere, the socialist society's deeds and intentions 'are directed towards supporting the people's striving for independence and social progress, and are subordinated to the main task of preserving and consolidating peace'.

As a description of Soviet society, this list is clearly deficient. However, as a set of principles, it is important for its normative rather than its descriptive qualities. If communism is to be achieved through the perfection of socialism, it is through the enhancement of these principles that that aim will be met.

The Program also provides an indication of what the future communist society will be like, although it adds that the party 'does not attempt to foresee in detail the features of full communism'. The picture presented by the Program is the same as that outlined in 1961:

Communism is a classless social system with one form of public ownership of the means of production and full social equality of all members of society; under it, the all-round development of people will be accompanied by the growth of the productive forces through the continuous progress of science and technology; all the springs of social wealth will flow more abundantly, and the great principle 'from each according to his ability, to each according to his needs' will be implemented. Communism is a highly organised society of free, socially conscious working people, a society in which public self-administration will be established, a society in which labour for the good of society will become the prime vital requirement of everyone, a necessity recognised by one and all, and the ability of each person will be employed to the greatest benefit of the people.[15]

Modern technology will enable productive activity to satisfy the 'reasonable requirements' of both individual and society. The elimination of the division of labour will make the society 'socially homogeneous'. Furthermore, 'with the maturation of the necessary socio-economic and ideological pre-conditions and the involvement of all citizens in administrative . . . [and] given appropriate international conditions . . . the need for the state as a special political institution will gradually disappear'. The activity of state bodies will become non-political in nature and their functions will be carried out by the public. The high levels of consciousness, discipline and self-discipline that accompany this mean that the desired rules of behaviour become internalised by all.

The key to the advancement toward this sort of society is the acceleration of socio-economic development. This is defined as the qualitative transformation of all aspects of life in Soviet society:

a radical renewal of its material and technical foundation on the basis of the scientific and technological revolution; perfection of social relations, above all economic; profound changes in the content and nature of labour and in people's material and cultural conditions; and invigoration of the entire system of political, social and ideological institutions.

It is to involve the shift from extensive to intensive economic development which in turn requires 'serious structural changes in the economy' and an improvement in productive relations. The Program gives little clear indication of the 'serious structural changes' being contemplated; the section of the Program headed 'Structural Reorganisation of Social Production' does not discuss any real organisational change. It talks about the need for increased mechanisation, automation[16] and flexibility[17] in the economy and the importance of heavy industry, particularly machine building. In agriculture, it calls for the transfer to an industrial basis and, in a development which reverses the emphasis of the 1961 Program, acknowledges the continuing role of the private plots in satisfying the country's food needs. The section also contains a call for increased production of consumer goods, improvement in the production infrastructure (mainly power and transport) and in construction standards, and for some geographical decentralisation of production forces.

47

Small- and medium-sized towns and workers' settlements are pinpointed as desirable locations for the establishment of specialised production facilities, while a generalised commitment is made to the accelerated development of productive forces in Siberia and the Far East.

There is greater suggestion of structural change in the discussion of the second pillar of economic strategy, the improvement of relations of production. Although the discussion here is vague, it does refer to the need for a 'dynamic correlation between demand and supply', increased use of 'commodity-money relations', the expansion of wholesale trade and of direct ties and contracts between consumer enterprises and product manufacturers, and increased influence by the consumer on product quality and standards. Such developments would be consistent with a move towards increased marketisation, but this is unlikely; the Program's failure to mention demand as a factor influencing price levels[18] alone is suggestive of this. So too is the failure, despite the positive reference to the private plots, to foreshadow any expansion of private ownership in the production sphere.[19] The measures specified above would also be consistent with the type of strategy that has been reflected in Gorbachev's speeches over the year prior to the congress and which is repeated in the Program (where it is directly associated with the principle of democratic centralism): an increase in the efficiency of planning as an instrument for the conduct of economic policy alongside a broadening of the rights and economic autonomy of production associations and enterprises and the expansion of their responsibility for the results of their production. Enterprises are to shift to full-scale cost accounting and the number of indices set at higher levels is to be reduced. Within the enterprises there is to be greater responsibility for decisions about the use of funds, while the shop floor workers are to play an increased part in management through the labour collectives. It is this sort of tinkering, involving a strengthening of central planning and local responsibility, even if the precise contours remain unclear, which seems to be on the agenda suggested by the Program.

The discussion of social policy is couched in the framework of acceleration and the transition to communism. Social policy is seen as 'a powerful means of accelerating the country's development, heightening the labour and socio-political activity of the masses, moulding the new man and affirming the socialist way

48

of life, and as a major factor of political stability in society'. The party's social policy is to be concerned with constant improvement in the living and working conditions of the people and with the fuller implementation of the principles of social justice. Echoing its predecessor, the Program speaks of the need for conditions which will enable 'a harmoniously developed, spiritually rich individual' fully to apply his or her abilities, gifts and talents in the interests of society as a whole. What is required is a 'qualitatively new dimension' of the people's wellbeing. The means whereby this new dimension is to come about are declared to be an improvement in working conditions, continuing supplies of high-quality consumer goods,[20] improved public health, a strengthened role for the family and improved status of mothers,[21] increased attention to the needs of the young, the disabled, labour and war veterans, the aged and war widows, and natural conservation. This is a somewhat incongruous list, but suggests attention to minimal economic conditions and some quality-of-life issues as major foci of social policy.

But social policy is also concerned with the divisions in society and their elimination. The Program confidently asserts that the divisions between different classes and among different national groups are disappearing, but its discussion of the future development of these two social categories involves an interesting difference. In discussing the differences between social classes (which are seen specifically in terms of differences between agricultural and industrial work, living conditions in rural and urban areas, and physical and mental work)[22] the Program declares that when communism is achieved, these differences will be completely eliminated, thereby creating a society without classes. Until then, the party will be sensitive to the interests of each class and social group in the policies it implements. Turning to national differences, the Program asserts that 'in the long-term historical perspective . . . [there will be] . . . complete unity of the nations'; individual national cultures are seen as drawing together a Soviet culture.[23] The Program does not, however, argue that the differences among national groups will ever fully disappear, thereby leaving open the possibility that some national differences will remain even after communism has been achieved. It is instructive in this regard that the term used in the Program is unity (*edinstvo*), not merging (*sliianie*). The Program also refers to a 'new social and international community — the Soviet people', and it eliminates the implication of Russian leadership over the other nationalities that was present in the 1961 document. The implication is that Soviet development is a partnership in which all national groups share, with none occupying a pre-eminent position.

The process of socio-economic acceleration requires continuing political guidance. The discussion of the political system in the 1986 Program differs substantially from that of 1961. In the earlier document, the focus was principally upon the state and the soviets; in 1986 it is overwhelmingly on the party and its role. The discussion of the state, still formally acknowledged as 'an all-people's socialist state',[24] and still expected to lose all of its functions to the public once communism has been achieved, is highly abbreviated and is couched largely in terms of the party's role. The party, which is 'the living embodiment of the fusion of scientific socialism with the working class movement', is projected as 'the nucleus of the political system'; it plays the leading role in Soviet society and that role will expand. The party's tasks are declared to be five-fold:

1. solution of the tasks of perfecting socialism and accelerating socio-economic development;
2. strengthening of democracy and socialist self-administration;
3. the further creative development of Marxism-Leninism and its application to current tasks;
4. enhancing the cohesion of the socialist countries and consolidating the unity of the international communist, working class and national liberation movements in opposition to bourgeois ideology, revisionism, dogmatism, reformism and sectarianism;
5. the conduct of foreign policy in the face of imperialist aggressiveness and the exertion of efforts to ensure that peace prevails.

Repeating the sentiment of the 1977 USSR Constitution, the Program declares that the party must act within the framework of that constitution. In general, it 'directs and co-ordinates the work of state and public organisations[25] and sees to it that each of them discharges its functions in full'. The party must ensure that there is no duplication between itself and these other organisations and it must continually concern itself with how they function in practice. It has a particular brief to encourage democratisation through an expansion of socialist self-administration and the exercise of socio-economic, political and personal rights and freedoms. Its role in channelling scientific investigation and development into socially useful areas,[26] in the promotion of economic development (particularly at the enterprise level), and in leadership of the Armed Forces all appear as significant aspects of the party's work. It is also to play a major part in the cultural sphere. Important here is the inculcation of a scientific world outlook based on Marxism-Leninism and a collectivist morality, which would provide a basis for combating religious prejudice,[27] 'manifestations of alien ideology and morals and all negative phenomena', such as procrastination, 'violations of labour discipline, embezzlement and bribery, profiteering and parasitism, drunkenness and hooliganism, private owner psychology and money-grubbing, toadyism and servility'. Education,[28] the media,[29] literature and art[30] must all contribute to this under party leadership.

As the party's leadership role expands, higher standards of performance are expected of party organs. They must exercise effective leadership, 'eliminate manifestations of formalism and red tape, bureaucratic and other distortions in the work of the administrative apparatus . . . intensify supervision over the implementation of party decisions and economic plans . . . strengthen state and labour discipline and order, and . . . raise organisational standards'. Such demands place a premium upon party personnel. The Program emphasises the need for high-quality personnel and for the promotion of those with talent and the right political, practical and moral qualities to positions of responsibility. Only if reliable people fill responsible positions can the party's leadership role be carried out effectively.

The demands on the party are also reflected in the discussion of the nature of leadership. By sketching the qualities desired in a leader, the Program effectively provides a profile of the desired model of a party leader. He (and following the Program's call for the promotion of more women) or she should demonstrate 'responsiveness to new ideas, readiness to take responsibility upon oneself, desire to learn to work better, an ability to understand the political meaning of economic management and of work with people, high demands on oneself and others'. This profile of the innovative, hard-working, demanding leader is consistent with both the criticism made of the Brezhnev period earlier in the Program and the stance adopted by Gorbachev since he was elected General Secretary in March 1985. Consistent with this, too, is the Program's emphasis upon accountability; all party members are to be made more responsible for their work and for the maintenance of discipline. In the words of the Program, 'not one party organisation, not one worker must remain outside supervision' (*kontrol'*). Party members are to be judged on the basis of how they carry out their responsibilities, of how they conduct the matters assigned to them. Indeed, in an interesting juxtaposition, the Program declares that party membership does not involve privileges but a higher level of responsibility.

Beside this emphasis upon the personal responsibility of party members, the Program also emphasises the need for the operation of the collective principle in all areas of party life. This is consistent with the more general emphasis upon the democratisation of the political system as a whole. Collectivism, which is directly associated with overcoming the shortcomings of the earlier party leaderships noted above, involves enhancement of the 'role and significance of party meetings, plena, conferences, congresses, party committees and bureau as collective bodies of leadership' and 'the free and businesslike discussion in the party of questions relating to its policy and practical activity'. Furthermore, it is associated with the deepening of inner-party democracy, observance of Leninist norms of party life, the promotion of criticism and self-criticism, and greater openness and publicity in party work. But balancing this emphasis upon collectivism and democracy is the continued concern for the strengthening of party discipline. The source of the party's strength and invincibility is declared to be the ideological and organisational cohesion of its ranks; its monolithic unity leaves no room for fractionalism or groupism. The long-established formula of democratic centralism formally remains the key organisational principle of the party.

The Program's handling of the party, officially described as a 'party of all the people',[31] thus reflects an institution which is to play a leading role in all spheres of life and which must, therefore, be attuned to its responsibilities and be able to carry them out. It is projected as an efficient organisation which will lead the society into its communist future. But at the same time it is an organisation that is solicitous for the welfare of the Soviet people. Caring but steadfast — is the image that is projected.

The achievement of communism, through a process of

accelerated socio-economic development, must take place within an international setting, and the Program accordingly devotes some attention to this context. The chief characteristic of the international situation remains the hostility of international imperialism, which, although past its peak and subject to serious contradictions,[32] remains a dangerous and implacable enemy. Although the Program sees it as moribund and decaying, unlike in 1961, the document does not suggest the imminent collapse of capitalism.[33] The USA is explicitly identified as 'the citadel of international reaction' and, as a result of its claims to world domination, the source of the main threat of war. The Program acknowledges that there would be no winners or losers in such a war, but that 'world civilisation would perish'. As a result, the Program emphasises the need for peace, for 'peaceful coexistence of states with different social systems',[34] and for an end to the arms race. Some quite specific proposals are made for moving towards this end.[35] In an interesting shift from the 1961 Program, disarmament and arms control are now seen as the principal guarantee against war; in 1961 the strengthening of the socialist bloc was the chief guarantee. Once again, the discussion is couched briefly in terms of the party's role in achieving these aims, thereby projecting it, rather than the state, as a major entity on the international stage.

But of course the Soviet Union is not alone in the hostile international environment. It is supported by 'the world socialist system', 'the socialist community' and the international working class and communist movement. The Program's discussion of bloc relations emphasises the need for tighter unity and integration among individual bloc members. It notes their 'common fundamental interests and aims', the 'extensive multifaceted cooperation' and the need to 'co-ordinate their actions in international affairs'. Furthermore, the higher the levels of development of the states, 'the richer and deeper' will be their co-operation and 'the more organic the process of their drawing together'. The Program explicitly calls for a 'further deepening of socialist economic integration as the material foundation for a drawing closer together of the socialist countries'. But the Program acknowledges that different levels of economic and political development, historical and cultural traditions and contemporary conditions can cause contradictions and difficulties between members. Referring to the 'organic interconnection' between national and international interests (a vague hint of the primacy of the latter over the former for other bloc members) the Program calls on bloc members to draw closer together in order to overcome any possible differences that may arise.

Turning to the international working class and communist movement, the Program specifically acknowledges the diversity of national paths and the way in which communists must take into account the specific conditions of their own situations and work out their own strategies and policies for the achievement of communism. This means that revolution (like counter-revolution) cannot be exported; it must come from within. However, the Program does not, like that of 1961, make explicit provision for the peaceful transfer of power from bourgeoisie to proletariat, the so-called parliamentary road to socialism. In acknowledging the possibility of different national paths, the Program recognises the possibility of disagreements occurring within the international movement. These should be resolved through comradely discussion. Should such disagreements concern matters of principle, 'the revolutionary essence of Marxism-Leninism, the substance and role of real socialism', the CPSU will firmly defend the position of principle.[36] Thus, while the Program recognises scope for differences within the international movement, it nevertheless asserts the principle of Soviet ideological hegemony as a whole and, with regard to the socialist bloc, by emphasising integration and unity, hints at organisational hegemony as well. Neither Yugoslavia, which was criticised in the 1961 Program, nor China, with which the USSR has been in open dispute for much of the past two and a half decades, are criticised in the Program.

The most important force opposing imperialism remains the working class which, being constantly replenished by highly qualified workers is growing stronger and waging a vigorous struggle against capitalism. The vanguard of the working-class movement is the international communist movement, while one of the major components of the world revolutionary process is the struggle of the former colonies to consolidate their independence and achieve social progress.[37] This is the only context within which the Program discusses the Third World, thereby seeing it in terms of the general East-West relationship rather than as an entity with its own intrinsic importance. Thus the view the Program offers of the relationship between reactionary imperialist forces and the progressive socialist forces supported by the broader world revolutionary movement is consistent with the long-standing official Soviet perception and with the picture presented in the 1961 Program.[38]

As well as the party Program, the congress adopted a revised version of the party Rules. The new Rules include a number of minor changes of party structure, while some of the other amendments reflect themes addressed in the Program and discussed above. Important in this regard is the increased emphasis given to the party's role in economic development. This is most clearly reflected in the discussion of the responsibilities of party organs at all levels, especially the primary party organisations, and the tasks of individual members. Also significant is the increased emphasis upon the need for high-quality performance by party organs and members and on the responsibility that they bear for their work. This is reflected in the call for higher party bodies to be kept regularly informed about the situation at lower levels and about the work of subordinate party organisations, and in the instruction that party organs must inform their organisations about any criticisms that are made of their performance. This is clearly an effort to overcome the practice of covering up mistakes which has been so common throughout the party's history. So too is the emphasis upon the openness of party operations, including the provision for open elections for some offices in small party organs[39] and the right of non-members to participate in the discussion about the entry of potential members to the party. This latter provision, along with the raising of the minimum entry age to 25, except for Komsomol members, also reflects concern to improve the quality of new party recruits.[40]

Two other changes to the Rules merit attention. Both have occurred in long-standing sections of the Rules. Since 1934 the formula 'democratic centralism' has consisted of four elements.[41] In the new Rules, the four principles of this formula have been joined by a new one. This emphasises the collectivity of party leadership at all levels along with the personal responsibility that each party member bears for the fulfilment of party assignments. The second section in which a significant change has occurred dates back to 1927 and relates to the grounds upon which party-wide discussion of an issue can take place. The original three grounds[42] have now been reduced to two by the omission of the provision which allowed such a discussion to resolve a difference of opinion within the Central Committee. The Rules have also omitted the statement that discussion was 'the inalienable right of a party member'. Both of these changes[43] were made between the publication of the draft Rules and the adoption of the final version at the congress.

What can one conclude about the programmatic documents adopted at the congress? Despite the important changes that have occurred in these documents compared with their immediate predecessors, especially in terms of the lowering of exaggerated expectations and extravagant claims, both possess strong continuities with those they follow. Many parts are repeated verbatim, others project essentially the same position but are couched in different language, while others are phrased in more general terms but not necessarily inconsistent with the former positions. No ideological innovations appear in either document, the introduction of developed socialism merely recognising the status that concept had achieved during the 1970s. Nor is much light shed on the future policy or development plans of the Soviet leaders. Apart from the overwhelming impression that the party is to play a much more extensive role than it has, the documents really add nothing to our understanding of possible future reform than could be gleaned from Gorbachev's speeches. In this respect, the Program in particular is immensely flexible, a quality which, in the eyes of party leaders, would doubtless have a high priority.

NOTES

1. *S''ezd kommunisticheskoi partii Sovetskogo Soiuza 23 fevralia–3 marta 1981 goda. Stenograficheskii otchet* (Moscow, 1981), vol. 1, pp. 97–8.

2. *Pravda*, 16 June 1983.

3. *Pravda*, 11 April 1984.

4. The Politburo meeting of 29 June 1985 discussed the Program and its content and appointed Gorbachev chairman of the drafting commission (*Pravda*, 30 June 1985). Other members of the drafting commission were G. M. Markov (first secretary of the board of the Union of Writers of the USSR), S. A. Shalaev (chairman of the All-Union Central Council of Trade Unions) and A. V. Vlasov (then first secretary of Rostov *obkom*), (*Pravda*, 15 October 1985).

5. The draft Rules were published at the same time. They were also published in *Partiinaia zhizn'*, No. 22–3, 1985, and *Kommunist*, No. 16, 1985.

6. *Pravda*, 7 March 1986. According to Gorbachev, over six million letters were received during the public discussion of the Program (*Pravda*, 26 February 1986). Discussion of the Program and its main

themes was also a major concern in the post-congress period. In particular, see the important series of five articles under the title 'Krupneishee dostizhenie sovremennoi marksistsko-leninsko mysli', *Kommunist*, Nos. 6–10, 1986.

7. For example, *Pravda*, 16 June 1983, *Kommunist*, No. 9, 1983, p. 21, and No. 7, 1984, pp. 4–8.

8. The structure of the 1986 Program differs from that of 1961. The earlier document had a brief introduction and two sections, the first concerned with placing the party and its tasks in the broad historical and geo-political context and the second with the party's domestic tasks. The latter section was related to 'Building a Communist Society'. The 1986 Program also has an introduction and sections devoted to these areas, although the second is now directed towards the party's tasks in 'perfecting socialism and making a gradual transition to communism'. There are also two other sections, relating to the party's tasks on the international scene and its role in Soviet society. Both of these had been subsumed within the broader sections of the earlier document.

9. There were three earlier programs, adopted at the 2nd Congress in 1903, the 8th in 1919 and the 22nd in 1961.

10. For discussion, see Alfred B. Evans, Jnr, 'Developed Socialism in Soviet Ideology', *Soviet Studies*, vol. xxix, no. 3 (July 1977), pp. 409–8, and 'The Decline of Developed Socialism? Some Trends in Recent Soviet Ideology', *Soviet Studies*, vol. xxxviii, no. 1 (January 1986), pp. 1–23. The decline of 'developed socialism' as a major organising principle is reflected in the lack of attention devoted to it in the post-congress discussion.

11. *Kommunist*, No. 3, 1983, p. 20.

12. *Kommunist*, No. 18, 1984, p. 8.

13. *Pravda*, 11 December 1984.

14. The annual growth rate required would be 4.7 per cent compared with a rate of 3.6 per cent in 1981–4. David Dyker, 'The New Party Program and the Future of the Soviet Economy', *Radio Liberty*, RL 363/85, 4 November 1985, p. 2.

15. Jan F. Triska (ed.), *Soviet Communism: Programs and Rules* (San Francisco: Chandler Publishing Co., 1962), p. 68.

16. The Program refers to the widespread use of electrification, chemicalisation, robotisation, computerisation and biotechnology.

17. In an immediate sense, this has been seen in terms of investment policy and the need to direct funds into those sectors of the economy which are 'essential for the acceleration of scientific and technological progress'. Emphasis has also been placed on the need to concentrate on the re-equipment and reconstruction of existing concerns rather than new projects.

18. Price formation must improve and price levels must reflect, *inter alia*, the quality of products and services. Rejection of market forces is more explicit in the discussion following the congress where it is declared that economic change will take place within the bounds of scientific socialism with no concessions to 'market socialism', anarcho-syndicalism or private enterprise (*Kommunist*, No. 7, 1986, p. 12).

19. The Program confirms the basis of public ownership in the

economy, in the process foreshadowing the drawing together in the agricultural sphere of collective-co-operative property and all-people's property. This refers to the future replacement of collective farms by state farms. The discussion of public ownership also includes a reference to 'the constitutional right of citizens to personal property'. This is an interesting innovation in 1986, but such personal property does not include, following Soviet usage, major productive forces.

20. This includes recognition of the continued role of the *kolkhoz* market.

21. The provisions relating to the role of the family include the parents' responsibility for their children's education and the children's responsibility for the welfare of elderly parents. The attribution of such responsibilities may have implications for the range of the state's social welfare obligations.

22. In an earlier part of the Program, there is discussion about the way in which social welfare funds may be used to improve services to the population (specifically, health, education and social security) which would assist 'in reducing the differences that are objectively inevitable under socialism in the material status of citizens, families and social groups, in evening out socio-economic and cultural conditions for the upbringing of children and in helping radically to improve the well-being of low income groups of the population'. This explicit recognition of the continuing existence of socio-economic inequality is consistent with the justification of wage differentials contained in the Program's linking of payment with 'the amount and quality of work and . . . the conditions and results of work'.

23. The handling of the language issue is interesting in this regard. The Program declares that all citizens have an equal right to use their native languages, the free development of which is to be ensured. However, it also points out that 'learning the Russian language, which has been voluntarily adopted by the Soviet people as a medium of communication between different nationalities, beside the language of one's own nationality, broadens one's access to the achievements of science and technology, of fatherland (*otechestvennoi*) and world culture'.

24. This is the term that replaced 'dictatorship of the proletariat' in the 1961 Program.

25. The organisations listed are the Soviet state, trade unions, Komsomol, co-operatives and other public organisations.

26. This instrumental approach to science is clearly reflected in the discussion of social science, which is mentioned for the first time in a party Program in 1986. This must 'provide scientific analysis of the objective contradictions in socialist society, work out sound recommendations on how to overcome them, and make dependable economic and social forecasts'.

27. The Program calls for 'strict observance of the constitutional guarantees of freedom of conscience', but condemns 'any attempts to use religion to the detriment of society and the individual'.

28. This must foster patriotism and internationalism, combining love for the Soviet Union and class solidarity with the international working people.

29. The media are called upon to be more forthright and interesting than they have been.

30. They are meant to serve the cause of communism and contribute to the individual's ideological development and moral education.

31. Although the party is described in this way, it is also declared to have remained in its class essence and ideology, a party of the working class.

32. The deepening crisis of capitalism is viewed in classical Marxist-Leninist terms and the description of it broadly follows that given in 1961, but in significantly less detail.

33. Nor is there the sort of optimism reflected in the following extract from the 1961 Program: 'The socialist world is expanding; the capitalist world is shrinking. Socialism will inevitably succeed capitalism everywhere. Such is the objective law of social development. Imperialism is powerless to check the irresistible process of emancipation'. Triska, *Soviet Communism*, p. 25. The closest the Program comes to this is the declaration that imperialism is 'parasitical, decaying and moribund capitalism, the eve of socialist revolution'.

34. Peaceful coexistence is defined as 'an international order under which good neighbourliness and co-operation rather than armed force prevail, and broad exchanges of the achievements of science and technology and cultural values are carried out for the good of all nations'. Compare this with the more extensive tratment of 1971. Ibid., pp. 65–6. Later in the Program a more extensive conception is given, one which combines the 1961 view with that in Article 29 of the 1977 state constitution.

35. The Program lists five main goals and directions of the party's international policy: 1) the establishment of international conditions facilitating the perfection of socialism and the achievement of communism in the USSR; removal of the threat of war; universal security and disarmament; 2) strengthening and expansion of Soviet co-operation with fraternal socialist countries and the consolidation and progress of the world socialist system; 3) development of relations of equality and friendship with newly-free countries; 4) maintenance and development of relations with capitalist states on the basis of peaceful coexistence and businesslike, mutually beneficial co-operation; 5) internationalist solidarity with communist and revolutionary democratic parties, with the international working class and with the national liberation struggles of the peoples. Proposals outlined in the Program aimed at achieving 'general and complete disarmament under strict and comprehensive international control' repeat positions already publicly announced by Gorbachev in the twelve months prior to the congress: 1) restriction and narrowing of the sphere of military preparations, more particularly the exclusion of military rivalry and weapons from space, non-proliferation of nuclear weapons, and the creation of zones free from weapons of mass destruction; 2) movement toward the complete elimination of nuclear weapons, including an end to their testing and production, renunciation of first use, and freezing, reduction and destruction of stockpiles; the Soviet Union is declared to be willing to limit or ban all weapons on a reciprocal basis with effective means of verification;

3) an end to the production of all types of weapons of mass destruction, their elimination, and a ban on new ones; 4) reductions in armed forces, conventional weapons and military spending; 5) freeze on and reduction in troops and armaments in the most explosive parts of the world, dismantling of foreign bases, and measures to build up mutual trust and lessen the risk of conflict. The Program also calls for the simultaneous dissolution of NATO and WTO, recognition of the post-war 'territorial and political realities' in Europe, and for 'zones of peace and good neighbourliness' in Asia, Africa, Latin America and the Pacific and Indian Oceans. This is by far the most detailed section of the Program.

36. In the draft it was declared that the party would wage a determined struggle against 'opportunism and reformism, dogmatism and sectarianism'. In the post-congress discussion, the party's relationship with other elements of the international working-class movement is declared not to be based upon a monopoly of truth possessed by any one party. *Kommunist*, No. 10, 1986, p. 50.

37. Passing reference is also made to the anti-war movements.

38. One omission compared with 1961 is that the Program does not include a section on the need to combat bourgeois and reformist ideology. This was a vehicle for attacks on right-wing socialists and social democrats in 1961.

39. This applies to party secretaries, deputy secretaries, party group organisers and delegates to district (*raion*) and city party conferences (Article 24).

40. It is interesting in this context that the 1986 Rules should exclude the moral code of the communist, which had been an important addition to the Rules in 1961.

41. These are the election of all leading party bodies from the lowest to the highest, periodical reports by party bodies to their party organisations and to higher bodies, strict party discipline and the subordination of the minority to the majority, and the binding nature of decisions of higher bodies for lower bodies.

42. These were recognition of the need for such a discussion by several regional or republican level party bodies, the absence of a sufficiently solid majority in the Central Committee on major questions of party policy, and if the CC considers it necessary to consult the party as a whole on some question of policy.

43. One other addition to the Rules is worthy of note: provision was made for the existence of a party apparatus at all levels of the party between national and district levels.

3

How Much of a New Elite?

J. H. Miller

'BEHOLD, I MAKE ALL THINGS NEW'

When M. S. Gorbachev came to power in March 1985 he
quickly became associated, by both Soviet and Western media,
with an expectation of reform; indeed it was easy for the two
media in combination to exaggerate the scope and pace of this
reform, and to obscure its specific thrust. Even some 18 months
later, when the slogan *perestroika*[1] (reconstruction) had become
firmly attached to Gorbachev's program, it was not easy to summarise all its specific themes and methods. In many ways people
have been reminded of Khrushchev — for instance, in the rapid
replacement of high officials, the reorganisation of top institutions,[2] or the appeal to popular enthusiasm implicit in the
campaign against alcohol, or in slogans such as *chelovecheskii
faktor* (the human factor). There are other ways, however, in
which Gorbachev is very clearly different from Khrushchev: his
use of public relations, for example, is incomparably more
sophisticated, and there is little sign that he would include
increased social mobility among the incentives of a restructured
economy.[3]

My broad aim in this chapter is to contribute to a clearer
picture of Gorbachev's program of *perestroika*, through
examination of the first of the above topics, namely the personnel of his administration.[4] Have the substantial changes of
bureaucratic heads led to qualitative changes of experience and
approach, such as might permit changed priorities and methods?
And supposing that this is the case, what may be their contribution to substantive socio-political reform; are a reformist

61

program at the top, and an elite committed to its realisation sufficient?

At the outset two objections to this kind of study must be met. The first of these would maintain that Soviet politics are so centralised that the characteristics of the persons who carry out orders make no difference to their outcome. The reply to this would point out that the Soviet system is not only centralised but also massive: it is difficult, despite major efforts, for central policy to transcend matters of general principle. This leaves considerable latitude for interpretation to officials on the spot as they disaggregate instructions for application to local conditions. This means in turn that unsympathetic or narrow-minded officials have wide opportunities to frustrate or deflect innovative policies. New leaders have always tried to ensure a co-operative elite — not because their contribution to policy-making is sought after, but because their co-operation is essential to policy implementation.

The second objection is more cogent: the kind of objective characteristics that outsiders can measure — age, sex, background, occupation and the like — tell us next to nothing about opinions and attitudes. This is something we cannot deny — or prove, quite simply because the sincere opinions of the Soviet elite are a closed book to us. We can do no more than point cautiously to numerous studies showing how the objective characteristics of politicians and officials change along with changes in announced policy, i.e. with changes in perception of the tasks officials should be tackling. Two illustrations of this relationship will be of relevance later in the chapter.

The first is the distinction initiated by F. J. Fleron between 'recruited' and 'co-opted' officials.[5] Recruited personnel are those who move fairly soon after training (which may be quite specialist in character) into party occupations, which virtually by their nature are more general in scope. Brezhnev's career is a good illustration. Co-opted officials, on the other hand, go on to develop their professional specialisation and are brought into party positions comparatively late, sometimes on the basis of a professional reputation. D. F. Ustinov, the armaments specialist and later Minister of Defence, is typical here. Sometimes specialists of this type do not join the communist party until late: L. N. Zaikov and N. V. Talyzin in the present Politburo are cases in point. A number of studies have shown that different Soviet administrations raise or lower the proportion of co-opted specialists among senior officials depending on their policy priorities.[6] In simple terms, the age at which one first entered a party post is a *prima facie* measure of one's position on the 'redness-expertise' spectrum.

Another illustration: observers have noted that under Brezhnev more senior provincial officials were locals who had made a local career, and fewer had been seconded from elsewhere.[7] Brezhnev in fact spoke about this at the 24th Congress in 1971:

> Furthermore the Central Committee has systematically followed a policy of promoting local workers; only in exceptional circumstances have people been dispatched to these posts from the centre. This practice in the selection and deployment of staff *is meeting with approval and support* from party organisations and all communists.[8]

It is surely not far-fetched to read into the second sentence a hint that in the provinces local careers for local boys are preferred, and hence to infer that an increase in postings from outside denotes increased centralisation in policy.

In short, though we have no access to the attitudes of Soviet officials, it seems reasonable to draw on objective, measurable data for conclusions about the *capacities* by virtue of which they were appointed, and to that extent the analysis of such data is not a fruitless exercise.

I propose now to analyse changes in the political elite under M. S. Gorbachev by examining two groups called (somewhat loosely) the 'top fifty' and the 'top five hundred'.

THE 'TOP FIFTY' POLITICIANS

The fifty-or-so persons who are (i) members or candidate members of the Politburo, (ii) Secretaries of the Central Committee (CC), (iii) members of the Presidium of the Council of Ministers (PCM), and (iv) heads of Central Committee departments, have a fair claim to being a distinct and reasonably coherent group at the apex of Soviet politics. The Politburo always contains representatives from the Secretariat and the PCM, and many Central Committee departments are headed by someone who is either simultaneously a Secretary, or may in due time become one. Between the 1981 and 1986 congresses this 'top fifty' of the elite declined in exact number from 58 to about 51, in part because of increasing overlap in their membership of the four bodies, but more because these bodies, in particular the Presidium of the Council of Ministers and the apparatus of Central Committee departments, have become smaller and more streamlined along the following lines.

In 1981 the governmental Presidium contained the Chairman of the Council of Ministers (N. A. Tikhonov), one first-deputy chairman (I. V. Arkhipov), and 13 ordinary deputy chairmen. By 1986 there were four first-deputy chairmen and eight ordinary deputies, the supremos of economic planning (N. V. Talyzin) and of agriculture (V. S. Murakhovskii) having been singled out and raised to the status of first deputies, and a number of other portfolios not renewed. The Central Committee departments numbered 25[9] in 1981, five of them headed by people who were also Secretaries; after the 27th Congress the indications are that three at least of the departments have been abolished,[10] or rather merged with others, and that three at least, and possibly four or five now have Secretaries as departmental heads.[11] The details are in Table 3.1.

Of the 51 persons in one or other of these four top positions in April 1986 — their names may be found by combining Table 1.6 in Chapter 1 with Table 3.1 in this — a mere 16 were also in the analogous list for 1981; more than two-thirds of them have been replaced in the intervening five years, and almost all of these replacements occurred either under Andropov (November 1982–February 1984) or in Gorbachev's first year of office. Of the 1981 Politburo (members and candidates) 8 out of 22 are still in politics, of the Secretariat 3 out of ten, of the PCM 4 out of 14, and of the 24 Department Heads, two only (V. A. Karlov and N. I. Savinkin). These are changes — admittedly over a number of years — which can stand comparison with the most hectic periods of the Khrushchev era. And turnover at the very top has also been greater than among the 'upper-middle' echelons of the bureaucracy, as will emerge below.

After the 27th Congress the group as a whole had a mean age of 62 years and two months, almost four years younger than it had been in 1981. Rejuvenation was greatest among the Central Committee Secretaries, who had an average age of 60 compared with 68 in 1981, and it was least among the PCM whose age had fallen from almost 65 to 61.[12] Viewed in this light the changes,

Table 3.1: Central Committee department heads

Department	April 1981[a]	April 1986[a]
Organisational-Party Work	I. V. Kapitonov[f]	G. P. Razumovskii[f]
General	K. U. Chernenko[f]	A. I. Luk'ianov
Administrative Organs	N. I. Savinkin	N. I. Savinkin
Letters[b]	B. P. Iakovlev	abolished?
Main Political Administration, Army and Navy	A. A. Epishev	A. D. Lizichev
Party Control Committee	A. Ia. Pel'she[g]	M. S. Solomentsev[g]
Heavy Industry[d]	V. I. Dolgikh[f]	I. P. Iastrebov
Defence Industry	I. F. Dmitriev	O. S. Beliakov[e]
Machine Building	V. S. Frolov	A. I. Vol'skii[e]
Chemical Industry	vacant	V. G. Afonin[e]
Construction	I. N. Dmitriev	A. G. Mel'nikov
Transport and Communications	K. S. Simonov	V. S. Pasternak
Light and Food Industry[d]	F. I. Mochalin	L. F. Bobykin[e]
Trade and Everyday Services	Ia. I. Kabkov	N. A. Stashenkov[e]
Planning and Financial Organs[d]	B. I. Gostev	?
Agriculture[d]	V. A. Karlov	V. A. Karlov
Agricultural Machine Building	I. I. Sakhniuk	abolished?
Propaganda	E. M. Tiazhel'nikov	Iu. A. Skliarov?
Science and Educational Institutions	S. P. Trapeznikov	?
Culture	V. F. Shauro	Iu. P. Voronov[e]
International	B. N. Ponomarev[f]	A. F. Dobrynin[f]
Liaison with Communist and Workers' Parties of Socialist Countries[c]	K. V. Rusakov[f]	V. A. Medvedev[f]
International Information	L. M. Zamiatin	abolished?
Cadres Abroad[c]	N. M. Pegov	S. V. Chervonenko
Administration of Affairs[b]	G. S. Pavlov	N. E. Kruchina

Notes:

a. The date April was chosen to allow administrative changes immediately after the Congress to become clear.

b. The Department of Letters deals with complaints and other 'feedback'; that translated 'Administration of Affairs' with the internal business management of the CC.

c. These two departments are not, to my knowledge, given titles in the Soviet media.

d. Four departments have been renamed since 1981: Heavy Industry has become Heavy Industry and Energy since April 1984; Light and Food Industry became Light Industry and Consumer Goods in May 1983; Planning and Financial Organs became Economics (December 1982); and Agriculture became Agriculture and Food Industry in May 1983.

e. For these six persons data are incomplete in the statistics which follow.

f. Incumbent simultaneously Central Committee Secretary.

g. Incumbent simultaneously Politburo member.

though substantial in number, scarcely amount to the 'change of generations' which had been forecast. Rejuvenation has not however been quite as cautious as the averages suggest: the most common year of birth of the group in 1986 was 1929 — well on the way to a 'generation' younger than the 1981 leadership whose most common birth year was 1914.[13]

Not much has changed, as Rigby observes in Chapter 1, in the educational background of the 'top fifty': as before, nearly two-thirds of them have tertiary qualifications in some form of engineering, though the proportion of these in such more modern sectors as aviation or electronics has risen. Tertiary qualifications are now general: no one is left who embarked on an official or professional career without completing tertiary studies, as Andropov, Grishin and Martynov had done, or who had party training only (like Chernenko or Nuriev). The 1981 generation tended to be educated in a few prestigious centres, notably Moscow, whereas the 1986 leadership qualified in a wide variety of provincial establishments.[14] Four people in the 1981 group were educated at the Leningrad Polytechnical Institute, and three (among them Brezhnev) at the Dneprodzerzhinsk Metallurgical Institute; the most common source of qualifications in 1986 — and unrepresented in 1981 — is the Urals Polytechnical Institute in Sverdlovsk. More will emerge about these six persons below.

Nearly half of the 1981 leadership had seen military service in some form or capacity, usually during the Great Fatherland War, but a few before it. The proportion is slightly over a quarter for the 1986 leadership, and, particularly striking, none of them entered any form of full-time military service *after* 1945 (with the sole exception of A. D. Lizichev, a career officer). In the main this is to be explained by the fact that there was very little conscription in the 1946–9 period, when Gorbachev and his age group became eligible; there is no doubt that this generation had a distinct advantage over those just a few years older who experienced the trauma of the war and had their training and careers seriously set back. Nevertheless, it is also the case that very few Soviet officials of the generation younger than Gorbachev have been in the armed forces. It is ironical that an oligarchy increasingly without military experience should be presiding over a so-far unabated cult of military achievement and sacrifice.

The 1986 leadership, though younger, joined the communist

party at a slightly older age, almost 25 on average, as compared with 24 for the 1981 leadership. This reflects a general trend towards later admission into the party in the post-war period, and also an enhanced role of 'co-opted specialists' in the new leadership. Two-thirds of the 1981 group were already in the party before the onset of the Great Fatherland War, but by 1986 this figure had sunk to a quarter, whilst a third had entered the party in the Khrushchev period (1953–64). Indeed one member of the present leadership, the youngest, Iu. D. Masliukov, joined the CPSU as recently as 1966; he had risen to become deputy chairman of the Council of Ministers in less than 20 years.

From the late 1930s to the mid-1950s is a short time, not strictly speaking a generation: but people undergoing their formative professional experiences[15] in these two periods have been affected by profoundly different sets of circumstances — which may, in turn, have fostered differences in attitude. The latter period is characterised by Khrushchev's 'Secret Speech' and early attempts at domestic reform, by the supression of the Hungarian rising and the launching of the first sputnik — a world in which the USSR is expressing the confidence both of a superpower and of advanced technology, and at the same time questioning Stalinist verities.

If we look at the career-types represented in the Gorbachev leadership, we can note some new trends, against the general background in which engineering, industrial management and party office predominate. Careers based mainly on control of communications and public relations, without accompanying technical proficiency — of the type of Suslov, Ponomarev, Pel'she — are fewer in number, whilst 'co-opted specialists' (as Rigby also observes) are more common, and especially among the members and candidates of the Politburo (they were always important in the Council of Ministers). By the same token there is now less 'line' provincial experience than there was. The appointment of A. P. Biriukova as a Central Committee Secretary shows a wish to appear responsive to two long passive interest groups, women and (state-)organised labour. Particularly interesting are co-optees from the efficient, but also privileged, military sectors of industry; Ryzhkov, Zaikov, Talyzin, Silaev, Masliukov and Voronin are all more or less from this background;[16] their present responsibilities create the impression that defence industry is meant to set the tone for the rest of planning and engineering.

The final group of parameters which should be monitored are ethnic affiliation and regional ties. Notoriously the top leadership is dominated by persons from the three Slavic nationalities who make up 72 per cent of the population; indeed there seem to be *no* non-Slavs among the Central Committee Secretaries or department heads. And of the three Slavic groups, Russians are the overwhelming majority and have increased their share of leading personnel from about two-thirds to around three-quarters. Ukrainian and Belorussian representation has remained about the same, at 10 and 6 per cent respectively, and this amounts to a considerable under-representation of Ukrainians, compared with their share of the population or the party; moreover two of the Ukrainians in the Presidium of the Council of Ministers, Marchuk and Murakhovskii, have never been politically active in the Ukraine and one, possibly both, were not born there. This is a noticeable rebound from the practice of the Khrushchev and Brezhnev administrations, both of whom drew heavily on Ukrainian personnel.

Among non-Slavs, Kazakhs, Georgians and Azeris remain represented by one person each in the Politburo, the same persons as in 1981, though two of them, Aliev and Shevardnadze, are no longer first secretaries for their republics. In 1981 there were representatives of one other major nationality (Uzbek) among the 'top fifty', and of five less numerous ones (Armenian, Bashkir, Jewish, Latvian and Moldavian); such representation is absent from the 1986 leadership.[17] Although this change has entailed a rise in the Russian share of the leadership, it is probably premature to interpret it as a sign of Gorbachev's preferences: Gorbachev, when he came to power, did not dispose of an extensive clientele[18] of the kind that a General Secretary can develop over the years, and which led to the elevation of non-Russians like Bodiul and Nuriev to high office.

Brezhnev's reliance on old allies and subordinates from two provinces in the Dnieper Valley in East-Central Ukraine led to that region's acquiring the nickname *kuznitsa kadrov* ('cadre forge'). Some other regions were also disproportionately represented in his administration: Belorussia during the 1970s, and Moscow (though many of the Muscovites had survived from the still more powerful position of the Moscow party machine at the end of the 1950s). This pattern of regional representation has been altered drastically: from the Dnieper there survives only Shcherbitskii (and, in one sense, Chebrikov) and from Moscow only Demichev.[19] Instead, other regions have become more conspicuous. Most important of these is the Urals and especially Sverdlovsk, the provincial base of N. I. Ryzhkov; it is particularly interesting that the General Secretary has no past associations with the Urals. But Gorbachev's home territory in the North Caucasus has also increased its representation, as have West Siberia (E. K. Ligachev) and Leningrad (L. N. Zaikov and Iu. F. Solov'ev), the latter despite its association with Gorbachev's defeated rival Romanov.[20]

To sum up this profile of the 50 most important persons in Soviet politics after one year of the Gorbachev administration: Gorbachev has brought about substantial change in some senses, such as turnover of personnel and the regional origins of the newcomers. But in some respects — age, education and professional experience — the changes have been measured and cautious. What shines through everything is the concern for technical experience, expertise and efficiency, illustrated by the preference shown to military industry by a generation with decreasing wartime experience. The one surprise, and the one way in which Gorbachev has not followed classical methods of the consolidation of power, is the powerful position conceded or delegated to the Chairman of the Council of Ministers, Ryzhkov, and his circle, based on the Urals and on Gosplan, and on heavy and armaments industry. This situation becomes less surprising, however, when one takes two factors into account: Gorbachev's position as the youngest member of the Politburo, and the fact that Ryzhkov never held a party post before 1982, when he was aged 53. Gorbachev can therefore afford to wait, and Ryzhkov is not, for the near future, a threat to him as an alternative focus of party loyalties.

THE 'TOP FIVE HUNDRED'

How much do these features of the new administration hold true when attention is turned to the 'upper-middle' echelons of politics, say to the top 500 politicians rather than the top 50? To attempt an answer to this question I shall follow convention and analyse the three bodies which, *de facto*, form the three tiers of the Central Committee of the CPSU. Legally speaking the Central Committee (CC) has full and candidate members (as does the Politburo), and these two are quite distinct from the

Table 3.2: Composition and turnover of leading CPSU organs

	1956	1961	1966	1971	1976	1981	1986
Central Committee members	133	175	195	241	287	319	307
Central Committee candidates	122	155	165	155	139	151	170
Members, Central Auditing Commission	63	65	79	81	85	75	83
TOTAL	318	395	439	477	511	545	560
of which, new members (%)	45.2	59.7	36.9	33.1	28.0	27.9	46.1
of which, re-elected members(%)	54.8	40.3	61.3	66.9	72.0	72.1	53.9
of which: No change in status	43.4	29.4	54.2	53.8	58.5	59.0	44.1
Promoted to full or candidate membership	6.9	9.9	8.0	12.4	13.5	12.7	9.6
Demoted to candidate or CAC membership	4.4	1.0	0.9	0.6	—	0.4	0.2

Adapted and updated from Elizabeth Teague, *The Central Committee and Central Auditing Commission elected at the Twenty-Sixth Congress of the CPSU*, RL 171/81 (28 April 1981).

body known as the Central Auditing Commission (CAC); but Soviet political protocol seems to treat the CAC as if it were a probationary committee junior to CC candidates. Together these three committees contain some 550 people, and, whilst this group does not coincide exactly with any particular echelon of power[21] or definition of 'the' elite, it can be said to contain the 500 most powerful officials in the Soviet system. Membership of the three committees is largely *ex-officio*. Those who draw up its membership have a certain latitude in deciding whether to increase or decrease the numbers in each of the three tiers and in assigning personnel among them; but in general, in appointing senior officials since he came to power the new General Secretary, and those who advise him (or bargain with him), have been shaping the composition of the new CC. This is why its composition is a good gauge of the characteristics of the elite.

Table 3.2 gives the figures for the size and turnover of the three tiers of the CC over the last 30 years. Full members, it will be noted, are slightly fewer in 1986 than they were in 1981 — the first time this has happened — but candidates and CAC members are more numerous, making a grand total of 560, a slight increase on the 1981 figure. Some 46 per cent of these 560 are completely new to the CC at any of its levels. This is a far higher turnover than at any congress during the Brezhnev period (the era of 'stability of cadres'), yet it does not approach (despite some people's predictions during 1985) the scope of Khrushchev's clean-out of the CC in 1961. And indeed to surpass that post-war record would have been a difficult achievement, for Khrushchev's CC of October 1961 was the outcome of five and a half years of turbulent politics, including two crises between the General Secretary and his Politburo.[22] By contrast, Gorbachev has had less than a year in which to replace senior personnel;[23] moreover his intention of so doing did not give rise to a factional dispute, such as might have pushed people to take sides for and against him.

This message of substantial change, but not quite so dramatic as some of us supposed, emerges in a different way from the age data in Table 3.3.[24] The mean age of full CC members has fallen, for the first time in many years, and is now somewhat over 60.[25] (We might note that the hypothetical 'most common' CC member is old enough to have been in the war, but will have been conscripted at a time when the Germans were retreating.) But the mean age of candidates, and, especially of CAC members,

Table 3.3: CPSU leading organs: age and party seniority

	Mean year of birth		Mean year of joining party	
	1981	1986	1981	1986
CC members	1919.3	1925.8	1944.5	1951.1
N =	319	287	319	276
CC candidates	1924.3	1929.0	1950.3	1953.5
N =	151	143	151	120
CAC members	1926.6	1927.7	1952.9	1953.0
N =	75	53	75	42
TOTAL	1921.7	1926.9	1947.3	1951.9
N =	545	483	545	438

has *risen*, despite extensive replacement of personnel. Something would seem to be different about the more junior appointments Gorbachev has made. It is true that there are a good deal of missing data in the 1986 columns of Table 3.3., and it would not be difficult in the case of CC Candidates for full information to show that they too were younger than in 1981. But this result would be fairly improbable in the case of CAC members; we are left with a minor anomaly which requires investigation.

Turning to the party seniority of the personnel of these three committees, we find that in 1981 full CC members had been in the party on average since the latter part of the war, but in 1986 since the beginning of 1951. This transition is much less marked in the case of candidates and CAC members; indeed, among the latter there is hardly any change at all (on the incomplete data available).

The year 1951 is a date that prompts closer scrutiny. Admission into the party was not so very common in that year, or indeed for most of the late Stalin period. Is it possible that the statistical mean conceals the existence of *two* groups, who joined the party some time before, and some time after 1951? Yes, indeed. The years of birth and years of party admission of this sample of nearly 500 are *not* distributed normally about their mean. Instead we can discern two overlapping but still distinct groups: one born in the 1918–23 period and entering the CPSU during the war, and the second born 1927–32 and admitted into the party typically after Stalin's death. Similar features were noted about the leading 50 personnel.

Table 3.4: CPSU leading organs: some newly co-opted members in 1986

	Mean year of birth	Mean year of joining party
CC members	1931.3	1956.2
N =	73	62
CC candidates	1931.6	1956.1
N =	76	53
CAC members	1930.3	1956.8
N =	31	20
TOTAL	1931.2	1956.3
N =	180	135

Table 3.4 assembles some of the available data about people co-opted into the CC (at any of its three levels) for the first time in 1986, that is, in general, persons who have gained advancement with Gorbachev. What we find is a remarkably homogeneous group,[26] born on average in the same year as the General Secretary and entering the party about the time of the 20th Congress and Khrushchev's Secret Speech. The age of new members varies very little across the three committees, even though full CC members normally hold the more important posts and CAC members the less responsible ones; indeed people newly co-opted into the CAC in 1986 are slightly *older* than the rest.

Drawing on these observations and on earlier items concerning personnel turnover in this chapter, I think it is possible to venture three inferences concerning the way Gorbachev has consolidated his power. First — an obvious point, which would hardly need making were it not for the contrast it offers with appointments of the late Brezhnev period — he has shown a preference for his own generation, meaning people born in the late 1920s and early 1930s, and has presided over appointments from this generation across the board to posts of very different seniority. It is as if he thinks of these people as like-minded, or, at any rate, predictable. If the question is raised, what is particularly distinctive about this age group, the answer must of necessity be speculative; but a prime possibility is that this is the generation which had (by Soviet standards) a good education, and made a smooth, relatively undisturbed transition from school to tertiary institute to professional career.[27]

Second, he has started from the top downwards. The Politburo, and the four types of position considered under the rubric of the 'top fifty' show a higher rate of turnover than does the Central Committee. Within the Central Committee the greatest changes in characteristics (though not in turnover) have been amongst the full members (whose numbers, incidentally, were *not* allowed to expand).

Third, and more speculative, is an interpretation of the fact that new entrants into the CAC are older than entrants into the CC, when under Brezhnev they would typically have been five or six years younger. Among Gorbachev's supporters there must be many who feel they were cheated of their expected promotions under the late Brezhnev gerontocracy. It would make sense for the new administration to satisfy these people's aspirations by moving them into the sort of posts that earn CAC membership — whilst deploying as full CC members more of Gorbachev's personally-approved 'high-fliers', people who were often virtually unknown five years ago.

To turn now to a personnel sector in which platform promises have so far fallen short of fulfilment. Table 3.5 gives details of female membership of the Central Committees in 1981 and 1986.

Table 3.5: Female membership of leading CPSU organs

	1981		1986	
	Females	of whom, officials	Females	of whom, officials
CC members	8	(6)	13	(6)
CC candidates	10	(2)	8	(2)
CAC members	14	(2)	19	(3)
TOTAL	32	(10)	40	(11)
%	5.9		7.1	

Female membership of the three tiers of the CC is indeed up from 32 to 40 (or from 5.9 to 7.1 per cent), but this increase seems to be almost all from among the 60 or so ordinary workers and peasants in the CC; the number of women holding political office, even quite junior office, is, on my count, one more than it was in 1981.[28]

Distribution of CC personnel by ethnic group cannot, unfortunately, be done with the precision that was possible in the case of the top leadership, and, in particular, we have no means of establishing the precise number of Ukrainians and Belorussians among the large group with common Slavic surnames.[29] We can, however, with only a small margin of error, distinguish Slavic from several characteristic types of non-Slavic names, and this analysis is the basis of Table 3.6. The 'totals' columns at the right do not suggest that there have been important changes in the ethnic composition of the CC. But when the distribution of full CC members is compared with that of candidates or of the CAC, a subtle shift between 1981 and 1986 can be detected — to the effect that non-Slavic representation has declined among full members and increased among the two junior tiers. As was the case with the top leadership, the suggestion of preferment for Slavs (and, implicitly, for Russians) is evident, though its precise mechanisms are somewhat less direct than might appear. A number of posts in the Union-Republics whose incumbents would normally be non-Russians have been downgraded from member to candidate, or from candidate to CAC status. Intertwined with this, a number of posts in Central Asia represented on the CC now have Slavic incumbents in place of the natives who occupied them in 1981; this can plausibly be connected with the corruption scandals of the last few years, and the increase in Moscow's intervention in Central Asian personnel deployment predates Gorbachev. But the essential trend is clear: a small but perceptible increase in the already great preponderance of Slavs in the upper echelons of politics.

The final table, 3.7,[30] compares occupational and institutional representation on the three tiers of the CC for 1981 and 1986. And the striking feature of the data it presents must surely be the *stability* of the internal structure of the CC, a stability all the more impressive when one considers that nearly half the persons here classified have changed in five years. It is difficult not to believe that the representation of, say, the Military, Rule Enforcement or Foreign Affairs is a carefully fixed quota, and this leads one to infer that changes to these quotas, even quite small ones, are also matters of deliberate policy.

In numerical terms the biggest of these changes has been an increase in representatives from ordinary farming and manufacturing, from 48 to 61. No commentator has doubted in the past that the worker and peasant component of the CC is placed there out of 'tokenism' — to give a show of representation whilst minimising or controlling input into policy.[31] If this is the reason for their presence, then that reason is growing stronger. Before the congress the Soviet media aired for the first time in many

75

Table 3.6: CPSU leading organs: nationality

% of total personnel who are	CC members		CC candidates		CAC members		Totals	
	1981	1986	1981	1986	1981	1986	1981	1986
Slavs[a]	87.1	89.9	82.1	82.4	73.3	72.3	83.9	85.0
Balts	2.2	1.3	2.0	1.8	2.7	6.0	2.2	2.1
Transcaucasians	2.2	2.0	4.6	3.5	6.7	6.0	3.5	3.0
Central Asians	4.4	2.9	6.0	8.2	6.7	9.6	5.1	5.5
	8.2	6.2	12.6	13.5	16.0	21.7	10.8	10.7
Others, unknown	4.1	3.9	5.3	4.1	10.7	6.0	5.3	4.3

Note: a. The Slav category is determined by surname in default of information; it will contain a small number of perople from the non-Slavic nationalities of the Volga and Siberia.

Table 3.7: Central Committee membership, 1981 and 1986, distributed by occupational base

	1981				1986			
	M	C	A	Total	M	C	A	Total
Party Officials								
At All-Union level	31	14	5	50	31	10	6	47
In RSFSR	66	13	1	80	62	19	2	83
In other republics	41	24	4	69	40	29	6	75
	138	51	10	199	133	58	14	205
State officials[a]								
At All-Union level	74	26	13	113	65	33	8	106
In RSFSR	10	8	3	21	9	7	4	20
In other republics	10	11	13	34	6	14	13	33
	94	45	29	168	80	54	25	159
Foreign Affairs	16	6	4	26	14	9	3	26
Military	23	13	4	40	23	13	4	40
Rule Enforcement[b]	7	2		9	7	2		9
Media	4	7	6	17	3	8	6	17
Academy of Sciences	9	4	1	14	8	6		14
Trade Unions	5	3	4	12	4	2	4	10
Ind. management	3	1		4	3	3		6
Voluntary organisations	4	4		8	4	3	1	8
Retired					4		1	5
Workers and peasants	16	15	17	48	24	12	25	61
	87	55	36	178	94	58	44	196
Grand totals	319	151	75	545	307	170	83	560

Notes: a. Includes Supreme Soviets.
b. KGB, MVD and Courts.

years what amounted to complaints against social stratification.[32] And Gorbachev in his Political Report seemed to go out of his way to allay doubts about the meritocratic nature of Soviet society and to emphasise that honest initiative and hard work are rewarded.[33] Furthermore, the Soviet authorities are still analysing and drawing conclusions from the rise and survival of Solidarity in Poland.

The worker and peasant component is half female, and the increase in the female presence on the CC has occurred principally in this group. As was noted above concerning A. P. Biriukova, the bid to increase representation (or the show of it) is aimed at several traditionally passive groups simultaneously.

The second striking change in the 1986 CC is the retention in membership of a small group of retired senior politicians: N. A. Tikhonov, B. N. Ponomarev and N. K. Baibakov are the most familiar. For a long time Soviet politics lacked provisions for honourable retirement. Andropov began to redress this lack by initiating published notes of appreciation (from the Politburo) when some (not all) senior officials retired. This has now been taken further with a signal to bureaucrats facing retrenchment that they can hope to retire with dignity or even be retained in an advisory capacity.[34]

Two other trends over the past five years are a slight decrease in the proportion of 'state' posts (mainly ministries, but with a few in the executive committees of Soviets) and a slight decrease in the proportion of central, i.e. All-Union echelon posts as compared with posts at the republican or provincial echelon. The first of these is probably a simple consequence of the merging of ministries (for instance; to form *Gosagroprom*).[35] The second, though, may well be another 'signal', meant to reassure provincial officials and remind the central *apparatchiki* that they are, after all, the party's servants. Representation of the All-Union instrumentalities on the CC reached a high point at Brezhnev's last congress,[36] and the balance between centre and regions has now been restored to something like what it was in 1976. The increase in regional representation, when scrutinised closely, turns out to be particularly an increase in provincial (*oblast'*) first secretaries; in addition, the Ukraine and Belorussia have done better than other republics out of the increase.[37]

When the new General Secretary came to power there was speculation to the effect that he had closer ties with some policy sectors than with others — with the KGB rather than with the military or foreign affairs for example, — and that he might lean more heavily on his early allies for support, or seek to play one sector off against another. The striking continuity of CC representation of such sectors as Foreign Affairs, the Media, the Military, or Security and Rule Enforcement, suggests that, whatever the truth of the matter, he is anxious to avoid any such appearance; this is all the more the case when it is considered that some of these sectors, notably Foreign Affairs and the Media, have undergone substantial reshuffles of personnel. And if we look within the representation of particular sectors for changes that might reflect shifts of policy, we can find them —

but none which reveal anything specifically about the new administration. Thus the Ministry of Foreign Affairs group shows a shift away from ambassadors towards Moscow-based deputy-ministers; the Academy representation shows a swing towards cybernetics and computing whilst the number of defence and atomic scientists remain the same; among the 40 soldiers, commanders-in-chief of large regions[38] have displaced some of the military district commanders; and KGB representation is up by one, at the expense of the MVD. All of these, with the possible exception of the last, can be explained in terms of organisational rationality, or of policy trends which predate Gorbachev; and the MVD representative displaced, former first deputy minister Iu. M. Churbanov, was a relative by marriage of Brezhnev — so that the case is not simply that of a set-back for the MVD. In all this, it would be convenient if changes in CC composition provided some clear evidence for or against Professor Rigby's conclusion that Gorbachev has quickly become supreme in the oligarchy; but they do not; the evidence is highly ambiguous.

How can we characterise Gorbachev's reforms of the elite? It is substantially new in terms of its personnel, and in terms of its age, and of the characteristic background and experience that goes with it, very nearly a new generation. But in other respects it is surprisingly little altered; changes have included some which are minor, even if significant, others in which public relations have masked lack of substance, still others which represent a continuation or acceleration of trends already under way; altogether they convey a sense of cautious and deliberate planning.

Nevertheless, it is possible to offer a profile of the typical 'New Man' of Gorbachev's generation. First, he is Russian and male — both of which characteristics have been true of the country's government for decades, indeed centuries, but which are still the case, in part because of the narrowness of Gorbachev's initial power base. Second, he was born sometime in the late 1920s or early 1930s, was educated in the late Stalin period and joined the CPSU sometime in the mid-1950s. He has high educational qualifications, usually technical, and his education and career have been, comparatively speaking, uncomplicated and undisturbed by social or political vicissitudes. He is energetic and confident, maybe indeed frustrated by the inactivity of his elders as the Brezhnev era drew to a close. Major

formative experiences in his professional life will include
Khrushchev's Secret Speech, the latter's struggle with the 'Anti-
Party Group', his populist enthusiasms and the administrative
gimmickry that led to his fall, the launching of the first sputnik
in 1957, and the Cuban missile crisis in 1962. He tends to be a
manager-turned-politician, and it is perhaps not fanciful to
picture him learning the importance of mobilisation and leadership in reaction to Brezhnev, and of organisation, discipline and
efficiency in reaction to Khrushchev. Implicitly (sometimes
explicitly) he is attracted by the military model for domestic
management and development (as so often in Russian history)
but is not himself a man of military experience. He has matured
in a world of evenly-balanced competition between two super-
powers; the United States must look like a bafflingly dynamic
and resilient rival, but it will be difficult to picture American
society in diabolical, or his own in messianic terms.

THE NEW ELITE AND BUREAUCRATIC CULTURE

The above thumbnail sketch is not, I would submit, implausible,
but it can take us only so far towards an assessment of the
chances of reform. Can anything further be argued about the
kinds of attitude and behaviour the new elite might bring to
governing? Simply to raise that question is to remind ourselves
that bureaucrats operate in a context and a climate — things
which are products of their own and their predecessors' education, experience and behaviour, and of assumptions and
expectations concerning bureaucrats on the part both of rulers
and ruled. Such a climate can be remarkably durable, and can
impose constraints remarkably difficult to shake off. As R. J.
Hill has pointed out, there is an intimate connection between
this 'bureaucratic culture' and the problems of successful
reform.[39]

Two things can be said about the bureaucratic culture which
draw on recent evidence (rather than being merely a prioristic);
both serve to modify any impression that may have been created
that the *energy* of the new elite entails greater *independence*
from the prevailing ways of doing things. Both can be illustrated
from a relatively perceptive and specific newspaper article,
which yet is misconceived, and probably representative of a
widespread misconception:

Quite simply, Mr Gorbachev has not been picking his men the way they used to be picked. In the past and, indeed, in present-day politics, in many large countries including the US, leaders have tended to choose for their entourage people with whom they have had past links, often from their home regions.

A large group in Mr Brezhnev's Government was even known as the 'Dnepropetrovsk Mafia'. Mr Brezhnev also used to reward friends and relatives with important political posts unrelated to their competence.

This so far is not true of Mr Gorbachev's team where cliques have had little time to form. Just four years ago, Mr Gorbachev did not even know most of them and almost none of them knew each other.[40]

Now there is a good deal of truth in this picture of the Brezhnev period, but not the whole truth. What is overlooked is that an increasing observance of conventions was just as much a hallmark of Brezhnevian conservatism as was nepotism: in the personnel field these were the conventions of 'stability of cadres', such things as virtual life-tenure, promotion by seniority and promotion within one's local region. These elements of convention are, of course, not incompatible with corruption, but frequently connected with it; and in its campaign against corruption the new administration has taken the option — a rather natural one in Soviet circumstances — of seeking to undermine the conventions and to heighten the unpredictability of political life. The policy of 'stability of cadres' has been repudiated, and the indications are that a continued high rate of turnover is planned for the future.[41] An aspect of this is that there will be a deliberate attempt to rotate officials from one place to another, rather than promote them up the ladder in one locality; this was explicitly advocated concerning the non-Russian republics by a number of congress speakers,[42] and its practice can already be observed in the RSFSR. There has also been a return to a practice, used only rarely under Brezhnev, of withdrawing provincial officials back to Moscow for a period of retraining in the CC apparatus and then of dispatching them on a new tour of duty.[43] Among the officials who entered the CC for the first time in 1986 this pattern can be noted in approximately 40 cases, and the true figure is probably more.

Now some of the officials just mentioned went back from

Moscow to the province from which they had originally come. Nevertheless, the implications of this increased use of its powers by the centre are clear. Officials will be rather more beholden to central authority than they were under Brezhnev, and this fact will affect not only who is chosen, but how they perform their tasks.[44] To be sure, that is not necessarily an obstacle to a program of reform (as students of the military and of military regimes will point out); but it serves to highlight the way in which this reform program is influenced by the long Russian tradition of modernisation from above.

A similar conclusion emerges from examination of the statement that 'Gorbachev has not been picking his men the way they used to be picked'. It is correct that the present administration has been impatient with the 'Dnepropetrovsk Mafia'. But a corollary of this, in Soviet conditions, has to be distrust of Brezhnev's personnel deployment institutions (above all the CC Department of Organisational-Party Work) and of the emergent conventions they were encouraging or tolerating. That in turn means that Gorbachev had to depend more than ordinarily on people in whom he had personal trust. He had, in fact, little alternative but to 'choose people with whom [he] had past links', if he was to make an impact on the self-protective bureaucracy.

There is a twist to this story. Gorbachev's own network of trusted associates was, in comparative terms, small and weak. He was a fairly recent arrival on the Moscow scene, and agriculture does not usually foster powerful careers. In this sense it is true, as the newspaper article says, that 'four years ago . . . Gorbachev did not even know most' of the new team. But what he did — and there may have been no other way to power — was to ally himself with others who had extensive and powerful networks of associates, often with ambitions frustrated under Brezhnev. Foremost among these was Ryzhkov, the present Chairman of the Council of Ministers; the list of people who have been promoted to high office either from Sverdlovsk, or from Gosplan (Ryzhkov's two power bases) is an impressive one,[45] one that is comparable in length to the list of those who seem to be direct protégés of Gorbachev.[46] A lesser clientele can be associated with E. K. Ligachev's time in Tomsk.[47] It is interesting to note that these two alliances — with Ryzhkov and with Ligachev — are likely to have been forged in late 1982 or early 1983, that is when Andropov was General Secretary; Andropov may well have organised the coalition.[48]

In this light it is by no means correct that 'almost none of them knew each other' in 1982. If anything the advance of identifiable patron-client groupings has been more rapid since then than was the rise of the Dnepropetrovsk faction in the first four years of the Brezhnev administration.[49] This point can be illustrated another way. It would be characteristic of a faction trying to break a bureaucratic mould from the outside that it would recruit support from casualties of that bureaucracy. Examples of this in the present administration are V. I. Vorotnikov and A. N. Iakovlev, both of whom suffered setbacks to their careers in the 1970s, and who seem to have allied themselves readily with the Andropov-Gorbachev group. We might also note that the mid-1980s is not the first occasion in recent Soviet history when a group of impatient young politicians has tried to put pressure on their elders; another, unsuccessful, attempt was made 20 years earlier by a group headed by A. N. Shelepin and based on the Komsomol and State Security. One of the new CC department heads is a restored 'political casualty' precisely from that group: Iu. P. Voronov succeeded A. I. Adzhubei as chief editor of *Komsomol'skaia pravda*, and was a member of the Komsomol Bureau between 1959 and 1965.[50] And when one looks at other members of the Komsomol Bureau for those years, an interesting number of them have appeared in the latest CC, or have been promoted by Gorbachev.[51]

Now it would be absurd to treat this as unusual: today's successful politicians can almost always be found among yesterday's Young Turks. It might also be risky to discern any particular cohesion or organised character in the Komsomol leadership of the early 1960s; after all, some others from that group did well under Brezhnev and not so well since 1982.[52] But on the other hand, in the light of this knowledge, it would be idle to treat the new administration simply as issue politicians, unsullied by factional fights, without political grudges or debts.

Now the bearing of all this on my argument is twofold. First, Gorbachev's consolidation of power has not been so very novel; indeed both in Russian and in communist terms it has followed a time-honoured recipe. And, second, officials who succeed as part of a patron-client arrangement are not simply products of talent, hard work and achievement, and their conduct of administration will be subject to special pressures and limitations, for instance those stemming from factional interests, past, present and future. If the personalist element in their appointment affects dealings with their superiors and their equals, why should it not also affect dealings with inferiors?

Despite the infusion of new persons and experience, then, the signs are that reform has not yet extended as far as reform of the bureaucratic culture in which the new elite work.

NOTES

1. It is noteworthy that a term like this was preferred to the obvious one (at least to outsiders) of 'reform'.

2. This is especially the case when it takes the form of amalgamation, as for instance with the creation of a 'super-ministry' like *Gosagroprom*; or when it takes the form of devolution to regional or territorial instrumentalities. The best example of the latter is the creation of four regional ministries in the construction field, see *Pravda*, 20 August 1986.

3. I draw this broad conclusion from his Political Report to the 27th Congress. See *Political Report of the Central Committee to the 27th Congress of the Communist Party of the Soviet Union* (Novosti, 1986), especially pp. 40–46, 49–52.

4. My thanks go to Mr Russell McCaskie who compiled the bulk of the data for this chapter.

5. See 'Representation of Career Types in Soviet Political Leadership', in R. B. Farrell (ed.), *Political Leadership in Eastern Europe and the Soviet Union* (London: Butterworth, 1970), pp. 108–39.

6. For instance R. E. Blackwell in *Soviet Studies*, vol. XXIV, no. 1, July 1972, pp. 24–40, or in *Comparative Politics*, vol. 6, no. 1, October 1973, pp. 99–121.

7. For instance J. F. Hough, *The Soviet Union and Social Science Theory* (Cambridge, Mass.: Harvard UP, 1977), p. 30, or the present author in T. H. Rigby and B. Harasymiw (eds), *Leadership Selection and Patron-Client Relations in the USSR and Yugoslavia* (London: George Allen & Unwin, 1983), p. 81.

8. *XXIV S"ezd KPSS. Stenograficheskii otchet*, vol. 1 (Moscow, 1972), p. 124 (my italics).

9. The total was 25 if one included the Main Political Administration of the Soviet Army and Navy, and the Party Control Committee.

10. These are International Information, Letters and Agricultural Machine-Building. The head and first deputy head of International Information, L. M. Zamiatin and N. N. Chetverikov, were both transferred elsewhere in April 1986 (*Izvestiia*, 27 April 1986, 19 April 1986), without any indication of replacement. There has been no mention of the Department of Letters, or of Agricultural Machine-Building, nor of their personnel, in the central press since, respectively November 1984 and September 1985. B. N. El'tsin (in *Die Zeit*, 9 May 1986), said that International Information and Agricultural Machine-Building had been

closed down; it had been El'tsin who had called for reorganisation of the CC departments at the Congress (*Pravda*, 27 February 1986).

11. G. P. Razumovskii and A. F. Dobrynin would seem both to be simultaneously CC Secretaries and department heads — respectively of Organisational-Party Work, and the International Department.

The situation regarding the headship of four other departments is, at the time of writing, as follows. In the *Department of Propaganda* it seemed, immediately after the 27th Congress, that A. N. Iakovlev was head as well as being a CC Secretary; but a new head of the Propaganda Department, Iu. A. Skliarov, was identified by *Pravda*, 10 August 1986. The activities of V. A. Medvedev after the congress made it clear that he had been transferred from the headship of the Department of Science and Educational Institutions to that of '*Liaison*' (*scil.* with ruling communist parties); on this see Archie Brown, 'Change in the Soviet Union', *Foreign Affairs*, vol. 64, no. 5, Summer 1986, pp. 1050–51. No successor to Medvedev in *Science and Educational Institutions* has been identified; it is possible that the functions of department head are being carried out by one of the two CC Secretaries in the ideological field, Iakovlev or M. V. Zimianin. Finally, for the *Economics Department* (formerly Planning and Financial Organs) no head has been attested since B. I. Gostev left to become Minister of Finance (*Izvestiia*, 15 December 1985). Either A. P. Biriukova or V. I. Dolgikh — or, possibly, L. N. Zaikov — might be supervising it.

12. It should not be forgotten that the process of renewal and rejuvenation began first in the Presidium of the Council of Ministers, with five newcomers entering it in late 1980, after A. N. Kosygin's retirement.

13. Elizabeth Teague in 'Turnover in the Soviet Elite under Gorbachev: Implications for Soviet Politics', *RFE/RL Supplement*, 1/86, 8 July 1986, has a neat way of illustrating the ambivalent quality of this change: the current age of the top politicians may be lower now than it was in 1981, but their age on appointment has been almost exactly the same as it was under Brezhnev (in fact slightly higher). It could be said that we are witnessing the 'normal' procedures of co-optation and promotion — but at the beginning, rather than at the end, of an administration.

14. There is probably no particular significance to this, other than that a network of training establishments, founded in the 1930s, made their real impact on education after the war.

15. Discussion of political generations is necessarily inexact because there is no 'normal' age for formative experiences. See Peter Frank in Archie Brown and Michael Kaser (eds), *The Soviet Union since the Fall of Khrushchev* (London: Macmillan, 1975), pp. 100–3.

16. To this list of persons promoted from defence industry to more general administration might be added A. A. Reut, V. I. Smyslov (successors to Voronin and Masliukov as first deputy chairmen of Gosplan), Iu. V. Konyshev (first deputy chairman, Council of Ministers Bureau for Machine-Building), and G. D. Kolmogorov (Chairman of the State Committee for Standards). A similar priority underlies the appointment of G. A. Iagodin, a nuclear physicist, as Minister of

Higher and Secondary Specialised Education.

As Teague ('Turnover in Soviet Elite', in note 13) points out, this is not a development of the Gorbachev leadership but can be traced back to the late Brezhnev period. It seems to be connected with greater weight given to defence industry in the selection of Gosplan first deputy chairmen, coupled with a greater readiness to move senior Gosplan personnel into the Council of Ministers.

17. The retirement of V. E. Dymshits marks the exit of the last really prominent Jew in Soviet politics.

18. See my chapter 'Putting Clients in Place', in Archie Brown (ed.), *Political Leadership in the Soviet Union* (London: Macmillan, forthcoming). The appointment of the Tatar, F. A. Tabeev, to be first deputy chairman, RSFSR Council of Ministers (*Sovetskaia Rossiia*, 3 July 1986) may be treated, from one point of view, as the co-optation of a substitute for Nuriev.

19. Demichev's survival as a candidate member of the Politburo after the 27th Congress and his subsequent appointment as first deputy chairman of the Presidium of the Supreme Soviet (*Pravda*, 19 June 1986) are remarkable. It is hard to interpret this as a gesture to the Moscow party organisation at the same time as its new first secretary, B. N. El'tsin, has been replacing so many of its officials. Both N. V. Talyzin and A. P. Biriukova have based their careers in Moscow, but not in the Moscow party like V. V. Grishin or I. V. Kapitonov.

20. Recent Leningrad politics are instructive in the pitfalls of argument about patronage. Both Zaikov and Solov'ev got accelerated promotion in Leningrad under Romanov, and continued successful careers both during Romanov's two-year period in Moscow and since his downfall. In this case there seems little alternative to the interpretation that Gorbachev wished to signal to Leningrad that Romanov's disgrace was an isolated matter, without implications for his protégés or the Leningrad organisation.

21. The CC and CAC do not include *all obkom* first secretaries from the Ukraine, Belorussia, Kazakhstan or Uzbekistan, and, in 1986, apparently not quite all members of the Council of Ministers. They do include about 60 ordinary workers and peasants, for whom see below.

22. This seems a fair way of describing the short, sharp crisis of June 1957, and the prolonged period of tension in 1960–61.

23. Perhaps it would be more accurate to include Andropov's period as General Secretary, and say two and a half years; rapid personnel turnover is one of a number of striking continuities between the Andropov and Gorbachev periods, sometimes giving the impression that the new regime began in November 1982 and experienced a hiatus between February 1984 and March 1985.

24. Data for this and subsequent tables were almost all collected at the ANU. A small amount of help is owed to the Radio Liberty Research Bulletins (Russian series), nos. 47/86, 51/86, 54/86, 63/86 and 69/86.

25. It might be noted that the dismissals have not been simply the retirement of the oldest officials. The two oldest members of the Council of Ministers at the time of Gorbachev's accession, namely

E. P. Slavskii (born 1898), and P. F. Lomako (born 1904), were retained as full members of the CC and remained ministers until late in 1986 (*Pravda*, 2 and 23 November 1986).

26. Thus for newly co-opted CC members, the standard deviation of birth years is 5.1, compared with 8.3 for members carried over from the 1981 CC.

27. On this theme see J. F. Hough, *Soviet Leadership in Transition* (Washington, DC: Brookings Institution, 1980), pp. 57–9.

28. This figure includes as an 'official' V. N. Golubeva, promoted to the position of factory director around the time of the Congress; see *Pravda*, 2 May 1986.

29. Many Soviet sources give ethnic affiliation as part of biographical reporting, but sources explicitly on the CC do not. In cases of unknown nationality, therefore, one is forced back to surname analysis, which does not allow one to distinguish Ukrainian and Belorussian names reliably from Russian ones. Slavic-sounding names are also borne by a small number of people from the non-Slavic but highly assimilated groups of the Volga and Siberia. This is why the 'Others, unknown' category in Table 3.6 is larger for 1981 (where we possess fuller information) than it is for 1986; in the case of the latter date some 1 per cent of the total will have been included among Slavs when they are in fact non-Slavs with Slavic surnames.

30. This table has been updated to reflect the situation as of early June 1986. The reason is that the composition of the CC in March clearly reflected plans for personnel changes that were not completed for several months. One example among many: the Soviet ambassador to Yugoslavia is someone we should expect to find in the CC at some level; N. N. Rodionov, however, ambassador since 1978, was not retained in the new CC. The obvious explanation — that he was scheduled for replacement — turned out to be correct, but his retirement (and replacement by V. F. Mal'tsev, a full CC member) was not announced in *Pravda* until 9 June 1986.

On the other hand major personnel changes of *late* June have not been included. The promotion of G. G. Vedernikov to deputy chairman of the USSR Council of Ministers (*Izvestiia*, 20 June 1986) entailed appointing a successor as first secretary, Chelyabinsk *obkom* (N. D. Shvyrev) who was not in the CC. The probability is that *this* move had not been planned prior to the congress.

31. It should be pointed out that the contribution of CC personnel to policy formation seems to be mainly informal. With the exception of a few well-known cases under Khrushchev, no one has been able to discern a function of policy formation in CC plenary meetings.

32. See in particular 'Ochishchenie' by T. Samolis in *Pravda*, 13 February 1986.

33. For instance in the section of the report on social welfare and justice: see *Political Report*, pp. 51–2.

34. Baibakov now has the title 'State Counsellor with the Council of Ministers' (*Gosudarstvennyi sovetnik pri SM SSSR*) (*Pravda*, 29 April 1986).

35. Membership of the USSR Council of Ministers appears to confer

a place *ex officio* on one of the three tiers of the CC. The exceptions to this rule are significant. They are, first, persons such as A. V. Kovalenko, D. L. Kartvelishvili or A. D. Duisheev who retired or were replaced shortly after the congress, and whose replacement, it may be inferred, was planned at the time CC membership was drawn up (see also note 30). Second is V. V. Kulov, chairman of the State Committee for Safety in Atomic Energy, who was dismissed in the aftermath of the Chernobyl' disaster (*Pravda*, 20 July 1986), but whose replacement (perhaps by A. G. Meshkov?) may well have been contemplated earlier. Meshkov was also among those punished, but prior to that he was the only *first deputy* member of the Council of Ministers to have a CC place. Another possibility is that he was being groomed to replace E. P. Slavskii. (See above, note 25).

36. See J. H. Miller in Archie Brown and Michael Kaser (eds), *Soviet Policy for the 1980s* (London: Macmillan, 1982), pp. 26–7. However I am less confident that I was that All-Union and regional echelons can always be distinguished precisely; hence the observation that one or the other job type occupies half the CC positions is probably insignificant.

37. *Obkom* first secretaries from the RSFSR are all in the CC or CAC, and the RSFSR has no republican party *apparat*. So if representation of non-central party officials is to be boosted, and the Central Asian republics snubbed, the Ukraine and Belorussia are a natural source for the increase.

38. There are four of these, covering apparently the North-West (commanded by N. V. Ogarkov), the South-West (I. A. Gerasimov), the South (i.e. Transcaucasia and Central Asia) (M. M. Zaitsev) and the Far East (I. M. Tret'iak). Their proper title may be Theatre of Operations (*Teatr Voennykh Deistvii*), for which see *Voenno-entsiklopedicheskii slovar'* (Moscow Voenizd., 1983), p. 732 . The title commander-in-chief has been attested, as far as I know, only in the case of Tret'iak's predecessor V. L. Govorov.

39. See R. J. Hill, 'Soviet Political Development and the Culture of the Apparatchiki', *Studies in Comparative Communism*, vol, XIX, no. 1 (Spring 1986), pp. 25–39.

40. 'Knives sheathed as Soviet leaders debate the issues' in *Canberra Times*, 31 March 1986.

41. See Gorbachev's concluding remarks concerning amendments to the Party Rules, in the Novosti edition of his *Political Report*, p. 109.

42. Ligachev's congress speech (*Pravda*, 28 February 1986) contained perhaps the most explicit statement of these policies. On inter-republic transfers, the policy was endorsed by others such as the Central Asian first secretaries I. B. Usmankhodzhaev and K. Makhkamov in *Pravda*, 28 February 1986, 1 March 1986.

43. See, for instance, Dawn Mann, 'New Trend in Party Personnel Policy', in *Radio Liberty Research Bulletin*, RL 385/86 (9 October 1986).

44. An example may be found in the *Pravda* editorial *Pervyi sekretar'* ('First Secretary') of 22 July 1986. This names the names of regional party first secretaries, both those who are promoting *perestroika*, and those who are allegedly dragging their feet. Criticism of the performance

of named officials, especially ministers, was of course common under Brezhnev; the charge of failing to *support* a current program would seem to be rather a new development.

45. Promotions which would seem to show the influence of Ryzhkov since he became a CC Secretary in November 1982 are those of L. F. Bobykin, E. A. Varnachev, L. A. Voronin, B. N. El'tsin, G. V. Kolbin, Iu. D. Masliukov, Iu. V. Petrov, Ia. P. Riabov and N. N. Sliun'kov. Sliun'kov's is particularly interesting: he was transferred from being deputy chairman of Gosplan to be first secretary in Belorussia less than two months after Ryzhkov became Secretary. It is difficult to think of his name occurring but for Ryzhkov's sponsorship, and the latter's authority must indeed have been great for that name to have been accepted.

46. A comparable list, with use of similar, rather exacting criteria, might be: V. G. Afonin, M. V. Gramov, A. I. Ievlev, V. A. Kaznacheev, V. I. Kalashnikov, A. A. Khomiakov, N. E. Kruchina, V. S. Murakhovskii, V. P. Nikonov, G. P. Razumovskii, A. V. Vlasov.

47. G. V. Aleshin, N. S. Ermakov, Iu. I. Litvintsev, F. I. Loshchenkov, A. G. Mel'nikov, P. Ia. Slezko. Note that this, and the previous two lists are not attempts to list members of a clientele, but merely those members who have been promoted since Brezhnev's death.

48. Of the 26 promotions just referred to, eight occurred under Andropov, and three under Chernenko. This is another reason for dating the new administration back, *de facto*, to late 1982.

49. I summarise some other ways in which the rise of the Andropov-Gorbachev group differed from that of Brezhnev's group in 'Putting Clients in Place' — see above, note 18.

50. I am indebted to A. Rahr in RL (Russian series), no. 100/86, for drawing my attention to Voronov's history.

51. First N. E. Kruchina and E. A. Shevardnadze, who may well have stood sponsors for others such as A. N. Aksenov, A. I. Kamshalov, A. D. Lizichev, V. P. Loginov, N. F. Rubtsov.

52. For instance B. N. Pastukhov, or G. A. Kriulin.

4

The Mass Party Membership: Steady as She Goes

J. H. Miller

The party congresses and conferences of early 1986 probably devoted less time and publicity to matters of mass party membership than on any previous occasion since the death of Stalin. As recently as under K. U. Chernenko there had been a lively discussion of party recruitment policy in *Pravda*,[1] but this was not pursued once M. S. Gorbachev took office. In place of questions of the mass membership, the stress under Gorbachev has been conspicuously on questions of leadership — the selection, training, deployment and performance of officials. The main reason for this shift in emphasis would seem to be the following: Gorbachev is clear, in a way the older generation were not, that a profound change has affected party membership since the early 1970s. The era is past in which the party strove to *establish* its presence in all walks of life, the era, in fact, of *partiinoe stroitel'stvo* ('party *construction*'); the party presence in society is probably considered to be close to its optimum,[2] needing only routine maintenance and fine-tuning. Far more important now is the more efficient and intensive *utilisation* of the party in social management; hence the pre-occupation with leadership.

The main features and profile, then, of CPSU membership have been remarkably stable in the 1980s. Which is not to say that interesting things cannot be observed in its development under four General Secretaries.

Table 4.1[3] gives an overall picture of the size and demographic tendencies of the CPSU over the last 15 years.[4] The party now contains more than 19 million members and candidates, or 9.7 per cent of the 'adult' population (by which is meant, almost

Table 4.1: CPSU: size, growth, admissions and losses, 1971–86

Congress	1971 (March) 24th	1976 (February) 25th	1981 (February) 26th	1986 (February) 27th
Size of party				
Members	13,810,089	15,058,017	16,763,009	18,309,693
Candidates	642,232	636,170	717,759	728,253
	14,455,321	15,694,187	17,480,768	19,037,946
Percentage of adult population	9.2	9.3	9.5	9.7
Net growth		1,238,866	1,786,581	1,557,178
% per annum		1.66	2.18	1.72
Admissions to candidacy		2,593,824	3,162,372	3,305,956
Total losses		1,354,958	1,375,791	1,748,778
% per annum		1.81	1.69	1.93
Expulsions		435,000	c.300,000	c.430,000
Non-promotions		?	91,000	101,000 +
Deaths?		(c.900,000?)	c.985,000	c.1,218,000
% per annum		(1.2?)	1.22	1.36

Note: Figures in brackets are estimates.

certainly, those aged 18 and over). It was growing quite briskly, at more than 2 per cent per annum, in the later years of the Brezhnev administration, but this growth rate has been cut back, to the unusually low figure of 1.39 per cent, in Gorbachev's first year of office. Candidate membership, at less than 4 per cent, is also close to a record low level. Both of these low figures suggest a policy of increased selectivity towards party recruitment, and it would be plausible to connect this selectivity with the new administration's campaigns for discipline and against official corruption. The intention may well be to return to party growth rates 'stabilizing at a point not greatly above the growth-level for the population at large'.[5]

If this is so, let us note that it entails a planning operation of some complexity: the officials who plan party recruitment and distribute instructions to effect these plans must aim for a rate of admission which, net of deaths and expulsions of party people, keeps approximate pace with the rate of growth of the adult population. We can assume that these officials are well informed about prospective disciplinary policies; they are also going to need reliable demographic data for both population and party (the latter are a closed book for us). As can be seen from the lower half of Table 4.1, to achieve a net growth of 1.5 million over five years, it has been necessary to recruit more than twice that number (3.3 million).

There is an oddity about these party recruitment figures (or their public presentation) which emerges from close scrutiny of pages 20–22 of the most recent source. Anyone who divides 1,659,000 by 0.594 (these being, respectively, the absolute figure for, and the fraction of, party admissions who come from the working class), or, alternatively, 277,000 by 0.099 (the same for collective farmers), will not arrive at a grand total of 3.3 million admissions; instead the figures seem to entail a total in the region of 2,790,000. We seem to be missing something in the order of half a million newly recruited communists. The clue lies in the subtitle to the table at the top of p. 21: the percentages are those of party recruitment '*by the territorial organisations*', and they omit entry into party organisations under direct central subordination. The latter are, above all, those in the Armed Forces, but also those of the KGB, and, more recently, in the MVD and Aeroflot.[6] We can say, with some assurance, that about half a million candidates have entered these branches of the CPSU in the recent quinquennium. If the same exercise is done on earlier editions of *KPSS v tsifrakh*, it will be found that admissions to centrally subordinate party organisations have varied around this average of c.100,000 per annum since the early 1960s.

It is tempting to proceed to two further hypotheses: first that the great majority of these 100,000 are being admitted into the party organisations of the Armed Forces. The latter maintain a party presence of more than 20 per cent.[7] Given the turnover that must occur, among officers as well as among NCOs and conscripts, this might well require as many as 100,000 new party candidates every year. A complication (which I cannot resolve) is a source which sets admissions into the party organisations of the Armed Forces (in the early 1970s) at half this figure.[8]

The second surmise is that the majority of these 100,000 per annum should be recorded in party statistics as white collar (*sluzhashchie*) by background — simply because that is what officers (police as well as military) are.[9] The data on the 'social position' of entrants to the party — for the 1981–86 period, that

59.4 per cent of them were workers, and only 30.7 per cent white collar — have prompted scepticism among some Western scholars. We can now discern one way in which the figures for *sluzhashchie* should be amended upwards.

We know very little about people who *leave* the CPSU — in consequence of their deaths, or for various other reasons. In fact the full extent of our knowledge concerning the 1981–86 quinquennium is (a) the figure for total losses, 1.75 million, derived by subtracting net growth from admissions, and (b) the facts that 'more than 101,000' candidates were not promoted into full membership, and that 430,000 persons were excluded 'for various misdemeanours'.[10] Concerning the 101,000 persons not promoted, some may have retained their candidate status, though this is not supposed to happen.[11] It is quite unclear whether the figure of 430,000 exclusions is supposed to include the 101,000 failed promotions, or not. Further, we are given no information, as we were in the early 1960s, about a third category of withdrawal, people who have 'lost contact with the party organisation'.[12] So the attempt in the bottom rows of Table 4.1 to separate out deaths from the various forms of deliberate annulment of party affiliation must be treated with caution; but *if* it has merit, we arrive at a figure of not more than 1.2 million for deaths in the CPSU in the 1981–86 period. This entails a death rate for the party which is apparently somewhat lower than the death rate for the adult population as a whole[13] — a conclusion which invites tantalising questions about party life styles.[14] Again, the speculative nature of this chain of argument must be emphasised: not only are the party figures unsatisfactory, but we possess neither age distributions nor age-specific death rates for the relevant period.

Table 4.2 gives some idea of the regional distribution of party membership and of its net growth. It can be noted first that party membership in *all* the 'non-Russian' Union Republics is increasing faster than in the RSFSR. In republics such as the Ukraine or Georgia this growth is close to the national average, but in a good number of others, notably the republics of Central Asia, it is very much higher. Analogous figures are available for 1983 as well as the 1981 and 1986 ones shown in Table 4.2, and it is noticeable from the former that growth rates in Central Asia (also in Azerbaidzhan and in Estonia) have fallen steeply in the latter part of the quinquennium; Kazakhstan, however, with a growth rate virtually unchanged before and after 1983 does not

Table 4.2: Party membership in the major regions 1981–86

	1981	% growth per annum	1986
Ukraine	2,933,564	1.68	3,188,854
Belorussia	595,311	2.33	667,980
Lithuania	170,935	2.91	197,274
Latvia	161,264	1.91	177,258
Estonia	97,923	2.28	109,599
Moldavia	163,902	2.93	189,403
	4,122,899	1.90	4,530,368
Georgia	350,435	1.82	383,472
Azerbaidzhan	330,319	2.67	376,822
Armenia	164,738	2.53	186,637
	845,492	2.29	946,931
Uzbekistan	568,243	2.47	642,025
Kazakhstan	729,498	2.14	810,776
Kirghizia	126,402	2.71	144,466
Tadzhikistan	108,974	2.45	122,985
Turkmenistan	93,556	3.32	110,141
	1,626,673	2.39	1,830,393
Non-Russian Union Republics	6,595,064	2.07	7,307,692
13 largest provinces of the RSFSR	4,424,686	1.49	4,765,176
Rest of RSFSR	5,310,663?	(1.45??)	(5,707,000??)
	9,735,349?	(1.47??)	(10,472,000??)
Armed Forces	1,100,000?	(2.17??)	(1,224,700??)
Grand Total	17,430,413	1.74	19,004,378

Note: Figures in brackets are estimates.

share this trend. Again it is appropriate to mention the corruption scandals and purges of local officials which have been a feature of many of the southern republics; Kazakhstan was not at first so deeply implicated in these as some other republics, and this, and the continued momentum of its party membership may both be linked to the striking political longevity of Kazakhstan's First Secretary, D. A. Kunaev, who was not removed from this position until December 1986.

Table 4.3: Men and women in the CPSU, 1976–86

	Females			Males		
	1976	1981	1986	1976	1981	1986
No. in CPSU	3,793,859	4,615,576	5,475,145	11,900,328	12,865,192	13,562,801
Net growth		821,717	859,569		964,864	697,609
% p.a.		4.00	3.47		1.57	1.06
Admissions		1,017,940	1,127,742		2,144,432	2,178,214
Losses		196,223	268,173		1,179,568	1,480,605
% p.a.		1.01	1.14		1.91	2.20

We do not know, nor have we ever known, the size of the party in the largest republic, the RSFSR. This is because *KPSS v tsifrakh*, and similar sources, routinely present figures for the 14 'non-Russian' republics only, and for their 'territorial' (i.e. civilian) party organisations. The very large residual (11.7 out of 19 million in 1986) embraces the party organisations both of the RSFSR and of the Armed Forces. The apportionment in Table 4.2 of party personnel between the RSFSR and Armed Forces in 1981 may be treated as fairly reliable;[15] the growth rate adopted for the RSFSR between 1981 and 1986,[16] and the absolute size that flows on from this for the 1986 party in the RSFSR and the Armed Forces, is no more than informed guesswork. But whatever figure is adopted (within reason), party membership in the Armed Forces will be found to have increased more than the national average. The size of the military organisations of the CPSU — well over a million, or one in fifteen of all members and candidates — as well as their contribution to party recruitment and ultimately to the civilian party (as ex-officers and others are released into the labour force) all deserve to be stressed; they are so easily overlooked in analysis of CPSU data and internal politics.

Our source does provide data on the 13 largest party organisations of the RSFSR, and, among these, four are worth singling out. The party organisations of Gor'kii, a major industrial province, has continued its established pattern of unusually slow development; less than 1 per cent per annum. The organisations of Kemerovo, Cheliabinsk and Sverdlovsk (respectively 2.32, 2.04 and 1.98 per cent p.a.) are, by contrast, well above the RSFSR mean. It is tempting to recall here that Sverdlovsk and Cheliabinsk have strong connections with the new Chairman of the Council of Ministers, N. I. Ryzhkov, and Kemerovo with the new 'second' secretary of the party, E. K. Ligachev.

Table 4.3 sets out much the same information as Table 4.1, but with men and women distinguished. Women are now 28.8 per cent of the party, and constitute 34.1 per cent of new candidates; comparable figures for 1976 were 24.3 per cent and 32.2 per cent. It will be seen that (for the first time) net increase in female members and candidates in the recent quinquennium exceeds that of males. This is due in part to the unabated emphasis on recruiting women, which in turn can be linked with the expansion of the party in the service and distribution sectors (see below); but much more to the substantially lower attrition

Table 4.4: Age distribution of communists, 1977–86

	1977		1981		1986	
Admissions to CPSU through Komsomol		1,873,131 (= 73.4%)		2,397,791 (= 72.5%)		
Age groups						
Up to 25	929,408	= 5.8%	1,129,559	= 6.5%	1,155,010	= 6.1%
26 to 30	1,729,738	10.8	1,930,121	11.1	2,194,127	11.5
31 to 40	4,134,166	25.9	3,693,195	21.2	4,501,662	23.7
41 to 50	4,229,078	26.4	4,542,863	26.1	4,239,015	22.3
51 to 60	2,897,398	18.1	3,631,789	20.8	3,693,409	19.4
Over 60	2,074,688	13.0	2,502,886	14.3	3,221,155	17.0
Total	15,994,476		17,430,413		19,004,378	

rate among women. Women not only live longer, but are, almost certainly, younger on average than male party members, simply because more of them are of recent recruitment.

The distribution of communists by age (Table 4.4) reveals a change in recruitment policy which distinguishes the late 1970s from the early 1980s; (it is unfortunate that no age distribution was published for 1976, so that we cannot make comparisons over an exact decade). In the late 1970s two age groups in particular — those under 26 and those over 50 — were increasing faster than the others; by the early 1980s it is the 26–40 year old age group which is showing fastest growth. One is also struck by the fact that the 41–50 age group in 1986 is larger than was the 31–40 age group nine years earlier; this can have occurred only if there was fairly substantial recruitment during the period among people over 30. The changed policy is in fact attested in the 1981 and 1983 sources: '. . . party organisations are conducting more actively the selection for the party of people of a more mature age, people who have undergone good schooling in production and in life'.[17] At the same time admission of people up to 30 is being channelled more and more through the Komsomol,[18] and a fifth of all candidacies are now in the over 30 age group, principally among those aged 31–40.[19] The outcome of this concentration on mature, but not yet middle-aged recruitment, and also of a more stable demographic structure in the party (with consequently increased death rates), is that the mean age of party personnel seems not to be rising any more, but to

Table 4.5: Original class background of communists

	All members and candidates			Newly admitted candidates		
	'Blue-collar' workers	Collective farmers	'White-collar' workers	'Blue-collar' workers	Collective farmers	'White-collar' workers
1956	32.0	17.1	50.9			
				41.1	22.0	36.9
1961	33.9	17.6	48.5			
				44.7	15.0	40.3
1966	37.8	16.2	46.0			
				52.0	13.4	34.6
1971	40.1	15.1	44.8			
				57.6	11.3	31.1
1976	41.6	13.9	44.5			
				59.0	10.3	30.7
1981	43.4	12.8	43.8			
				59.4	9.9	30.7
1986	45.0	11.8	43.2			

have stabilised at about 44; this seems to be a mean age slightly above that of the population over 20, though, for reasons already noted, that calculation is a hazardous one.

Table 4.5 reviews the trends in class background (*sotsial'noe polozhenie*) of party personnel over the last 30 years. It should be borne in mind that this is a categorisation assigned to new candidates at the time they are first admitted to the party, and one which (presumably) stays unaltered on file thereafter. It is assigned on the basis of 'relationship to the means of production', i.e. of current or most recent job of the candidate (or of his or her parents) at the time of joining the party, and class background figures thus bear only a very indirect relationship to the current 'class' composition of the party at any given time. Classifications of CPSU personnel by current type of work (*po rodu zaniatiia*) are sometimes published for individual republics or provinces, but not for the party as a whole.

Putting *that* problem aside for the moment, we can note that party personnel who are by origin 'blue-collar' workers (*rabochie*) have recently become the largest of the three social groups in the party, for the first time since the late 1930s — edging out the 'white-collar' workers (*sluzhashchie*). The latter — described at the time as the 'best people'[20] — had come to dominate the party in the latter half of the Stalin period, and it has been an unremitting priority of the leadership since Stalin (at least in public relations) to get this dominance reversed and to present for inspection a party which is unambiguously 'proletarian'. (This is presumably one reason why statistics *po rodu zaniatiia* are not offered.) Concerning the third category, collective farmers (*kolkhozniki*), there are few problems: their declining share in the party has reflected the decline in the collective farm sector of the labour force; collective farmers are nowadays about a tenth of the latter, and are only very slightly overrepresented in the party.

The data on blue- and white-collar workers, by contrast, present considerable difficulties. It is hard to see why *sluzhashchie* have retained their position so intractably, and *rabochie* made such slow gains, if the latter have been more than half of all recruits over the past 20 years.[21] The difficulty can be resolved, I believe, if one accepts two hypotheses. The first has already been mentioned: figures on recruitment pertain to the territorial organisations only, and do not include people who join the party in the Armed Forces, the latter being classified principally as white-collar.[22] Second, the figures can be made to fit quite neatly, if one also assumes a higher rate of attrition among *rabochie* and *kolkhozniki* than among *sluzhashchie*.[23] It is perfectly plausible that the former two groups should have a lower life expectancy, and should be more vulnerable to party penalties like expulsion.

A different problem is that of the current 'class composition' of the CPSU. It is well known that the CPSU membership improves one's career chances and has promoted social mobility; indeed some outsiders would see this as the principal motive, and social significance of CPSU membership. It would follow that a lot of people originally registered as *rabochie* or *kolkhozniki* have moved into white-collar occupations.[24] Most interpreters have assumed, therefore, that the figure for blue-collar workers *po rodu zaniatiia* would turn out to be substantially lower, and that for white-collar workers substantially higher than the class background figures. In a previous analysis[25] I presented data and arguments suggesting that about 55 per cent of employed communists are *sluzhashchie*; there seems no reason to change this conclusion. If it stands, we should think now in terms of about 10.5 million communists being in, or retired from, white-collar occupations (including the military); this can be contrasted with the 8.2 million who are *sluzhashchie*

Table 4.6: Party membership and levels of education

Communists with qualifications:	1976		1981		1986	
Tertiary	3,807,469	= 24.3%	4,881,877	= 28.0%	6,045,653	= 31.8%
Incomplete tertiary	382,556	2.4	391,216	2.2	398,059	2.1
Secondary specialist	3,806,087	24.3	4,355,465	25.0	4,836,347	25.5
Secondary general	2,216,310	14.2	2,941,624	16.9	3,615,133	19.0
Incomplete secondary	3,175,163	20.3	2,973,839	17.1	2,601,613	13.7
Primary	2,251,306	14.4	1,886,392	10.8	1,507,573	7.9
Total	15,638,891		17,430,413		19,004,378	
N.B. 'Specialists'	7,613,556	48.7	9,237,342	53.0	10,882,000	57.3
'Non-specialists'	8,025,335	51.3	8,193,071	47.0	8,122,378	42.7

by social origin; that is, about a fifth of white-collar communists are 'parvenus', whose current occupation does not correspond to their registered class background.

In practical terms this would entail that between a quarter and a fifth of the white-collar labour force are in the party, about 7 per cent of blue-collar workers, and about 12 per cent of collective farmers. This last figure may seem surprising. It is explained in part by the lack of any white-collar/blue-collar distinction among *kolkhozniki*. But it is also the case that farming (state and collective) has now achieved a higher party presence than many sectors of industry and distribution.

By contrast with class, data on the education levels of the CPSU (Table 4.6) present few ambiguities. The most striking fact, and one whose socio-political implications do not need spelling out, is that almost a third of the CPSU has tertiary qualifications, and these six million persons amount to more than 40 per cent of all employed graduates. The role of tertiary graduates is especially pronounced in the party bureaucracy: two-thirds of party secretaries in primary organisations have these qualifications, and virtually all officials at echelons higher than this.[26] Party, economic and educational public relations have long stressed the importance of 'specialists' — people with tertiary or so-called 'secondary specialist' qualifications; as can be seen, nearly 60 per cent of the party are now specialists in this sense. It is not implausible that this category and the category of *sluzhashchie* by type of employment coincide to a considerable degree. But most important is the fact that the disproportionate growth in the specialist sector is due almost entirely to the increase in tertiary graduates in the party. When we turn to the category of 'non-specialists' (which has begun to decline for the first time), we notice another area of dynamic growth — that of party membership among those with completed secondary general education. More and more people are completing secondary school rather than leaving it as soon as legally possible, and party recruitment of workers and peasants is concentrated on these.

Employment of people in the CPSU is the subject of Table 4.7.[27] The Soviet sources which form its basis refer to deployment in 'branches of the national economy', and it will be apparent that 20 per cent of the CPSU are not employed 'in the national economy', and that this category has been growing quite rapidly. The term 'national economy' is a technical one, and in this

Table 4.7: Employment of communists in branches of the economy

Communists employed in:	1976		1981		1986	
I Material Production						
Industry	3,881,519	= 24.8%	(4,408,000)	= 25.3%	(4,713,000)	= 24.8%
Construction	1,048,492	6.7	(1,145,000)	6.6	(1,220,000)	6.4
Transport	934,225	6.0	(996,000)	5.7	(1,061,000)	5.6
Communications	(123,000)	0.8	(134,000)	0.8	(146,000)	0.8
Agriculture	2,611,698	16.7	(2,834,000)	16.3	(3,017,000)	15.9
State farms	1,020,018	6.5	(1,142,000)	6.6	(1,228,000)	6.5
Collective farms	1,373,654	8.8	(1,424,000)	8.2	(1,500,000)	7.9
Trade, catering, supply	(548,000)	3.5	(626,000)	3.6	(696,000)	3.7
Miscellaneous	(153,000)	1.0	(192,000)	1.1	(229,000)	1.2
Subtotal	(9,300,000)	59.5	(10,335,000)	59.3	(11,081,000)	58.3
II Non-material branches of economy						
Science	(548,000)	3.5	(620,000)	3.6	(637,000)	3.4
Education, health, culture	(1,580,000)	10.1	(1,650,000)	9.5	(1,743,000)	9.2
Administration	(1,096,000)	7.0	(1,227,000)	7.0	(1,379,000)	7.3
Housing and services	(217,000)	1.4	(268,000)	1.5	(319,000)	1.7
Subtotal	(3,440,000)	22.0	(3,764,000)	21.6	(4,078,000)	21.5
Total employed in national economy	(12,739,000)	81.5	(14,099,000)	80.9	(15,159,000)	79.8
Not employed in national economy	(2,900,000)	18.5	(3,331,000)	19.1	(3,845,000)	20.2
Total CPSU	15,638,891		17,430,413		19,004,378	

Note: Figures in brackets by calculation from percentages, or by interpolation, extrapolation, or subtraction. Inaccuracies in totals due to rounding.

context a handy euphemism for directing attention away from important aspects of the CPSU; almost certainly it does *not* include employment in the Armed Forces or security. If then we subtract from the 3.8 million not employed in the national economy in 1986, the figure of 1.2 million communists in the Armed Forces (Table 4.2), we reach a figure of 2.6 million as the maximum estimate for communists who may genuinely not be in employment: retired and invalid pensioners, non-earning house-wives, etc. And it will be noted by reference to Table 4.4 that this number is considerably less than the number of communists aged over 60, the legal retirement age for males. The conclusion, which fits with other evidence,[28] is that a great many communists continue to work after reaching pensionable age, and that the number engaged in 'home duties' is probably quite small.

When attention is turned to specific sectors of employment, it is noticeable that the proportion of the party in heavy industry and transport has begun to decline (after many years of steady increase), whereas the proportion in the much smaller sectors of trade, catering and supply, housing and everyday services is now increasing; both these trends are also reflected in the figures for distribution of new candidates by employment,[29] which have not so far been analysed. They reflect the growing emphasis on con-sumer goods, distribution and services which dates back to the late Brezhnev period, and the realisation that these were occupa-tional sectors where the party presence, and hence its mobilis-atory capacity, were at their weakest.[30] Further, the relative buoyancy of party recruitment among women will surely be con-nected with the expansion of the party presence in these sectors.

Another interesting development is the declining share of the party employed in science, education, health and culture, whilst that employed in administration is rising. Both these tendencies can also be detected in the figures on *sluzhashchie* by type of employment.[31] The background to this divergence is undoubtedly a policy of concentrating party admissions among the real decision-makers and supervisory personnel, at the expense of professional people less clearly in a position to affect politics. This has sometimes been interpreted, inside as well as outside the USSR, as a policy of 'discrimination against the intelligentsia'. It certainly represents discrimination among white-collar and professional employees, but use of the word 'intelligentsia' here conveys, I suggest, a misleading impression in English.

Table 4.8: Ethnic composition of the party

	1981 No.	% growth per annum	1983 No.	% growth per annum	1986 No.
Russians	10,457,771	1.67	10,809,066	1.32	11,241,958
Ukrainians	2,794,592	1.85	2,898,757	1.62	3,041,736
Belorussians	651,486	2.50	684,492	1.99	726,108
Moldavians	89,680	4.64	98,195	4.08	110,715
	3,535,758	2.04	3,681,444	1.75	3,878,559
Lithuanians	126,704	3.17	134,866	2.93	147,068
Latvians	71,911	1.60	74,225	1.75	78,193
Estonians	55,957	2.11	58,341	1.65	61,277
	254,572	2.49	267,432	2.33	286,538
Georgians	290,227	2.17	302,947	2.05	321,922
Azeris	280,498	4.26	304,915	3.48	337,904
Armenians	261,572	2.16	272,965	2.17	291,081
	832,297	2.87	880,827	2.58	950,907
Kazakhs	332,821	3.31	355,213	2.97	387,837
Uzbeks	393,770	4.31	428,446	2.80	465,443
Tadzhiks	74,987	3.48	80,293	3.01	87,759
Kirghiz	62,694	5.81	70,195	3.61	78,064
Turkmen	61,430	5.79	68,744	3.76	76,786
	925,702	4.09	1,002,891	3.00	1,095,889
Others	1,424,313	1.81	1,476,243	1.65	1,550,527
Total	17,430,413	1.95	18,117,903	1.61	19,004,378

Finally the ethnic composition of the party: Russians continue to be by far the largest ethnic group in the CPSU, and are represented well beyond their share of the population; they are 59.1 per cent of the party and about 52 per cent of the population. At the same time Russian party membership is growing more slowly than that of any other major nationality, so that they are the only ethnic group whose share of the party is declining (from 60.0 per cent to 59.1 per cent in the last quinquennium). A few groups — Ukrainians, Latvians, Estonians and 'Other' nationalities (i.e. those not associated with a 'titular' Union Republic) — are maintaining a reasonably steady share; all the others are increasing faster than the national average, and hence increasing their share of party membership. This is especially true of the Islamic nationalities of the south of the USSR; the number of communists among these groups was increasing at more than 4 per cent per annum, twice the national rate, at the beginning of the decade.

In Table 4.8 it is worth while to insert the figures for 1983 between those for 1981 and 1986, for they point up changes that have occurred in the latter part of the quinquennium, almost certainly policy changes to be associated with the Andropov and Gorbachev administrations. Annual growth rates have fallen (as was evident in Table 4.2), but there has been surprising variation in this fall. It has been steepest in Central Asia, especially among Uzbeks, Kirghiz and Turkmen; and shallowest among the Baltic and Transcaucasian nationalities, two of whom, Latvians and Armenians, have actually increased their growth rates, against the national trend, in 1983–86. To complicate the pattern still further, Kazakhs have not shared in the deceleration of recruitment as much as other Islamic nationalities, whilst Estonians have been much more affected by it than other Balts; and the number of Moldavian communists is now increasing faster than that of any other titular nationality!

The tendency among the 'Other', non-titular nationalities may give a clue to what is going on. It has long been thought that Union Republican leaderships take such opportunities as are available to favour the 'titular' nationalities,[32] with the result that party recruitment among 'non-titulars' has never been particularly dynamic. Yet we can see that growth rates for these other nationalities have not fallen very much by the 1983–86 period, and are now higher than the national average. This suggests the hand of central party authorities, and the reining in of republican leaderships. Pointers in the same direction are the steep decline in growth rates among Islamic groups (coinciding with purges in those republics), and the more stable increase among Latvians, Armenians and Georgians (all nationalities whose party membership grew only sluggishly under Brezhnev). Concerning Kazakhs and Moldavians it might even be noted that the leadership in these two republics had particularly close ties with Brezhnev, and remained (until late 1986 at least) relatively 'unreconstructed' by the new administration.

To sum up: the watch-words for the mass party membership

are 'steady as she goes' and — as with the economy — more intensive utilisation of available resources. This is why matters of party recruitment and composition have become very much overshadowed by questions of political leadership and style. We are nowadays in a position to tease rather more out of party statistics than used to be the case, and some of this is interesting, even important; but little of this concerns major, recent change; the advent of Gorbachev's reconstruction has not so far affected the mass party membership in any radical or significant way.

NOTES

1. Entitled 'Razgovor o prieme v partiiu' (Conversation on admission to the party), this began in *Pravda*, 3 June 1984, and seems to have ended with the contribution in *Pravda*, 3 February 1985.

2. I argued this in 'The Communist Party: Trends and Problems', in Archie Brown and Michael Kaser (eds), *Soviet Policy for the 1980s* (London: Macmillan, 1982) pp. 1–34, especially pp. 4–7.

3. The principal source for this and subsequent tables is 'KPSS v tsifrakh' (The CPSU in Figures) in *Partiinaia zhizn'*, 14/86, pp. 19–32. 'KPSS v tsifrakh' is an intermittent series, and comparisons over time may draw on articles with the same title in *P.zh.*, 1/62, pp. 44–54; 10/65, pp. 8–17; 19/67, pp. 8–20; 14/73, pp. 9–26; 10/76, pp. 13–23; 21/77, pp. 20–43; 14/81, pp. 13–26; 15/83, pp. 14–32. These will not be cited further, unless the material concerned is elusive or ambiguous.

For earlier academic analysis of 'KPSS v tsifrakh', see T. H. Rigby, *Communist Party Membership in the USSR 1917–1967* (Princeton NJ: Princeton University Press, 1968), and 'Soviet Communist Party Membership under Brezhnev', in *Soviet Studies*, vol. XXVIII, no. 3, July 1976, pp. 317–37 (plus comment and a rejoinder, ibid., April 1977, pp. 306–16, and July 1977, pp. 452–53; Boris Meissner in *Osteuropa*, 8–9/71, pp. 596–609; 8–9/76, pp. 634–50; 9–10/81, pp. 766–68; also the present author cited in the previous note.

4. Some notes on points of detail in Table 4.1:

(i) Date: figures in this table pertain to the holding of the Party Congress typically in early March; elsewhere in this chapter figures for the beginning of January will be used;

(ii) Adult population: treated here as those aged 18 or over, in line with the Soviet sources; in my chapter cited in Note 2 I used figures for those aged 20 and over. Percentages are from 'KPSS v tsifrakh', except that for 1971 which is calculated;

(iii) Total losses = Admissions minus Net growth;

(iv) Expulsions and non-promotions: we have figures for expulsions for all three quinquennia, in *P.zh.*, 14/81, p. 19, 14/86, p. 25; for failure to be promoted no information is known for 1971–76, but for 1976–81 and 1981–86, see *P.zh.*, 14/81, p. 14; 14/86, p. 20.

5. See Rigby, *Soviet Studies*, July 1976, p. 322.

6. See *Radio Liberty Research Bulletin*, RL 5/84 (30 December 1983), and RL 23/86 (10 January 1986).

7. This figure has been cited with little variation for the last 30 years; the most recent reference known to me is S. A. Tiushkevich, *Sovetskie Vooruzhennye Sily: istoriia stroitel'stva* (Moscow, Voenizd, 1978), p. 486.

8. *Krasnaia zvezda*, 17 March 1976, p. 2.

9. This has always been the most plausible classification, but it is confirmed by N. S. Igrunov in *Pravda*, 26 September 1983, p. 2 — who indeed refers at this point, not to officers, but to *soldiers* (*voennye*).

10. See *P.zh.*, 14/86, pp. 20 and 25.

11. See article 16 of the *Rules of the CPSU*.

12. For 'loss of contact' in the early 1960s see *P.zh.*, 10/65, p. 10. It may have been realized that reliable figures on this category are almost impossible to keep. A common way of 'resigning' from the party must be failure to re-register with a new party organisation when one moves to a new job.

13. If this exercise is repeated for *members* only, i.e. ignoring the complicating factor of non-promotions, it gives approximately the same results. Indeed it leads to the finding that the apparent 'death' rate among candidates is higher than among members; which in turn suggests that voluntary withdrawals are hidden somewhere in this residual, and real deaths correspondingly fewer. Death rates for those over 20 in the mid-1980s will be more than 1.4 per cent per annum, for those over 25, more than 1.6 per cent.

14. This suggestion depends on the fact that communists have approximately the same mean age as the eligible population — see below. Because the CPSU contains more men than women, and perhaps a higher proportion of war invalids than the adult population, one might have expected CPSU death rates to be higher, not lower than those of the eligible population.

15. It is based on scrutiny of provincial data from more than 13 provinces, and on counts of delegates to the 1981 congress.

16. It is not implausible that the growth rate for the rest of the RSFSR should be a bit smaller than for its largest provinces; the growth rate for Russians, as an ethnic group, was 1.46 per cent p.a. (see below).

17. *P.zh.*, 15/83, p. 20; a similar passage in *P.zh.*, 14/81, p. 16, adds *kadrovye rabotniki* (responsible employees) to the list.

18. The Komsomol admits members between the ages of 14 and 28. The recent congress raised from 23 to 25 the age up to which only Komsomol members are admitted to the party.

19. The proportion of candidates aged more than 30 is given in *P.zh.*, 14/86, p. 22. My judgement that these are mainly in the 31–40 age group is based on detailed comparison of the 1983 and 1986 age distributions.

20. See Rigby, *Communist Party Membership*, p. 221.

21. That this is a problem can be verified in the following way: apply the class background percentages for newly admitted candidates (the right-hand portion of Table 4.5) to the number of surviving communists who entered the party at the relevant period (material from the

distribution of party members by seniority or *partiinyi stazh*). From this a predicted distribution by original class background can be obtained for the 1986 party membership. The prediction confirms one's intuition that *rabochie* ought to be close to 50 per cent of the party.

22. See above. My own belief is that *total* admissions are currently *about* 55 per cent *rabochie*, 9 per cent *kolkhozniki*, and 36 per cent *sluzhashchie*.

23. There is empirical evidence for this: see Table 17, p. 337, in J. F. Hough and M. Fainsod, *How the Soviet Union is Governed* (Cambridge, Mass. and London: Harvard University Press, 1979).

24. It is also possible that *rabochie* statistics have been inflated by the temporary redefining of jobs at the time application for party membership is made. There is anecdotal evidence for this practice.

25. Brown and Kaser (eds), *Soviet Policy*, pp. 12–13.

26. *P.zh.*, 14/86, p. 31.

27. A note on the sources for Table 4.7: we have absolute figures, as well as percentages, for a good many employment sectors (enough to enable reliable calculation of the rest) for the years 1976 and 1983; see *P.zh.*, 15/83, p. 26. For 1981 and 1986, we have (a) percentages, and (b) the absolute increase in certain employment sectors since some previous date; see *P.zh.*, 14/81, pp. 19–20; 14/86, pp. 25–26. In consequence the figures in Table 4.7 are rather less reliable for 1986 than for the other dates.

28. See, for example, *Radio Liberty Research Bulletin*, RL 387/86 (10 October 1986), p. 2.

29. *P.zh.*, 14/86, p. 21, and comparable material in earlier editions.

30. This is illustrated by the 'party saturation' estimates in Brown and Kaser (eds), *Soviet Policy*, p. 10.

31. *P.zh.*, 14/86, p. 23. This and comparable tables are difficult to use because it is not at all clear whether they really concern *sluzhashchie* by background, or by type of current employment. But whatever absolute numbers lie behind the percentages, we may note that 21 per cent of *sluzhashchie* are unaccounted for. Once again party personnel in the Armed Forces come to mind.

32. See M. McAuley, 'Party Recruitment and the Nationalities in the USSR: a Study in Centre-Republican Relationships', in *British Journal of Political Science*, vol. 10, part 4, October 1980, pp. 461–87.

5

The Soviet Economy: Problems and Solutions in the Gorbachev View

Robert F. Miller

INTRODUCTION

One of the most noteworthy features of M. S. Gorbachev's 'Political Report' to the 27th Congress was its stress on the centrality of the economic factor in national power. As Marxists, to be sure, Soviet leaders have always formally reckoned on the decisive role of the economic 'base' in the formation and functioning of the political, social and military 'superstructure' of a society or social formation. Under Stalin the consciousness of that relationship had become blunted by the latter's increasingly voluntaristic political manipulation of the economy to achieve specific internal and external political goals.

That practice was continued, with greater or less uneasiness, by his successors, reaching its culmination in the last years of the Brezhnev era, when the actual performance of the economy seemed to become less salient in official thinking than the preservation of the appearance of general power, stability and welfare. There was widespread recognition among specialists, not to mention, the population at large, that the actual economic situation under 'real socialism' was far from satisfactory. In the words of a noted American specialist on the Soviet economy, Robert W. Campbell, writing in the early eighties:

Soviet leaders face unprecedented conditions of resource stringency in the 1980s, as growth of the economy slackens and as resource expectations and demands of the various claimants on the nation's output expand. A number of adverse trends will combine to bring the rate of economic growth well below recent experience. Soviet GNP growth has generally been decelerating in the years since the Second World War: it was 6 to 7 percent per year in the 1950s, and 5 percent in the 1960s, declining to 4 and then 3 percent in the 1970s. In the 1980s, output is unlikely to grow at more than 2 percent per year.[1]

Nevertheless, the regime continued to maintain a façade of 'wellbeing' (*blagopoluchie*), behind which a tacit agreement between leaders and led was allowed to operate. The leaders got enough out of the economy to satisfy their priorities — a high level of military security for the Soviet state and power, deference and material comfort for themselves and for the lower ranks in the *nomenklatura* on whose support they relied; meanwhile, the more enterprising among the led were allowed to grab what they could from the rest of the economy by general corruption and the operation of variously 'coloured' markets for scarce goods and services.

The new group of party leaders brought into the Politburo and Secretariat of the Party Central Committee by (and/or along with) Gorbachev represents a change of generations in several senses of the term. The political details of the change are treated in Chapters 1, 3 and 4 by T. H. Rigby and J. H. Miller. Here I wish only to note the apparent metamorphosis in the psychology with which they seem to be approaching problems of the economy. The fact that the generational change has come about much more precipitously than many of us had expected places this difference in approach in specially bold relief. From their verbal utterances and policy directives before and since the 27th Congress it is much less easy to argue the case for simple continuity with the past than is ordinarily true of a succession period in the Soviet Union, although the rhetoric of change is far from unusual. The new leaders have obviously gone out of their way to differentiate their style and policy orientations from those of their predecessors. How much of this is, again, mere rhetoric and how successful they will be in overcoming the powerfully entrenched structures and forces of resistance to change remains to be seen. It is clear, however, that even in their rhetoric they have left themselves little room for backtracking — except perhaps in the face of some overriding external danger. Yet, paradoxically, it is their consciousness of one particular long-term external danger, namely, strategic vulnerability arising out of accumulated technological backwardness, that has given Gorbachev and his colleagues their principal motive and justification for change. For they have understood that the relative stagnation and immobility of the Soviet economy in a period of international stress and renewed competitiveness by the rival superpower have, in a sense, changed the parameters within which Kremlin decision-making takes place. Chernobyl' was merely the most dramatic symbol of a disturbing pheno-menon which they had come to recognise: namely that even in those areas where they had decided to concentrate their scientific and technological talent, Soviet performance was not up to con-temporary world standards. The disaster of 26 April 1986 must have profoundly undermined those Soviet scientists who have been arguing since the mid-70s that Soviet technology could go its own way, generating its own innovations and standards with-out regard to what the rest of the world is doing.[2]

Chernobyl' does not mean, of course, that Gorbachev & Co. will be turning their backs on the home-grown R&D establish-ment. It is certainly much too good for that, and there is more than a grain of truth to the views of the former president of the USSR Academy of Sciences, A.P. Aleksandrov and his cronies that Soviet R&D ultimately loses more than it gains by being dependent on imported technology for innovations. It means, rather, that Soviet scientists, engineers, economists and the politicians they advise will continue to have to take account of the scientific, technological and managerial experience of the advanced Western countries, notwithstanding current cam-paigns in the media to encourage Soviet scientists and engineers not to be satisfied with meeting world technological standards but to strive to surpass them and become pace setters in their own right.[3]

In short, Gorbachev and his colleagues have come to power largely on the strength of a program to 'get the Soviet Union moving again', with the economic base cast in the role of the main engine for doing so. They have adopted a particular strategy for accomplishing this objective, based on a combina-tion of traditional centralised direction and means-ends selection, on the one hand, and local flexibility guided by a system of economic signals and standardised input coefficients (*normativy*), on the other. Some of the choices of instruments are informed by the experience of other socialist countries — most notably East Germany and Hungary — as interpreted and 'sanitised' by a few favourite academic quasi-liberalisers, such as Abel Aganbegian and Tat'iana Zaslavskaia.[4] Notably absent among their prescriptions is a categorical acceptance of the kind of market determination of prices and supply allocations which most Western students of the Soviet economy suggest is essential for its effective modernisation. In Chapter 6 Victor Zaslavsky presents the theoretical debates over this argument and considers their significance for the success of Gorbachev's reform program. Besides ideological conviction, which may or may not be genuine for individual Soviet leaders, the latter have serious political constraints to consider in choosing their institutional economic alternatives. Paradoxically, they may have substantially less room for manoeuvre than their East European junior partners, who are relatively free to experiment with market processes.

Before examining the conceptions of the problems of the economy presented by Gorbachev and others at the time of the Congress and the solutions they have been proposing, it will be useful to look at some of the main elements in the lexicon of economic discourse they have employed in their recent pronouncements. More often than the word 'reform' Gorbachev tends to use the 'reconstruction' (*perestroika*) to characterise his efforts to transform and modernise the Soviet economy. The key concept is *acceleration* (*uskorenie*), that is, increasing the tempo of change in various sectors of the system, from the introduction of state-of-the-art technology to the timely completion of capital construction projects and the long delayed build-up of infrastructural elements such as housing and transportation. Along with acceleration one often finds the term *intensification*, or the shift to fuller exploitation of existing productive factors — e.g., economies in the consumption of materials and energy per unit of manufactured output, the systematic use of shift-work in enterprises, training of workers in multiple skills, etc. Even under Brezhnev verbal acknowledgement was given to the idea that the extensive methods of development associated with the Stalinist mode of industrialisation would have to give way to new, intensive methods, but little was done to identify the essential differences between the two methods, let alone to shift substantively from the former to the latter.

Quality is another buzzword of the Gorbachev offensive against 'stagnation' (*zastoi*), 'inertia' and 'complacency'. There is general recognition that the products of Soviet industry are not internationally competitive in terms of durability, technical sophistication, productivity or appearance. These shortcomings, of course, also affect their serviceability in domestic production and constitute a major reason for the declining rate of return on investment in recent years. Now the objective is to raise the quality of Soviet producer and consumer goods to the best world standards . . . and beyond.[5]

Another key concept given renewed emphasis by the Gorbachev leadership is *integration*. Domestically the term refers to the concentration of planning and administrative direction of related R&D and production processes under unified management to overcome so-called 'departmental barriers', which are said to be the main obstacle to contralised control of the economy at the present stage. In intra-bloc relations integration ultimately implies Soviet direction or, in the short term, closer co-operation between Soviet and East European managers, production facilities and R&D organisations for the achievement of specific scientific or industrial tasks.

Finally, Gorbachev and his colleagues are laying particular stress on what they call the *human factor* ('*chelovecheskii faktor*') as a key to achieving the desired qualitative changes in the structure and performance of the economy. This emphasis on personal, attitudinal motors of change is not new, of course — it has always been at least nominally the focus of party activity in the economy. What has changed are the relative sophistication of the appeal and the persistence of its application, reflecting a recognition that positive efforts will be required, beyond material allocations, to channel the activities of individual actors in the economy and society into the desired directions.[6]

All of these concepts are being woven, since the Congress, into an elaborate propaganda garment for 'dressing up' the new program to revitalise the flagging Soviet economy. They are part of an impressive media 'blitz' which seems to be a major element of Gorbachev's political style and a reflection of his evident conviction that the program requires an early and sustained demonstration of success if the individual effort needed for the attainment of its difficult goals is to be effectively harnessed. Whether his prescriptions are correct for the concatenation of problems plaguing the economy, and whether there is much chance that he will succeed in having them implemented even if they are, remains to be seen. Before addressing these questions, however, it is necessary to have some understanding of the nature of the problems.

MAJOR PROBLEMS OF THE SOVIET ECONOMY

Even in comparison with the uneven performance of the Western capitalist economies, there seems little doubt that the Soviet economy has slowed down considerably in recent years. In the late 1950s, when the present writer was taking graduate courses on the Soviet economy, the main arguments tended to centre on when, not whether, the Soviet economy would overtake that of the USA in the principal measures of economic power. Indeed, Soviet growth rates at the time were such that N. S. Khrushchev could predict, and have his predictions incorporated into the official CPSU Program, that the 'overtaking' would have occurred, and the Soviet Union would be entering the stage of full communism, by the early 1980s. Gorbachev wisely avoided any such predictions in his 'Political Report' to the congress, and the new edition of the Party Program likewise eschews the setting of any deadlines for the achievement of communism. For, since the days of Khrushchev, there has been a marked decline in the rates of growth of the Soviet economy and in its responsiveness to remedial state intervention. Tables 5.1 and 5.2 show some important aspects of this entropic tendency.

The data given in Table 5.2 give a clear picture of the general slowdown in the rate of growth of the Soviet economy; they also show the tendency under the Brezhnev leadership to try to maintain consumption at the expense of accumulation and investment. Hopes that a decline in the previously high rate of investment would be compensated by a rise in labour and capital productivity proved to be illusory. In fact, what happened during the later Brezhnev years and their immediate aftermath was that the effects of a reduced level of investment growth were compounded by a reduction in the rate of return per rouble of investment. Indeed, during the last two years of the 11th FYP investment had to be increased above the original FYP targets in order to try to stem the decline in overall productivity. The modest recovery registered for 1984 and 1985 in Table 5.1 was, therefore, achieved at very high cost.

To understand the background of this deteriorating situation

Table 5.1: Selected indicators of Soviet economic performance, 1971–85 (in % per annum)

	1971–75	1976–78	1979–82	1983	1984	1985
Growth of GNP	3.7	3.7	1.6	3.2	2.0	—
of which,						
in Industry	5.9	3.8	2.4	3.4	4.3[a]	3.9[a]
in Agriculture	−0.4	5.2	−0.9	6.3	0	0
		(1976–80)	(1981)			
Growth of national income used in consumption and accumulation	5.1	3.8	3.2	3.1	2.6	3.1

Note: a. Industrial production growth rates as shown in the two TsU SSSR reports cited for 1984 and 1985.

Sources: Robert Gates, 'Soviet Economic Performance, 1983–84' in Joint Economic Committee, Congress of the United States, *Allocation of Resources in the Soviet Union and China — 1984* (Washington, DC, 1985), p. 43; Jan Vanous, 'Macroeconomic Adjustment in Eastern Europe in 1981–83: Response to Western Credit Squeeze and Deteriorating Terms of Trade With the Soviet Union', in Joint Economic Committee, Congress of the United States, *East European Economies: Slow Growth in the 1980s* (Washington, DC, 28 October 1985), p. 38; TsU SSSR reports for 1984 and 1985 in *Ekonomicheskaia gazeta*, No. 5 (January 1985), p. 5; ibid., No. 6 (February 1986), p. 11.

Table 5.2: Tempos of growth of national income by Five-Year Plans (in %)

	(1966–70) 8th FYP	(1971–75) 9th FYP	(1976–80) 10th FYP	(1981–84) 11th FYP
National income	139	134	124	116
of which,				
for consumption	131	134	127	117
for accumulation	142	133	117	113

Sources: 'Nakoplenie i intensifikatsiia', *Ekonomicheskaia gazeta*, No. 3 (January 1986), p. 1.

it is necessary to look a bit more closely at the spectrum of problems confronting the new leadership as it sought to restore the earlier high-growth capabilities of the system. For discussion purposes it is possible to divide them into four main categories: resource problems, labour problems, financial problems and structural-organisational problems. It scarcely needs mentioning that this taxonomy is somewhat artificial and that a number of the categories are interrelated and overlap to a considerable extent. Moreover, many of the problems are of long duration, and we address them here only as they concern the perceptions of the party leadership at the times of the 27th Party Congress.

Among the most frequently mentioned *resource problems* are the increasing costs of extraction of raw materials and fuels as the location of their principal sources moves to the east. In addition, the standard Soviet techniques of extraction, based on rapid initial output with little regard for the procurement of subsequent, less easily obtained supplies (as in the case of petroleum deposits), have proven incompatible with intensive development of resource deposits. Further along in the production cycle, the Soviet economy is notoriously wasteful in the use of material and energy inputs per unit of output. There are numerous reasons for such waste. For one thing, the incentive system tends to reward firms for inflating the value of inputs, which is reflected in higher sales prices and, hence, value of output. For another, the non-availability of high-strength materials and synthetics, at least in the civilian economy, compels Soviet designers to increase the volume of metals in manufacturing and construction to meet strength and safety standards.[7] Another source of wastefulness is the poor quality of the inputs supplied in the production process. The high proportion of rejected items represents a substantial waste of materials.[8] Another source of waste is the high level of concealed inventories of materials, fuels and semi-finished products that enterprise managers are more or less compelled to maintain in order to insure against shortfalls in centrally planned supplies or to barter for the inputs they need with other, similarly vulnerable enterprises.

At the macro-level *labour problems* are considered a major reason for the need to shift to intensive methods of development. According to Prime Minister Nikolai I. Ryzhkov, in his report on the economy at the congress, 'without the planned growth in labour productivity the national economy would need 22 million additional workers.'[9] Meanwhile, Campbell has shown that from 1980 to 1990 the working-age population of the USSR will have increased by less than 6 million, and of that total virtually all will come from the Central Asian and Kazakhstan regions, where industry is relatively underdeveloped.[10] As Campbell's data show, the shortage of labour is highly regionally specific. Unfortunately, those regions with surplus

116

labour are characterised by low labour mobility: Central Asians do not like to leave their home villages, or even to migrate to urban areas within their own republics, let alone resettle in Siberia or the Far East. One obvious solution is to site new industrial developments in these areas of labour surplus, and that is precisely what is now being contemplated.[11] From the standpoint of rational utilisation of available labour supplies some Soviet specialists are now arguing that a labour shortage does not really exist. The problem, they say, is rather to use labour more productively, avoiding the over-manning associated with the prevailing extensive modes of production.[12]

Another aspect of the labour problem is the inefficient use of skilled professional manpower in the economy. The Soviet Union is by far the most prolific producer of engineers and scientists in the world. Yet many professional graduates are employed in positions where their training is under-utilised or not used at all. Soviet research institutions and design bureaux regularly carry surplus specialists for 'insurance' during peak work periods or simply to carry out routine non-specialised jobs imposed upon them by local party and state bodies, such as helping with the harvest on local farms.[13] A corollary of this policy is the low salaries paid to Soviet engineers (although not to scientists with higher degrees) relative to skilled workers, especially in highly paid industries such as mining. The result is a general depreciation of the prestige of the engineering profession, which is seen as a reason for its declining morale and creativity.

The list of what can broadly be called *financial problems* stretches from the 'overhang' of cash holdings of the population relative to the supply of available goods and services, to the intransitivities of the material incentive systems and to the unmet needs of the growing number of sectoral claimants for increasingly scarce investment roubles. In the words of one recent commentator in the journal *MEMO*:

The high level of concentration of reproduction resources in capital intensive sectors of production has limited the possibilities of their allocation to other branches of the national economy. In particular, it has impeded the development of types of production, which are less capital intensive but have decisive importance for raising the effectiveness of labour productivity and the economic use of raw materials and energy.[14]

As we have noted above, in connection with Table 5.2, the requirements of Brezhnev's 'social compact' with the Soviet population necessitated the maintenance of an at least marginally increasing level of consumption in the face of a declining rate of growth of national income. Given the tacit commitment to maintain defence spending, that could only mean a declining rate of growth of investment at a time when the rate of capital productivity was declining, particularly in the vital raw materials, agricultural and energy sectors.[15] Something had to give. One of the first things Brezhnev's successors did was to pump up the level of investment, but that meant reducing consumption, something that could no longer easily be done for very long now that the Stalinist reliance on terrorising the population has been abandoned. Nor could past methods of concealed deficit financing and repressing inflation serve to bridge the current financial gap. Soviet leaders have come increasingly to understand that they live in a real world, where the rouble must eventually have some meaning in terms of goods and services if they are to have any hope of controlling the development of their economy, especially now that it is more heavily involved in world trade.[16]

The material incentive system is another area where the attempt to achieve 'control by the rouble' over the R&D-production-distribution process has often led to serious unintended and undesirable consequences. Success indicators and bonus payments frequently lead to the production of unwanted consumer items and technologically distorted producer goods. (The proverbial 'one-tonne nail' is the characteristic example.) the system of centrally determined supply channels results in a kind of producer sovereignty which makes any form of market assessment of product utility and quality impossible. When combined with the practice of centrally determined prices, which rewards almost any kind of modification of products, regardless of real economic benefit, this system virtually guarantees a waste of resources, of design activity and of industrial labour.[17] The system of arbitrarily determined prices, no matter how cleverly bolstered by 'scientific' coefficients and 'normatives', has long been recognised in the West (and tacitly in the East as well) as one of the chief obstacles to the rational allocation of resources in Soviet-type economies. But in the eyes of Soviet politicians any abandonment of the state's prerogative to set prices represents a grave threat to their control over the economy and society. They are probably right in believing so.

In a broad sense all of the foregoing problem areas are subsumed under our final category, *structural-organisation problems*. It is the basic structure of the economy, its rigorous separation into military and civilian (or, more accurately, 'closed' and 'open') sectors, and its administrative division into an array of quasi-autonomous, rigidly hierarchical ministerial empires that have given rise to many of the problems that we have been discussing. The notorious 'departmental barriers', which prevent the adoption of a useful innovation by the enterprises of one ministry because it was designed by the R&D institute or design bureau of another ministry, or the shipment of components urgently needed by an enterprise because they have been promised, perhaps with a lower intrinsic priority, to enterprises within the producer's parent ministry, have long been recognised as one of the primary obstacles to the smooth functioning of the Soviet economy. As a rule, it takes the interference of regional party organs to circumvent these barriers, but even that is not always successful. Narrow departmental interests are often cited as the cause of the proliferation of capital construction work, as each ministry seeks to have its pet projects included in the annual or five-year construction plan, even if there is no prospect that the given project can be fully funded or allocated the necessary equipment or labour resources.[18] Another central theme of the organisational debates involves the improvement of the linkage between R&D institutions and production enterprises in order to increase the responsibility of designers for the more rapid introduction of innovations into large-scale production. Many structural modifications of the basic relationship between R&D and production have been tried in the past decade, with only modest success.[19]

Given the prevailing rules of administrative structure, it is very difficult for a governmental organisation to co-ordinate the activities of bodies at the same horizontal level in the administrative hierarchy. This fact was well illustrated in agriculture by the inability of the new *oblast* and *raion* agro-industrial associations established in 1982 to get the local agencies of the state agricultural machinery committee (*Goskomsel'khoztekhnika*) to accept common agricultural production and service tasks. The same problem has existed for a long time in the operation in inter-farm production associations, but it has plagued other sectors as well. The various ministries jealously protect their legal and financial prerogatives despite obvious needs for co-ordinated effort. As we shall see in the next section, the new leadership team has 'bitten the bullet' on these structural problems with refreshing vigour. If necessary, they have simply abolished the offending agencies or placed them under 'super-ministries' or governmental co-ordinating bodies situated at a higher level in the administrative hierarchy.

These, then, are the major problem areas responsible for the slowdown in the Soviet economy as perceived by Gorbachev and his colleagues. In the following section we shall look at some of the major solutions they have devised to handle them.

PROPOSED SOLUTIONS

Perhaps the most common Western criticism of Gorbachev's Political Report, the new edition of the Party Program and Premier Nikolai Ryzhkov's presentation of the 12th Five-Year Plan at the congress was the vagueness of the prescriptions they contained. As the speakers themselves admitted, many of the details of the innovations to be introduced had yet to be worked out. That applied to the new administrative arrangements as well. The general strategy of 'acceleration' was set forth, but few concrete details were given. Thus, according to Ryzhkov,

> The strategy for administering the acceleration of scientific and technical progress worked out by the party consists in, first, while promoting science and technology on a broad front, to concentrate available resources on key directions. Secondly, to give scope for the massive utilisation of reliable, practically tested innovations in order to obtain a maximum payoff before they become morally obsolete. Third, quickly and persistently to carry on scientific and design developments which secure the creation and mastery of principally new techniques and technology, which manifoldly increase labour productivity.[20]

Among the more concrete measures announced for achieving these goals was the plan to increase capital investment during the 12th FYP by 36 per cent over the total for the 11th FYP. And the all-important machine-building industry, which has been singled out as the engine of 'acceleration' — the main factor for increasing the technological level of the Soviet economy as a whole — is to receive an 80 per cent boost.[21] Within the machine-building, or engineering, sector special importance is being placed on re-equipment of the machine-tool industry with state-of-the-art technology, using numerically controlled machines and complex machining centres based on microprocessors and a high level of robotisation, which are being touted as the key to enhanced labour productivity and higher quality output. Other sectors scheduled to receive disproportionate shares of investment are fuels and energy, the development of new materials (synthetics and composites), and biotechnology. Here and elsewhere throughout the economy special emphasis is being placed on microprocessors and other branches of advanced electronics, where the Soviet Union is acknowledged to have lagged seriously behind the West in the past two decades. In many ways the shift to highly automated, programmable machine-tools is precisely what the Soviet (or any other) economy needs in the modern age, allowing the substitution of flexibility for economies of scale in the determination of output assortment. The previous practices of extensive investment in large-scale equipment, which was subsequently used well beyond the point where it was both technically and physically depreciated, had locked Soviet industry into a set of obsolete technologies. The new computerised, modular machine-tool configurations could go some way toward alleviating this problem, provided the equipment itself is satisfactory and capable of the kinds of accuracy and quality of output required by modern technology. So far, this has not always been the case.[22] Modern machine-tools, it is anticipated, will reduce the quantity of metals and energy used in production by cutting down on the volume of machining required per unit of output.

They will also, of course, reduce the number of workers required to man industrial machinery. That is also the objective of the 'complex goal program' to increase the amount of labour-saving machinery in auxiliary operations, such as materials transfer, loading, etc. According to Ryzhkov, the goal here is to relieve some 20 million persons of unskilled, monotonous work by the end of the century.[23] If these persons can be appropriately retrained to upgrade their skills in conformity with the requirements of modern technology, that would be a major contribution to solving the present labour shortage. Once again, that is a very big 'if' indeed.

This orientation toward technology is also to apply in agriculture. The 'agro-industrial complex' — farming and its backward and forward linkages — will continue to receive a third of all capital investments. The main change envisaged now, however, is to shift the principal focus of investment from agriculture *per se* to the commodity storage and food processing industries. Eliminating losses from the farm to the retail shop would be equivalent, according to Gorbachev, to making available an additional 20 to 30 per cent of commodities for public consumption.[24] The equally crucial problem of the economic infrastructure — transportation, roads, communications, energy transmission, etc. — is also scheduled to be 'solved' (*reshaetsia*) during the 12th FYP, but no actual investment targets for them are set down, which may mean that they will be handled as a residual, as in the past.[25] The traditional, ideologically determined attitude toward these sectors as 'non-productive' seems at last to be changing, however, and more attention is being given to viewing them as an integral 'complex', vital to the performance of the overall economy.

One of the most interesting features of the plan for capital investments, under the 'intensification' rubric, is that, by 1990, fully 50 per cent of all investments are to go into the reconstruction and re-equipment of existing enterprises, as compared with 37 per cent in 1985.[26] Furthermore, virtually all of the expected growth in national income and industrial output is to come from increased labour productivity. (Additional labour supplies, as has already been pointed out , will simply not be available in any case.) Indeed, in a report of the Politburo meeting of 13 June 1986, it was noted that measures had been adopted to achieve the 'programmed task' of reaching 'the highest labour productivity in the world in the foreseeable future!'[27]

Similarly, 60–65 per cent of the planned growth in consumption of energy and raw materials is to be obtained from economies in their use. Now, the wastefulness of most Soviet-type economies in the utilisation of labour, energy and raw materials is well known, and there is undoubtedly plenty of room for improvement in this regard. But one wonders whether changes of the magnitude demanded are in the realm of serious practicability. The rate of growth of capital investment is to be increased to 25 per cent over the 12th FYP, as compared with 16 per cent during the 11th FYP, which will require a sharp reversal of the trend toward a decline in the share of national income going to accumulation noted above in Table 5.2. That means a proportional decline in the share of consumption, unless the 'acceleration' of the economy is such as to reduce the latter to politically insignificant dimensions.[28]

The Soviet leaders are obviously placing most of their bets on science and technology to provide the requisite quick and durable 'fix' for the economy. Judging from past performance, the prospects for more than limited success do not appear very bright, particularly if the leaders insist on a rigid import substitution approach. The main problem is not the lack of competence or talent in the Soviet scientific and engineering community, but rather the inordinately long lead times in translating the results of R&D into large-scale production. It is not uncommon for Soviet discoveries to find their first practical applications in the West and to be obsolete by the time they can be incorporated into Soviet production schedules.[29]

In addition to the higher rates of investment in strategic sectors of the economy, the solutions proposed for what we have broadly called financial problems include measures for rationalising the wages and incentive systems. Their main thrust is toward making wages and bonuses more responsive to the quantity and quality of final output. In the R&D-production cycle this will mean tying the remuneration of scientific collectives and design bureaux to the ultimate production and sale of the new items they have designed and developed, rather than to the completion of intermediate stages of the cycle as in the past. The objective is to stimulate scientists and engineers to be more conscious of, and responsible for, the production requirements of new technologies. The goal — and the strategy for reaching it — are, of course, hardly new. Various experiments with 'Science Production Associations' and contract research have been in progress for over a decade now, without spectacular results.[30] Some improvement in their work can probably be expected under the more exacting conditions being created by the present leadership, but grounds for scepticism clearly remain. The current campaign to raise the prestige of the engineering profession and to increase their salary scales on the basis of actual contributions to work, rather than seniority and the possession of higher degrees, should address one other long-standing grievance and source of wastefulness.[31] But the continued insistence on maintaining overall wage limits and labour contribution standards (*normativy*) could easily lead to other problems of intra-group friction and other avenues for rule evasion in R&D collectives.

Somewhat more imaginative, although also not new in the Soviet context, is the re-emphasis on self-financing (*khozraschet*) at various levels of the system, but especially within production-type organisations. Efforts to introduce 'elements' of *khozraschet* date back to Lenin's day and were formally eschewed in agriculture under Stalin only in 1938 with the transfer of the machine-tractor stations to the state budget. The principle was revived in earnest by Khrushchev, and it became one of the pillars of the so-called 'Liberman reforms' of the later 1960s under Khrushchev's successors. Accordingly, the idea of making individual enterprises, production associations and farms responsible for financing their own capital investments, infrastructural development and material incentive programs by allowing them to retain a larger part of their earned income and by encouraging them to seek repayable bank credits for working capital needs and to cover temporary cash-flow problems is not really an innovation in Soviet economic thinking. What will be new is if the regime can muster the will-power to maintain its commitment to the universal introduction of self-financing in the face of certain predictable problems. What will happen, for example, to the explicit pledge not to syphon off the profits of successful organisations to compensate for the losses of others, especially of the former are the recipients of extraordinary profits that are at least partly the result of genuine entrepreneurial skill or extra effort? And what is likely to happen in cases (sure to be widespread) of enterprises and farms that are unable to marshal the resources to meet the regime's demands for technological modernisation or to repay the bank credits obtained to do so? Are the unsuccessful firms or farms to be allowed to declare bankruptcy and go out of business? That hardly seems likely, even in agriculture, where the incidence of failure is bound to remain very high. Gorbachev's catchy appropriation of the idea of the tax in kind (*prodnalog*) — Lenin's forced innovation in the methods of extraction of peasant grain by which the NEP was launched — as a symbol of the new approach to farm obligations to the state should be regarded as more a matter of style than of substance. Treating *kolkhoz* and *sovkhoz* deliveries of grain to the state as a tax, rather than a quasi-commercial transaction, if that is indeed what he has in mind, would represent a step back to the bad old days of Stalin and the MTS, when compulsory deliveries and *naturoplata* brought the farms next to nothing by way of compensation. What Gorbachev evidently intends is to continue to require the farms to produce (and deliver) a sufficient quantity of basic grains to cover essential state requirements — for which they would be paid a fixed, generally adequate price, with the possibility of earning higher prices from additional grain sales — while leaving the farms greater leeway to plan their own assortment of other commodities and to dispose of limited quantities of the latter through the co-operative network or even on the free market. Much depends on the mandatory *prodnalog* assessments and on the degree of genuine freedom from local control in the sales of any substantial surplus. In any case, the original experience with the *prodnalog* showed that it was not sufficiently stimulative and had to be replaced by a cash tax within three years. Were the farms now to be allowed to pay the state entirely in cash and permitted to grow what they wanted, that would be a truly revolutionary reform. It could conceivably succeed in generating the kind of increases in output Gorbachev desires. Unfortunately, it would also mean a loss of state control over the assortment of commodities produced — unless the state were willing to pay much higher prices for less profitable items, which would, in turn, undermine the politically sensitive policy of keeping the prices of bread and other staples artificially low.[32] The Chinese have apparently been able to handle these problems successfully, albeit with some difficulty. It is interesting to note, by the way, that Gorbachev has taken a page out of Deng Xiaoping's book in suggesting that individual families be permitted to register as 'contract' teams for carrying out farming operations under the new system of work organisation in agriculture.

The larger issues of structural administrative change affect all areas of the economy and, potentially, the political system as well. The dominant motivation is to break down the traditional administrative and bureaucratic barriers to the co-ordination and implementation of policy, particularly where technological innovation is concerned. Nevertheless, there is no inclination to do away with centralised direction of the economy. On the contrary, while greater initiative is to be allowed to enterprise management (in line with the new stress on self-financing), equal emphasis is being placed on the strengthening of centralised control, although the central agencies are supposed to avoid detailed interference in management and confine themselves to global, strategic issues of development, the choice of technology policy, and the monitoring of compliance. Thus, at the same time that the All-Union Industrial Associations (VPOs — really the old *glavki*) are being liquidated in favour of a two-stage administrative system (ministry-production association or enterprise) — actually, three-stage where union-republican ministries are concerned — a number of 'super-ministries' or governmental co-ordinating bodies are being established. First, in October 1985, there was created a Biuro of the Council of Ministers of the USSR for Machine-Building; then, in November, came 'Gosagroprom USSR', replacing five former ministries and a state committee in agriculture; then, a week after the 27th Congress, came a Biuro of the Council of Ministers of the USSR for the Fuel and Energy Complex; finally, a week later, an All-Union State Committee of the USSR for Computer Technology and Information Sciences. Subsequently a major reorganisation of the construction industry was announced, greatly strengthening the centralised control of Gosstroi, while decentralising the operational construction ministries on a regional basis. What is of interest is the evident contradiction between the relative flexibility in administrative thinking reflected by the new agencies, and, on the other hand, the tendency to resort, again, to traditional practices of 'bureaucratic layering' in addressing perennial problems of co-ordination. In some respects the creation of these super-agencies recalls Khrushchev's approach to overcoming bureaucratic obstacles to his policies. But there are important differences as well. Whereas Khrushchev was constantly searching for the 'holy grail' of a perfect administrative structure to pinpoint responsibility, the new leaders seems to realise that such a quest is illusory.[33] With the exception of Gosagroprom, which is very 'Khrushchevian' in its conception, the various Biuros of the Council of Ministers are evidently regarded as temporary organs, headed by very high-ranking government officials (first deputy or deputy chairmen of the USSR Council of Ministers), explicitly charged with bringing order and harmony out of the existing chaos in strategic *points d'appuis* of the national economy. Unlike the Gosagroprom case, where the previously contending ministries and state committee were simply abolished and their functions transferred to the super-agency, the Biuro format retains the existing ministries, but more specifically subordinates their activities to the co-ordinating agency. In the past many of the inter-ministerial disputes were referred to the Council of Ministers, or its Presidium, on an *ad hoc* basis. Now this process has been regularised.

Another important development, again reminiscent of the Khrushchev era and re-emerging from time to time during the late Brezhnev era, is the re-emphasis on territorial principles of organisation, most notably in so-called 'Territorial-Production Complexes'. Most of these, such as the BAM railroad scheme, the Kansk-Achinsk brown-coal energy development scheme, and the West-Siberian oil and gas field complex, have been under development for some time now. They are evidently seen as a model of more or less efficient co-ordination work (by Soviet standards), and the territorial focus is to be applied to major resource projects elsewhere.[34]

Another indication of flexibility that is unusual in the Soviet context is the encouragement for setting up well equipped, small-scale enterprises. Obviously, Western experience with the superior innovative characteristics of smaller enterprises, more willing and able to take the associated risks, has been taken into account here, in the face of the traditional, quasi-ideological Soviet belief that 'big is beautiful' — that large-scale manage-ment of productive forces and economies of scale are the hall-mark of efficient socialist production. How the new emphasis squares with official injunctions to complete the consolidation of related enterprises in production associations (which was sup-posed to be accomplished by the late 1970s!) remains unclear. What does show is the relative openness of the Gorbachev team to questioning of heretofore accepted principles of economic management. As yet we have no way of knowing just how far this tendency will extend. An interesting sidelight on the matter, perhaps, is the renewed interest in questions of socialist property. Although the debates on property in the specialised literature are couched in highly abstract terms, it is evident that the concept is being used, among other things, to relieve the state of the obligation to continue to finance industrial costs out of the state budget.[35] Another sign of possible change in this direc-tion is the recent renewal of interest in the formation of small project groups of specialists to carry out contract R&D for industry on a one-off basis. Since the groups would be non-permanent, the scheme would require a degree of administrative and material flexibility heretofore absent in the Soviet system.[36]

Finally, at the congress, as well as in the preliminary discussions, Gorbachev and his colleagues gave their endorsement to new, large-scale 'Inter-Branch Scientific and Technological Complexes' (MNTKs), a quintessential organisational device for breaking down departmental barriers to technological innovation. In Ryzhkov's words, 'they are situated along the main directions of scientific and technical progress and are a new, effective form of the unification of science with production'.[37] By the end of 1985 there were already 16 MNTKs in operation, the majority of them headed by institutes of the USSR Academy of Sciences.[38] Obviously the new structures are an offshoot of the previous concept of 'Complex-Goal Programs', the operations of which have been criticised by Stephen Fortescue and others.[39] Presumably, given the heavy artillery being brought to bear on them now, their efforts will be somewhat more successful than in the earlier prototype, which, incidentally, will continue to work on problems of lesser complexity.

As in the past when science has been singled out for special attention, the administrative and co-ordinating role of the USSR Academy is to be strengthened, this time by involving Academy institutes directly in production-development ventures. Similarly, the State Committee for Science and Technology (GKNT), which Ryzhkov justifiably criticised at the congress for having 'not yet found a place for itself . . . and not reconstructed its work in the light of contemporary requirements',[40] is being asked to upgrade its work on the 'co-ordination of scientific and technical progress', including direct management of MNTKs (presumably in co-operation with the USSR Academy). The GKNT is also to supervise the 'national information economy', an area where it has already acquired a good deal of experience.

There is a strong aura of *déjà vu* around most of these structural changes. Many of them have been tried before, at least on a piecemeal basis, without having significant long-term effects on performance or the general way of doing things. If there is anything new, it is in the relative consistency and the sense of urgency which Gorbachev and his colleagues are trying to instill in leadership cadres and in the workforce in general. Here is where the emphasis on the 'human factor' enters the picture. Individuals are being pressured by both moral and material incentives to intensify their activity for innovation and extra effort at their places of work. On the surface at least,

Gorbachev seems to be taking a page out of Zaslavskaia's book, with her emphasis on the importance of social justice as the key to activating the human factor.[41] His pledge of greater mass participation in decision-making, self-management in the work-place, greater attention to payment according to work, emphasis on the collective, rather than the individual, as the basis of the value system of developed socialist, etc., are all verbally tailored to the kind of social mobilisation that Zaslavskaia, and evidently Gorbachev himself, regard as essential — and possible — for the achievement of the goals set forth at the 27th Congress. It is worth noting that barely a week after the Congress Gorbachev held a meeting in the Central Committee with leaders of the Soviet mass media and the propaganda apparatus to lay down the guidelines for a long-term campaign for maintaining popular enthusiasm at the highest possible pitch. The reports of Gorbachev's personal remarks at the meeting make him sound more like a Madison Avenue ad-man or a football coach than a Soviet politician 'of the Leninist stripe', as they used to say about Brezhnev.[42] How far this reliance on greater atmospheric openness, sincerity and Gorbachev's personal, boyish enthusiasm, particularly in the wake of Chernobyl', will take the Soviet system down the path of genuine economic reform and rationalisation remains to be seen. Gorbachev is undoubtedly right in pulling out all the stops to achieve plan targets from the very beginning of the 12th FYP, since any sign of failure is bound to have a depressant effect on popular and official morale and, perhaps even more seriously, on how he goes about implementing his mobilisational ideas in the future. Chernobyl' does not seem to have diverted him from his original strategy, but it is too early to tell just what effect it has had on popular perceptions of the new leader and his worthiness of confidence.

CONCLUSIONS

Gorbachev's efforts to pull the country out of the slough of complacency and muddling through which is said to have characterised Brezhnev's handling of the economy in his last years are an interesting illustration of the cyclical pattern of Soviet political leadership and policy-making style. The Khrushchevian parallels are as numerous as they are superficial;

history never does repeat itself exactly, especially in the Soviet Union. It is often forgotten that Stalin, too, was successful against his opponents largely on a campaign to 'get the country moving again'. He, too, seemed a refreshing change from his main rivals, with his no-nonsense rhetoric and his businesslike attitude. It is by no means excluded that a frustrated Gorbachev, fascinated by discipline and the 'human factor' (read: '*kadry reshaiut vse*'), will in time resort to the methods of the *krepkii khoziain* upon whom many Soviet citizens evidently look back so fondly! I am not predicting such an outcome, only citing it as one possibility which the Western sovietological fraternity, with its lamentably short memory and attention span, have failed to consider. For, in addition to being obviously intelligent, sophisticated and alert to the shortcomings of the system, Gorbachev is equally obviously a believer in the basic tenets of Marxism-Leninism. It would be difficult to argue that his analysis at the congress of the 'eight groups of contradictions' in the world today[43] or his persistent endorsement of the essentials of central planning and direction of the economy are merely cynical word play or political opportunism.

The massive shift of investment priorities, bolstered by tighter controls over capital construction, increasing the share of national income going to accumulation and the reliance on prescribed standards ('normative') of labour and resource expenditure per unit of production as a means of increasing productivity and efficiency — all of these measures represent a typically Soviet approach to economic management. There is little about them to suggest a significant movement toward market mechanisms that would alter the basic nature of the system. Many critics, as Victor Zaslavsky shows, argue that such a movement is essential for genuine improvement of Soviet economic performance. One possible harbinger of change in that direction is the recommendation of the establishment of wholesale trade in producer goods, which would appear to be unavoidable if enterprises are to enjoy the kind of freedom they are being promised to invest their retained earnings in expanded production capacity. This would be a major change indeed, but it would require a good deal more slack in the economy than is likely to be available in the foreseeable future. At least the issue has been raised in the highest circles, which indicates an important change in official thinking. The same thing cannot, unfortunately, be said about price determination, one of the most important causes of irrationality and distortion in the economy. Prices will continue to be determined centrally or at any rate by centrally defined criteria of quality and production-cost 'normatives'.

The crucial question remains where all the funds will come from for the ambitious targets for accelerated development in key sectors. There are really quite a number of such priority target areas — machine-building, electronics, food processing, energy, biotechnology, to name only the most prominent. Without a rapid increase in national income other important sectors will necessarily be left to stagnate or worse. At present it seems that consumption is the most likely target for belt-tightening. As noted, Birman argues that there is almost no margin for further stringency in that area.[44] Gorbachev evidently thinks that there is, and his wager on the 'human factor' is designed to instil a feeling that shortfalls in consumption can only be blamed on the failure of the individuals involved to work hard enough. Higher salaries and bonuses, it will be recalled, are to come largely at the expense of the less successful or assiduous members of the collective. It remains to be seen how readily the average Soviet worker or specialist will accept these changes.

Foreign trade and credits are one possible way out of this dilemma. Birman contends that shortages of tradeable commodities limit the potential of this source,[45] but he may be too pessimistic. Recent Soviet foreign policy initiatives designed to split the European Community from its American ally have considerable foreign trade overtones, particularly in the areas of high technology. Nevertheless, the Soviets themselves have pointedly asserted that they do not intend to become dependent on the capitalist economies for strategic imports, which can be suddenly cut off for political reasons. That is one reason for their recent re-emphasis on scientific, technological and production co-operation with their East European junior partners. Just how much real help Moscow will be able to count on from that quarter must remain questionable.

In short, the Soviet economy is indeed at a crossroads. Gorbachev is probably correct in believing that a total psychological, as well as material shift in the management and operation of the economy are required to reverse the declining fortunes of the systems. The stakes are higher than merely economic. It will be interesting to see in the next few years just how appropriate are the recipes the Gorbachev team has chosen for the attainment of their goals.

NOTES

1. Robert W. Campbell, 'The Economy', in Robert F. Byrnes (ed.), *After Brezhnev: Sources of Soviet Conduct in the 1980s* (Bloomington, Indiana: Indiana University Press, 1983), p. 69.

2. President of the USSR Academy of Sciences A. P. Aleksandrov has been one of the most consistent proponents of this view. See, for example, his speech at the 27th Party Congress, *Pravda*, 28 February 1986, p. 5.

3. See, for example, the campaign under the rubric *Dogoniat'? Net, operezhat'* (Overtake? No, Surpass) on the pages of *Sotsialisticheskaia industriia*, especially 26 April 1986, when an article with that title by Vitalii Kovalenko launched the campaign. The date of its appearance was something short of felicitous. The unique RBMK nuclear reactor used at Chernobyl' is precisely an example of Soviet standard-setting. In fact, Chernobyl' illustrated the tendency of Soviet managers, operating under ultimately political pressures, to violate even their own standards. The US space agency NASA behaved very similarly, and for analogous reasons, in the case of the 'Challenger' space shuttle disaster. Indeed, there is evidently a certain commonality in the approaches of the two superpowers to problems of technological complexity and associated concerns with safety. For both, considerations of national prestige seem to impel decision-makers to cut corners in the effort to achieve successes and meet deadlines. Combined with this political factor is a probably normal tendency toward the erosion of safety consciousness in the use of technologies, no matter how dangerous, once they have become routine. The latter factor, which is obviously not confined to the super-powers, is undoubtedly reinforced in their case by the national prestige factor.

4. One of the most famous of the recent proposals for changes was Zaslavakaia's 'Report on the Need for the More Thorough Study in the USSR of the Social Mechanism of the Development of the Economy' (*Doklad o neobkhodimosti bolee uglublennogo izucheniia v SSSR sotsial'nogo mekhanizma razvitiia ekonomiki*), delivered in Moscow in April 1983 and subsequently circulated in samizdat. See Radio Free Europe/Radio Liberty, *Materialy samizdata*, Issue No. 35/83, 26 August 1983.

5. See, for example, Vitalii Kovalenko, 'Dogoniat'? Net, operezhat'', *Sotsialisticheskaia industriia*, 26 April 1986, p. 2.

6. See, for example, the Decree of the Central Committee of the CPSU, 'O stat'e "Skol'ko brat' na sebia?'', opublikovannoi v gazete "Pravda" za 20 aprelia 1986 goda', in *Sots. ind.*, 18 May 1986, p. 1, where the removal of a plant official by local party and administrative officials for displaying too much initiative in rationalising work practices is reversed and the guilty punished.

7. See, for example, D. Pipko, 'Vremia navodit' mosty', *Sots. ind.*,

1 April 1986, p. 2, where the difficulty of getting equipment for the modern vacuum processing of steel is recounted. See, also, G. Khabalov, 'Rekonstruktsiia: tochki oslozhnenii', *Sots. ind.*, 30 May 1986, p. 2, where the author shows that new capacity for the production of thinner walled steel pipes is being held up because the product is 'not profitable' to the enterprise under the existing incentive system.

8. See, for example, E. Chernova, ' "Don": proverka nadezhnosti', *Sots. ind.*, 11 May 1986, p. 1, where tests on the new 'Don-1500' combine harvester have shown that only 20 per cent of defects were the result of design faults and 80 were caused by faulty components. An analogous problem, potentially even more serious in light of Gorbachev's priorities, are shortcomings in some of the new programmable machine-tools coming on stream, which are often ineffective because of weaknesses in the electronic processor units. A. Pasechnik, 'Ugovorili na . . . ubytki', *Sots. ind.*, 5 April 1986, p. 2.

9. Doklad tovarishcha Ryzhkova, N. I., *Sots. ind.*, 4 March 1986, p. 3.

10. Campbell, 'The Economy', p. 82, table.

11. 'Doklad tov. Ryzhkova', p. 4.

12. G. Sarkisian, 'K aktivnoi sotsial'noi politike', *Sots. ind.*, 4 April 1986, p. 3.

13. For an analysis of power relationships within Soviet R&D institutions during the 1970s, based on emigré interviews, see Robert F. Miller, 'The Role of the Communist Party in Soviet Research and Development', *Soviet Studies*, vol. XXXVII, no. 1 (January 1985), pp. 31–59.

14. V. Kirichenko, 'Strategiia uskoreniia sotsial'no-ekonomicheskogo razvitiia SSSR', *Mirovaia ekonomika i mezhdunarodnye otnosheniia*, No. 3 (March 1986), p. 17.

15. Ibid.

16. For an excellent, if controversial, treatment of Soviet financial methods and practices see Igor Birman, *Secret Incomes of the Soviet State Budget* (The Hague: M. Nijhoff, 1981).

17. See, for example, D. Shatilov, 'Effekt uslovnyi i real'nyi', *Sots. ind.*, 18 May 1986, p. 2, where the fraudulent receipt of bonuses for innovations on the basis of unsubstantiated claims of economic benefit is condemned.

18. The problem of inter-departmental co-ordination of equipment deliveries has been especially serious in nuclear power plant construction. See, for example, the article on problems at the Chernobyl' AES published a month before the disaster. Liubov Kovalevs'ka, 'Ne privatna sprava', *Literaturna Ukraina*, 27 March 1986. Similar problems have been encountered in the construction of the Rostov AES. B. Gordeev, 'S otvetom ne skhoditsia', *Sots. ind.*, 13 April 1986, p. 1.

19. For a good illustration of some of the co-ordination problems involved see Stephen Fortescue, 'Project Planning in Soviet R&D', *Research Policy*, No. 14 (1985), pp. 267–82. See also, I. Peshkov, 'Most na styke vedomstv', *Sots. ind.*, 29 January 1986, p. 2.

20. 'Doklad Predsedatelia Soveta Ministrov SSSR tovarishcha Ryzhkova N. I.', *Sots. ind.*, 4 March 1986, p. 2.

21. Ibid., p. 3.

22. See, for example, V. Dunaev, 'Dva shaga nazad', *Sots. ind.*, 13 May 1986, p. 1, where automatic forming machinery for metals casting does not work; also, A. Pasechnik, 'Ugovorili . . .', where high-precision machining centres show lower than expected productivity because of the unreliability of the electronic brain of the system.

23. Ryzhkov, *Sots. ind.*, p. 2.

24. *Izvestiia*, 26 February 1986, p. 4; see, also, Ryzhkov, *Sots. ind.*, 4 March 1986, p. 4.

25. Ryzhkov, *Sots. ind.*, 4 March 1986, p. 4.

26. Ryzhkov, *Sots. ind.*, 4 March 1986, p. 3.

27. 'V Politburo TsK KPSS', *Sots. ind.*, 14 June 1986, p. 1.

28. The well known Soviet emigré economist, Igor Birman, argues that there is very little margin for cuts in consumption and that the decline in overall national income is, without truly major reforms, well nigh irreversible. Igor Birman, *Ekonomika nedostach* (New York: Chalidze Publications, 1983), esp. pp. 189–99.

29. For example, the case of the anti-friction metal depositing process allegedly invented in the USSR some 30 years ago, which is being widely used in the West and was rapidly adopted in an East German engine plant, but has yet to be approved for industrial application in the USSR. N. Il'inskaia, 'Spros za iznos', *Sots. ind.*, 5 March 1986, p. 4.

30. The existing system seems to favour trivial innovations and work on narrow dissertation topics for the advantage of the individual researcher, rather than national economic benefit. See, for example, A. Krainev and M. Khostikoev, 'Izobreteniia ne dlia vnedreniia?', *Sots. ind.*, 29 May 1986, p. 2.

31. In his Political Report Gorbachev noted that: 'The interests of society require the raising of the prestige of engineering work', *Izvestiia*, 26 February 1986, p. 6. On the further development of this campaign see the report of the Politburo session of 10 April, partly devoted to improving the training and utilisation of specialists in the economy. 'V Politbiuro TsK KPSS', *Sots. ind.*, 11 April 1986, p. 1. See also G. Ikilikian, 'Po real'nomy vkladu: Novoe v oplate truda uchenogo, inzhenera', *Kommunist* (Erevan), 30 April 1986, p. 2; and V. Zhuravlev, 'Kak vospitat' spetsialista', *Sots. ind.*, 12 April 1986, p. 2; also, E. Gontmakher and N. Denisov, 'Neprestizhnyi inzhener', *Sovetskaia Rossiia*, 29 March 1986, p. 2.

32. V. I. Kalashnikov, the First Secretary of the Volgograd Obkom, incidentally, suggested just such a rise in retail food prices, arguing that: 'The present policy of prices is such that even those kolkhozy and sovkhozy that successfully cope with planned procurements cannot work on a self-financing basis, and retail prices don't cover the costs of production of food products. '*Sel'skaia zhizn*', 1 March 1986, p. 2.

33. For example, in contrasting Gosagroprom and the Biuro for Machine-Building, Ryzhkov notes that, 'Their structure and function are different — they reflect the specificity of each complex. As experience accumulates, it will be expedient to move further along the path of improved management of groups of interrelated and homogeneous branches.' Ryzhkov, *Sots. ind.*. 4 March 1986, p. 4.

34. Gorbachev, *Izvestiia*, 26 February 1986, p. 5.

35. That is the sense in which Gorbachev used it at the Congress (Gorbachev, ibid., p. 5). Of course, the property debate has had other references as well, notably in the discipline and anti-corruption campaign. But the administrative and financial implications are the most interesting theoretically, since the proponents make a strong case, for the operational autonomy of enterprise managers. See, for example, S. N. Bratus, 'O sootnoshenii sotsialisticheskoi sobstvennosti i prava operativnogo upravleniia', *Sovetskoe gosudarstvo i pravo*, no. 3 (March 1986), pp. 19–26.

36. Note the experiment in Khar'kov, where periodic 'fairs' are held at which enterprises present specific design problems and select from tenders offered by groups of specialists. The project contracts are customarily for a maximum of 12 months. 'Iarmarka idei', *Sots. ind.*, 16 May 1986, p. 1.

37. Ryzhkov, *Sots. ind.*, p. 3.

38. See, for example, 'Mezhotraslevye kompleksy', *Sots. ind.*, 20 December 1985, p. 2. Examples given in this article are concerned with laser technology, industrial robots, 'reliability of machines' and corrosion resistance.

39. Fortescue, 'Project Planning . . .'

40. Ryzhkov, *Sots. ind.*, 4 March 1986, p. 3.

41. See, for example, her article 'Chelovecheskii faktor i sotsial'naia spravedlivost', in *Sovetskaia kul'tura*, 23 January 1986, p. 3.

42. 'Vstrecha v TsK KPSS', *Sots. ind.*, 15 March 1986, p. 1.

43. The theoretical quality of that analysis is another matter. See, for example, the criticism by A. Kurochkin, 'Kak by uluchshit' dela, nichego ne meniaia', *Russkaia mysl'* (Paris), 14 March 1986, p. 2.

44. Birman, *Ekonomika*, pp. 196–9.

45. Ibid., p. 195.

6

Soviet Reforms in the 1980s: Current Debate

Victor Zaslavsky

When in 1964 Khrushchev was ousted from the leadership, he was accused of 'voluntarism' and chaotic administration of the Soviet economy. The Brezhnev-Kosygin team which replaced him promised broad economic reforms and the introduction of the 'scientific management' of social affairs. Economic reforms began in 1965 but they did not last long, and the 1968 invasion of Czechoslovakia put an end to these attempts. Unsolved problems began accumulating while the leadership dedicated all its energies to an enormous military build-up and the maintenance of an unprecedented social stability.

Now the new Soviet leadership accuses Brezhnev's generation of bureaucratic immobilism, corruption and inability to discern unfavourable social trends and take necessary measures. The Soviet press writes about a 'dramatic accumulation of negative trends' in the seventies when social and cultural life was characterised by 'irresponsibility, mediocrity and demagoguery'.[1] These accusations are more than justified. An obvious decline of the Soviet economy started in the second half of the 1970s. It was somewhat slowed down by windfall profits from Soviet foreign trade because of very favourable prices on such major export articles as oil, gas and gold. In the 1980s, however, this decline accelerated.

The central goal of a Soviet-type economy consists in permanently increasing state-controlled surplus, while the major mode of economic co-ordination is centrally planned redistribution of this surplus appropriated by the state. A crisis in the Soviet system emerges when its economy stops achieving growth of the state-controlled surplus. In the early 1980s, the Soviet economy has come dangerously close to this. As Boris Rumer concludes, 'the Soviet economy is clearly in severe straits, although it may be premature to declare it in a state of crisis, if by that one means the imminence of structural collapse or conditions threatening the very survival of the system'.[2] The exhaustion of the policy of extensive development and the involution of the system of incentives are two major manifestations of the coming economic crisis in the USSR.

The Soviet economy, which still finds itself at the stage of extensive growth based on the increased use of labour, capital and raw material imputs, is substantially affected by the diminishing labour force, declining capital investments and overall exhaustion of favourably located resources. Labour force growth rates are falling, following a decline in the rate of population growth. According to demographers' calculations, during the 1970s the labour force would be growing at 1.8 per cent per year, but by the early 1980s these growth rates had fallen to 0.5 per cent and may fall even further, before rising slightly to 0.8 per cent towards the end of the century.[3] Moreover, from the qualitative point of view, a severe decline in numbers of the most industrialised and productive Slavic and Baltic populations cannot be compensated by the growth of the predominantly rural Central Asian populations.

Growth rates of the capital stock are also falling, and this decline is aggravated by a considerable decline in capital investment productivities. Now it requires twice as much capital investment as it did in the early 1970s to achieve the same increment to real national income.[4]

The extensive economic development still characteristic of the Soviet economy has another negative consequence. The economy, measured by standards of advanced industrial societies of the West, is extremely wasteful. Thus, according to Soviet statistical data, the Soviet economy in 1983 had to spend 2.2 times as much oil, 3.7 times as much cast iron, 3.0 times as much steel, 2.9 times as much cement as the American economy to produce a comparable unit of national income.[5] As Gorbachev has recently frankly admitted, 'we have already arrived at a point where such a waste is not only intolerable, but also simply unsustainable'.[6] In fact, taking into account the sheer volume of the Soviet GNP, this waste has begun exhausting even the enormous natural resources of the Soviet Union.

As a result of all these developments, in the past decade the

137

productivity and technology gap between Western industrial societies and the Soviet Union began growing.

Another aspect of the crisis of the Soviet economy is a changing balance between state-controlled and market-generated systems of incentives. One of the most important functions of the Soviet state is the engineering of social stratification. Up until recently the extent of social inequality in Soviet society was determined by the state, which organised the process of unequal distribution of valued resources through closely controlled systems of social, ethnic and territorial stratification. The state treats certain groups as strategically important by redistributing the social surplus in favour of these groups. Thus, Soviet ethnic policy is based on preferential treatment of territorially-bound ethnic groups. Similarly, policies of creating high-priority factories (closed enterprises) and privileged geographical locations (closed cities) can be cited as examples of the state-created system of incentives.[7] This particular system of unequal distribution was instrumental for encouraging higher productivity, for opening new channels of upward social mobility, for maintaining internal stability. In the past decade, however, its potential as a system of incentives has rapidly declined. Simultaneously, the 'second economy' began providing new and powerful incentives. Unable to suppress a certain amount of market activity, the Soviet state has had to tolerate it, which in turn substantially affects both the process of unequal distribution of resources and the incentive system. The effects of a free or semi-free labour market are especially noticeable. Workers make good use of their right to quit their jobs at will as a means of extracting concessions from the administration. As a result, wages often grow faster than productivity.[8] In the last years of the Brezhnev rule, the state, notwithstanding its enormous apparatus of coercion, proved unable to control many aspects of market relations in the USSR.

These domestic difficulties have been aggravated by the deteriorating economic situation of the East European allies, especially the 1980–1 Polish explosion and the continuing disastrous economic situation in Romania. The international position of the Soviet Union also weakened in comparison with that of the 1970s, while its international prestige suffered, especially after the 1979 invasion of Afghanistan. Having analysed the Soviet situation in the mid-1980s, Seweryn Bialer and Joan Afferica have concluded that 'the problem for the

Soviets has become not to catch up to the West, but to keep from falling further behind'.[9]

This fact is crystal clear not only for Western analysts but for the new Soviet leadership as well. In the 1980s such words as 'the turning point', 'radical change' and even 'radical reforms' have become the most popular expressions in the Soviet press. Their meaning, however, remains ambiguous because those who participate in today's debate concerning reforms use these expressions in a variety of ways. It can hardly be otherwise in the conditions of the leaders' repeated appeals for increased 'openness' about pressing economic problems and for 'profound changes' in the existing economic mechanism, when even staunch opponents of any meaningful change have to use the 'reform' language.

The change of attitudes towards economic reforms among the Soviet economic and political elite can be illustrated by the following example. In a 1975 survey of agricultural administrators and managers, of 545 respondents only 15, or less than 3 per cent, referred to the necessity of reforms. 'On the whole, administrators and managers were more inclined to analyse the concrete facts of rural life than to discuss the general problem of the nature and depth of economic reform in the countryside.'[10] In 1983 a Soviet sociological journal published results of another survey of attitudes towards reforms on the part of *apparatchiks*, high level economic managers and scientific administrators. Asked whether considerable economic and technological progress could be achieved *without* any structural transformation of the existing economic mechanism and management system, 48.5 per cent of the respondents answered positively, while 35.5 per cent of them denied such a possibility. The sociologists identified three groups of respondents according to their attitudes towards reforms: supporters of the 'stabilisation program' which reads 'improve everything without changing anything', 30–36 per cent of all respondents in different surveys; proponents of moderate reforms, 16–28 per cent; proponents of radical reforms, 15–20 per cent of all respondents.[11] Thus, in the last year of Brezhnev's rule, only up to 20 per cent of the political-managerial elite advocated radical reforms.

It has already been noted that when the Soviet leadership is receptive, new policy ideas come in a 'flood, unrefined, unintegrated and untested'.[12] It seems that after Gorbachev's advent all the Soviet administrators and academics to a man have been

139

converted into supporters of some 'radical change'. Today the Soviet press is rife with calls for economic reforms and severe criticism of the state of the economy. In many cases, they serve as a mere smokescreen to hide a pervasive resistence to serious changes in Soviet society. As Vasil Bykov has pointed out, 'the distressing fact is that people who for years preached and practiced their conservative views, after the 27th Congress started proclaiming the necessity of changes making believe that they always wanted nothing but reforms.'[13]

Under these conditions there is an understandable difference in the very use of the term 'radical reforms' between Western and Soviet publications. Western analysts usually single out several types of possible reforms in Soviet society and assert that the term 'radical reforms' should be reserved to a quite specific type of reform. Thus, Bialer and Afferica point to three major types of reforms: policy reforms directed at changing long-standing policies using as a main instrument the redistribution of resources; organisational-administrative reforms directed at changing and streamlining the decision-making process through reorganisation of the existing administrative units; finally, structural-institutional reforms directed at changing the existing basic political-economic structures. Only this latter type of reform can be called radical or fundamental because it must be implemented through fundamental reorientation of priorities and major shifts in the power of existing institutions and because it profoundly changes all the basic principles of the Soviet political-economic system.[14]

In the Soviet literature the concept of 'radical reform' is of a very recent origin. Even now the expression 'radical reforms' is often used purely metaphorically, referring simply to a rapid and resolute implementation of whatever reorganisation measures are being proposed by the leadership. For many years Stalinist political economy postulated that, unlike the capitalist economy where the process of perfecting production relations and harmonising them with productive forces was realised through a clash of interests and class struggle, the socialist economy was free from antagonistic contradictions, and the process of harmonising the growing productive forces with production relations was secured almost automatically without any serious clashes of interest, let alone class struggle. As a result there was no room and no need for radical reform in the Soviet economy. By the 1980s this dogma has finally been challenged, and there appeared a number of publications whose authors discussed antagonisms, contradictions and conflicts of interests in Soviet society which are not inherited from the pre-revolutionary period or infused from the capitalist West but are rather of its own 'socialist' making.[15] The authors of the unpublished Novosibirsk Report emphasised that, notwithstanding numerous resolutions recognising the urgent need for reforms, 'the present system of management of the economy stubbornly retains its existing features'.[16] Siberian sociologists ridicule the central theses of the dominant ideology which denies the existence of profound contradictions and conflicts among classes and groups in Soviet society. They insist that the failure of reforms is due to the fact that these reforms affected the interests of 'social groups that occupy a somewhat elevated position within this system and accordingly are bound to it through personal interest'.[17]

In the 1980s for the first time in Soviet history a heightened awareness of sharp social contradictions has spread among Soviet social scientists and members of the political elite. Many of them recognise that a successful introduction of meaningful structural reforms depends on the outcome of these internal antagonisms. Some Soviet specialists are now proposing changes and reforms so radical that, if implemented, they would challenge certain basic structural principles of Soviet-type societies.

Analysing Soviet reformist writings, a distinction must be made between radical system reforms aimed at qualitative change of society's basic structural principles and rationalising reforms which aim at adjusting the existing socio-economic mechanism without changing it qualitatively. The latter can also be called 'within-the-system' reforms which correspond to organisational-administrative and policy reforms discussed by Bialer and other Western analysts.[18] Some Soviet economists would claim that historically the Soviet economy has already experienced both radical systemic reforms and within-the-system, rationalising reforms. Thus one of the leading representatives of the reformist camp, Gavriil Popov, analysing interrelations between market and command principles in the history of the Soviet economy, singles out three successive periods.[19] During the NEP period enterprises were usually fully entitled to specify their product mix and their volume of production and to set their own prices. In some cases these rights of enterprises

141

were limited by orders issued by higher state authority, but the right to issue an order was in turn clearly connected to the economic obligations of the higher authority. In the mixed economy of the 1920s, therefore, enterprises and state management organs were commercially interconnected, and the economy was essentially structured along market lines.

After the well-known Stalinist reforms of the early 1930s, which represent a perfect example of radical systemic reforms, the situation changed dramatically. The command principle reigned supreme. In the command economy enterprises received from the central planners 'all instructions on what to do, when to do it, where to obtain materials, and where to deliver its products. Since orders came from above, they also guaranteed the basic wage. The enterprise's sole right was to decide whether to produce larger quantities or at a lower cost'.[20]

This command economy was rationalised in the mid-60s through a within-the-system reform which gave some room to the market principles, creating, in Popov's words, 'a hybrid of sorts in which administrative commands from above were combined with the right to disobey these commands'.[21]

A much more open and wide-ranging debate is now taking place in many areas of Soviet society. But those who remember the two previous periods of major leadership changes and the introduction of economic reforms — after Stalin's death and after Khrushchev's ousting — cannot fail to notice a substantial difference in the social atmosphere during the initial stages of the mid-50s and mid-60s reforms as compared to that of Gorbachev's reforms.

Decades ago economic reforms were presented to the population in fairly detailed party programs, resolutions and other official documents full of unbridled optimism. Accompanied by some real changes, they evoked, at least initially, considerable expectations and positive responses on the part of the population. In contrast to those periods, the present leaders' speeches and program documents — the proceedings of the 27th Congress being the best example — seem very vague and general on the problem of changes. A noted Soviet journalist characterising today's social atmosphere in the USSR concludes: 'in the past decade scepticism, lack of faith and cynicism have undermined social consciousness. Those who believed in a better future seemed to be out of their minds . . . When the economy is mentioned, the general pessimism is overwhelming'.[22] Moreover,

Soviet central planners appear to be unprepared to cope with the economic decline. Characteristically, in 1985 the Gosplan presented three successive variants of the 12th Five-Year-Plan for 1986–90, while the new leadership rejected them one after another because of their low efficiency and output growth rates. After replacing major Gosplan administrators, Gorbachev's leadership team finally approved, with a substantial delay, the fourth version of the plan.[23]

New forms of economic management which are now being introduced in the Soviet economy have already been and continue to be criticised in the Soviet press as insufficient or partial solutions, which may solve some problems but will raise new and different ones. It seems that the present political leadership is uncertain of the practicality of the measures it is adopting and is, therefore, ready to encourage contrasting trends and currents in economic thought. Under these conditions policy debates are concentrated primarily in specialised journals, but sometimes even in newspapers. Today there are hardly any economists or social scientists of stature who have not expressed their views on the present economic problems and the ways to solve them. Three sets of positions can be distinguished among the recent Soviet publications: those concerned with substantial reforms of the Soviet economy, in both radical systematic and within-the-system variants; those which, whatever their phraseology, belong to an anti-reformist camp; and those whose middle-of-the-road authors limit themselves to certain concrete measures promising some immediate, even if short-lived, improvements. But before we turn to a more detailed discussion of these currents among Soviet economists, it is important to summarise Soviet specialists' accounts of the present economic slow-down. The following arguments are especially popular.

1. The Soviet economy at the extensive stage of its development is characterised by a resource-consuming orientation which is still instrumental in guaranteeing full employment and job security to the population.[24] In the long run the command economy generates excessive demand and various shortages, especially as a result of its built-in tendency towards over-accumulation, aggravated by unmerited wage increases due to informal bargaining at the factory level and tacit compromise between workers and managers. Correspondingly, with the progressive exhaustion of labour and other resources the command economy has outlived its usefulness.

2. Today's Soviet economy is so complex that it can no longer be managed administratively from the centre. This argument suggests, however, that there was a golden period when the Soviet economy was simple and transparent, and central planning organs worked irreproachably. The argument tends to degenerate into assigning full responsibility for the economic decline to the poor performance of the central planners. But as Nikolai Fedorenko, the Head of the Institute of Mathematical Economics, has recently remarked, 'Gosplan is now planning the production of about 4,000 aggregated items. Ministries expand the list of products up to 40,000 or 50,000 items. The State Committee for Material Supply issues orders for one million items'. Given the enormity of the task and the shortage of time, 'we can only be astonished at the relatively good performance of these organisations and the relatively small number of errors made by them'.[25]

3. The authors of the Novosibirsk Report present yet another argument. The rigidly centralised, predominantly administrative Stalinist system worked satisfactorily when 'people were consistently regarded as "cogs" in the mechanism of the national economy and behaved just as obediently (and passively) as machines and materials'. Soviet workers of the 1980s are radically different from the poorly educated, obedient and terrorised workers of the 1930s and do not represent any longer 'a convenient object of management'.[26]

4. Both proponents of radical reforms who advocate a self-regulating economy and the anti-reformist economists who insist on curbing market relations in Soviet society agree that major difficulties of the present economic system are products of its inconsistent, contradictory character as it was shaped by the inconsistent economic reform of 1965. This reform, as we have already seen, brought about an uneasy coexistence between the dominant command principle and the subordinate but vital market principle. Very often an enterprise's economic interest runs counter to orders and directives from above, established as plan targets. 'Even a slight increase in independence proved to be an instrument in the performers' hands for lowering plan targets and for selecting those targets which offer an easier path of bonuses'.[27] As a result, industrial output between 1965 and 1980 increased 2.7 times, while enterprises' retained earnings (profit) increased 9.0 times.[28] It is worth noting, however, the significance and the degree of radicalism that today's Soviet

economists, with the benefits of hindsight, attribute to the 1965 within-the-system reform. This historical experience can be of help in evaluating the present round of reforms in the USSR. If both proponents and opponents of a self-regulating economy vigorously attack the existing economic mechanism resulting from the 1965 reform as well as its social consequences, they differ dramatically in their recommendations for the future direction of Soviet economic development.

The program of the radical reformers is now only taking shape, but some of its principal ideas are clearly spelled out in the present economic debate. Advocates of radical reforms try to find a structural basis for such proposed measures as strengthening the independence of the primary economic unit, increasing the role of the market mechanism, reinforcing commodity-monetary relations, and democratising the state administrations. They recognise the immense influence which the prevailing form of ownership exercises on the 'situation of different social groups, on their interests and behaviour'.[29] They recognise that the existing complete nationalisation of the economy and the absolute predominance of state ownership are structural prerequisites of the suppression of civil society by the party-state. As a result, numerous reform proposals, which seem to be radical (decentralisation, self-management) but which do not even mention existing forms of ownership and property rights, hardly stand a chance of being effective. Correspondingly, proponents of a self-regulating economy suggest certain important changes in property relations which might profoundly change the character of Soviet society. In a complete reversal of Stalin's dogma, a Soviet sociologist now writes that introducing a nationalised economy which does not guarantee higher productivity and development than a capitalist one does not signify social progress.[30] Obviously, no calls for a return to private property can be found in the Soviet press. But reformers propose, alongside dominant state ownership of the means of production, a large-scale introduction of group or collective ownership. Recommendations of this kind can still produce accusations of anarchism or petty-bourgeois deviations on the part of ideological hard-liners; but the present proliferation of articles on positive aspects of group, brigade and family contracts,[31] of collectively owned enterprises in East European countries[32] or of the mixed economy of the NEP period,[33] demonstrate that the idea of group ownership is gaining wider support.

Another proposal related to changes in property rights refers to the existing structure of state ownership in the USSR, where there emerged a strict division between the right to utilise and the right to dispose of the means of production and social surplus created by enterprises. Economists point out that the state, as the owner, makes the means of production available for use by enterprises, while the function of disposing of the product and material and financial resources is performed exclusively by economic management organisations acting in the name of the state. As a result, the state administrative organisations bear no economic responsibilities for their mistakes and counter-productive orders and at the same time they acquire 'certain possibilities for extracting benefits for themselves from the disposition process' simply by using their official position of power.[34] Restructuring state ownership in such a way that enterprises will be given the right to use and to dipose of both the means of production and a noticeable part of the created surplus will strengthen material incentives for direct producers, necessitate greater independence of enterprises, encourage repsonsible management and eventually transform the command economy into a self-regulating one.

Proponents of radical reforms insist on the reintroduction of enterprise self-management and of the market principle to regulate relations between cost-accounting enterprises, central planners and consumers. Thus if agricultural reforms proposed by the noted economist and principal author of the Novosibirsk Report, Tatiana Zaslavaskaia, were implemented, the collective farms would be divided into a number of smaller farms, each worked by families or by a voluntary co-operative of families, whose income would be determined basically by their output.[35] Gavriil Popov presents the following scheme of a self-managing enterprises' activity. Any enterprise has the right to choose orders rather than obey commands from above. Enterprises and central planning organs should become equal partners. 'The enterprises' own goals coincide with the interests of central planning only when the execution of directives is profitable for enterprises.'[36] It is up to central planners, therefore, to make their plan targets profitable for enterprises. General methods of price formation might be established centrally. But the price calculated centrally should be only the initial basis for forming the *agreed* price which, in turn, is to be determined by supply and demand. The wage fund should be formed from the income received from sales. Also, enterprises should use their income to pay for capital provided by the state and to pay the central budget for the central guidance of the economy in general. These are top priority payments, and the higher the income of a self-managing enterprise, the higher the centre's share.[37]

These ideas are now cautiously supported by some influential members of the economic establishment. Fedorenko begins his recent article on the necessity of increasing enterprises' self-management and introducing full cost accounting by saying: 'I emphasise that this path is fundamentally distinct from the prescriptions of "market socialism" and decentralisation. On the contrary, its goal is the strengthening of true democratic centralism'.[38] He continues by asserting that only a certain part of the enterprise production plan should be centrally formulated, while the central distribution of material resources should be limited to a small number of scarce, important resources. The rest should be planned and procured by the enterprise itself on the basis of direct contractual relations with other enterprises. Fedorenko even refers to the NEP experience to prove that relations of reciprocal material responsibility between state planning and administrative organs and enterprises are possible.

Proponents of reforms insist on restructuring the planning process on the basis of 'planning from below' rather than from above and on drastically reducing the power of the state apparatus over the day-to-day activities of enterprises.[39] They even propose a relaxation of the system's commitment to full employment and to price stability.[40]

Analysing the program of radical reforms presented by Soviet economists we can easily see how the limits to free discussion set by the one-party state grossly distort the very process of reformist thinking and debate. Reformers simply cannot touch certain principal social institutions and practices and have often to play down the degree of radicalism of their own proposals. Thus they do cautiously discuss the fact that the proposed reforms will contribute to a further strengthening of economic inequality and stratification in Soviet society. They stress that enterprises operate under objectively dissimilar conditions. Their natural conditions, technologies used, work force qualifications may be tremendously different. Self-management and full cost accounting will contribute to differentiation among enterprises, irrespective of their own efforts.[41] This fact has been confirmed by Hungarian and Bulgarian experiences. But radical reformers

147

somehow ignore the fact that under conditions of scarcity and shortages typical of the USSR, economic inequality at the initial stage of reforms may reach enormous proportions. Even the boldest reformers have to deal with an artifical construction enterprise-ministry — central planners (Gosplan) — and have to omit any mentioning of the role of the party apparatus, the military, the system of closed enterprises. They often seek to present their proposals as fairly innocuous measures which will not entail profound changes in the distribution of political power.

The radical reformers attract a lot of attention both by the essence of their proposals and sometimes by the very fact that their articles have been published. But it would be a mistake to overestimate their influence. As a Soviet dissident author Roy Medvedev has noticed, 'only a minority of the Soviet population understands the necessity of reforms; the majority simply quests for order and improvement of the standard of life'.[42]

Now the anti-reformist camp is also consolidating. Using reformist phraseology, anti-reformists suggest, in fact, a return to the principles of the Stalinist economy. They trace the origins of the present economic difficulties back to the 1965 reform which strengthened markets and commodity relations and resulted in growing shortages and a severe financial crisis, where the population's savings vastly exceed the volume of consumer goods available.[43] They propose a course of actions very different from that envisaged by radical reformers. They insist that the Soviet economy should be based on 'truly socialist principles' and should be purified of the elements of market economy and value indicators introduced by the Brezhnev-Kosygin reform. The idea that the existing economic mechanism does not require any other cardinal change but a resuscitation of the economic mechanism of the 1930s is both the starting point and the conclusion of numerous writings from the anti-reformist camp.[44] Anti-reformist authors stress the 'primacy of use value over exchange value in the socialist economy' and call for a return to physical indicators in planning. For example, Professor D. Valovoi, who in the mid-70s produced a stir by defending monetary-commodity relations in the USSR,[45] now defends the opposite thesis that value indicators and the reliance on profit distort the normal functioning of the Soviet-type economy.[46] Socialist enterprises are not independent commodity producers, and self-management, self-financing and contractual relations as well as price formation based on supply and demand will not work under Soviet conditions, assert the anti-reformists. Articles by Vladimir Iakushev which provoked a heated debate are very characteristic in this respect.[47] Iakushev seeks to demonstrate the practical incompatibility between the principles of central planning and the elements of market economy which emerged in the USSR after the mid-60s. According to Iakushev, the socialist state, acting in the best interests of society, forms prices which may strongly 'deviate from the cost of production'.[48] This practice is not an exercise of subjectivism and voluntarism on the part of central planners but it represents an objective necessity in a socialist society, its law of functioning. Iakushev and his supporters are reviving an old idea that a product's usefulness does not depend on its cost of production and, consequently, prices should reflect the product's use-value rather than its cost of production. Price formation, therefore, should remain a prerogative of state agencies rather than depend on the play of market forces.[49] These suggestions aim at perpetuating the conditions of total domination by the state over consumers. Since, from the point of view of use-value, a pair of fashionable shoes may not differ from that of an old-fashioned model, the state may continue producing the old model and force consumers to buy it using its monopoly of production and trade. Such proposals seem to reflect Soviet conditions in the 1930s and sound today out of touch with reality. As has been demonstrated, state agencies have already failed in controlling prices. Since today's product list contains around 25 million prices and rapidly changes, state agencies in the overwhelming majority of cases cannot help but approve prices suggested by producer enterprises.[50]

The most thorny problem for anti-reformists remains that of incentives. How can the state encourage workers to raise labour productivity? Iakushev and other anti-reformists answer that labour productivity in a socialist state should grow as a result of 'socialist competition', which is radically different from the struggle for survival in the market place. They are eager to stress that the proposed socialist competition qualitatively differs from the old-style *stakhanovism* of the Stalinist period. Each factory or, better, group of enterprises, should be given a fixed wage fund, and competitors will divide this fund in proportion to their real labour input. This practice, according to Iakushev, will increase wage differentials, create new incentives for work and

149

will not generate inflationary tendencies. But who is going to determine the real labour input of a worker or a factory? In the absence of market mechanisms, this will obviously be a task performed by huge state bureaucracies, engaged in non-productive control operations. Moreover, taking into account the extreme diversity of conditions and the heterogeneity of types of work in a modern industrial society, these bureaucracies, unable to arrive at impartial data on the real labour input, will inevitably use arbitrary and biased comparisons. Under these conditions wage differentials and incentives will continue to be state-engineered and reflect considerations other than workers' effort and productivity. There may even emerge a tendency to curtail or eliminate the worker's right to quit a job at will, as was the practice during the Stalin period.

Anti-reformist writings illustrate the state of mind of conservative officials and academics and provide clear evidence of the widespread resistence to change in the Soviet system. The most salient feature of these writings is that the ideological orthodoxy of the anti-reformist proposals is often combined with a sense of the impossibility of their practical implementation, of their sterility. What is interesting about the anti-reformist proposals is not their substance but the fact that they indicate the larger struggle between advocates and staunch opponents of reforms that is now going on in the USSR.

The public economic debate in the Soviet Union is not limited to articles by specialists elaborating on the virtues of radical reforms or insisting on the essential validity of the existing economic mechanism. There is also a variety of publications by authors who, far from suggesting comprehensive programs of reforms, advocate a 'moderate' or rationalising sort of change and propose certain limited but concrete measures of socio-economic reorganisation. In this motley collection of writings on economic change articles written by Soviet enterprise directors merit special attention.

In the 1980s the Novosibirsk management journal *EKO* published a number of articles by industrial managers and reported the results of a few surveys of managers' attitudes towards economic reforms. These attitudes are not only important because of the key role this particular social group will be playing in realising whatever reforms the Soviet leadership is going to adopt, but they are also indicative of basic attitudes and the mentality of many new leaders who were formerly plant directors and managers.

The image of the Soviet manager which emerges from the *EKO* materials is a far cry from that of an enterprising and innovative technocrat pressing for radical economic reforms and struggling with conservative party bureaucrats and central planners. The Novosibirsk Report is much more realistic in concluding that the social type of both workers and managers formed by the existing economic mechanism 'fails to correspond not only to the strategic aims of a developed socialist society, but also to the technological requirements of contemporary production'.[51]

In a survey of Siberian directors of large and medium enterprises the respondents were asked to specify factors which, in their opinion, contributed to the deteriorating morale and productivity of labour. Seventy per cent of them blamed the situation where workers could not be punished for poor work, and 68 per cent pointed to the workers' 'lack of responsibility', while such factors as inadequate organisation of production and bad working conditions, which depend mainly on the system of management, were mentioned respectively by 17 per cent and 21 per cent of respondents. In the same vein, when enumerating factors which prevent directors from extracting higher productivity from their workers, respondents started with the shortage of manpower and labour turnover which ensues when workers move from one enterprise to another seeking better pay and slacker discipline; next, directors pointed to the inadequacy of their rights to punish workers habitually violating discipline; they concluded by mentioning shortcomings of planning and general organisation as factors of decidedly lesser importance than those mentioned first.[52] Directors demand that their rights to discipline workers, to keep them under their employ and to control workers' wages be greatly enhanced. Their approach to workers and their ideals of industrial relations are paternalistic in the extreme. Some directors boast of farms attached to their factories which supply *their* workers with meat, dairy products or vegetables. Others seek to have construction brigades attached to their plant to provide their workers with housing. Some even suggest introducing special parent bonuses for each child who works at the parent's enterprise. Directors contemplate measures forcing workers to repay losses incurred by an enterprise as a result of their wilfully quitting a job. There have even appeared proposals to change from elections based on the territorial principle to elections based on the employment principle to make directors of enterprises simultaneously members (deputies) of local soviets.[53]

Directors would obviously like greater decision-making autonomy, but they are not interested in introducing a market environment with the ensuing competition and increase in responsibility. Characteristically, in a recent survey of 60 enterprise directors, only two of them mentioned price-setting as an area where their rights were inadequate. Philip Hanson, analysing this fact, suggests 'the lack of real understanding on the part of Soviet managers of how important prices would be in a genuinely decentralised system'.[54] But Soviet managers lack neither ingenuity nor understanding of the implications of a serious shift towards market relations. Soviet sociologists who supervised several surveys of managers' attitudes conclude that many of their respondents do not want decentralisation and increased decision-making autonomy, preferring a more centralised system with less power and less responsibility.[55]

Analysing the present debate on radical reforms in the USSR, the most important problem remains establishing the position of the Soviet leadership on radical reforms. It can be clarified taking into account previous records of those in the leadership who had been in the position of power for some time; theoretical views of those leaders who happened to express them publicly and, most important of all, evaluating the practical policy the present leadership is implementing in order to improve economic performance and accelerate the growth of the Soviet economy. As Bialer and Afferica point out, 'radical *economic* reforms, in the normal sense of the term "reforms" are impossible in the Soviet Union. What is possible are radical *political* reforms that have fundamental economic consequences'.[56] There is no indication whatsoever that the new leadership has even slight doubts concerning the basic soundness of the Soviet political system or has any intention to introduce any serious political change. In all their pronouncements Soviet leaders stress that what is needed is the 'radical reconstruction of the economy, the cardinal reorganisation of structural and investment policy, the radical reform of the whole economic mechanism, the activation of the human factor, and the intensification of the social thrust of our plans'.[57] 'Radical reforms' in this case mean, as we have already seen, nothing else but within-the-system rationalising reforms. There is quite a sharp contrast between the leaders' statements about the forthcoming reorganisation of the economy and the ideas of Soviet radical reformers. In his recent book Vadim Medvedev, who has emerged as one of the major theoreticians within the present Politburo, concludes: 'it is impossible to avoid shortages and improve economic efficiency through such measures as curtailing the centralised management of the economy, as strongly developing independence, cost accounting and self-reliance of enterprises, as strengthening the market mechanism. This road is unacceptable in principle for us'.[58] Moreover, no person in the highest leadership, Gorbachev included, can be associated with any radical proposals or original approach to economic changes. As Weickhardt concludes his study of Gorbachev's record on economic reform, 'while Gorbachev's record demonstrates that the Soviet system is not moribund, his reforms prior to his appointment as General Secretary were neither new nor radical nor were they his original ideas'.[59]

But whatever the theoretical positions, previous records and emotional preferences of the present Soviet leaders, their practical steps point in the direction of an ongoing within-the-system reform which in all likelihood will be more profound and consequential than the 1965 or any other within-the-system reform since the Stalinist radical reform of the early 1930s. It is obvious that in the heated debate between marketeers who respect the working of the profit motive and autonomy of enterprises within the context of central planning, and non-marketeers who believe in the strictest control of commodity-monetary relations, the higher echelons of the party have of late begun to side with marketeers. These days *Pravda* repeatedly warns its readers to 'stop underestimating the role of commodity-monetary relations, economic interest and profit if we are to achieve a considerable acceleration of economic growth'.[60]

There is no doubt that the leadership is trying everything in its power to preserve the dominant role of the party bureaucracy and its ability to control all aspects of the socio-economic system. But in order to achieve an acceleration of economic growth the leadership has to liberalise the way the economy is run. The government's course of action is of necessity contradictory. On the one hand, the leadership adopts measures which add up to even stronger centralisation. It plans a higher growth rate of productive investments, while the share of investments in the machine-building and energy sectors is supposed to grow by one-third in one year. To further centralisation Soviet leaders have just established super-ministries or cluster administrations to supervise these increased investments and to redistribute investments and raw materials among different sectors of the economy. But where are these drastically increased investments in heavy industry to come from? In order to avoid a war-style mobilisation and massive cuts of investments in social infrastructure, Gorbachev's leadership is simultaneously implementing a limited decentralisation. Programs and rationalising reforms which promise an increase in productivity without additional capital investments have strong political support. Agriculture is a sector in which returns to serious organisational change would be especially high. Correspondingly, a more radical approach is being taken precisely in this sector. Collective farms and state farms are given five-year delivery targets which supposedly will not be changed from year to year. (Such promises were given and broken under Khrushchev and Brezhnev.) Small, semi-independent working teams operating on a contractual basis are encouraged, and there are even attempts to return to family farming in the form of leases of the collective farm land to peasant families. The chairman of the new agricultural super-ministry calls for a considerable strengthening of market relations in agriculture, asserting that it would not endanger the Soviet socio-economic system as long as 'the limits of the market are set by the socialist system and the state keeps holding its key positions in the system of production and distribution'.[61] In the service sector Soviet administrators have also begun experimenting with decentralisation by permitting contracts between the state and groups of workers or individual workers who may now rent premises and equipment from the state in exchange for paying taxes.[62] These measures may amount to a partial legalisation or, at least, decriminalisation of the 'second economy'. Soviet leaders hope that they will result in the renewed growth of the state-controlled surplus without increased inputs of resources.

As to the heavy industry sector, initial measures seem to be fully in line with the strategy of reforms suggested by one of Gorbachev's chief economic advisors, Abel Aganbegian.[63] In the beginning, improvements are to be achieved through vigorous discipline and an anti-alcohol campaign directed against workers' violations of discipline and extensive personnel changes at the managerial and administrative level. Later,

various organisational changes aimed at restructuring the existing economic mechanism should strengthen these initial
improvements and accelerate economic growth.

While campaigns for greater discipline and personnel changes
are underway, the Soviet leadership is now taking the first steps
in the direction of a large-scale economic reorganisation. Along
with a drastic increase of productive investments, the Soviets
have started introducing what can be called 'simulated market
relations' (the scheme known as the Sumy experiment) based on
principles of self-financing and economic accountability. Profit
and the fulfilment of contracts are to become major indicators
against which industrial enterprises' success or failure is to be
measured. The initial reaction of managers and economists to
the large-scale introduction of the system based on sharing
profit, in a proportion known in advance, between the state
budget and the plant is mixed.[64] Changes seem to be real and
may actually solve certain problems, even if at the cost of
creating some new, equally serious ones. It is clearly understood
that such reforms require, in turn, economically meaningful
prices. According to the statements of Soviet leaders, major
restructuring of planning and pricing will be taking place in
1987–8. The result will be seen by the 1990s at the earliest.

In 1985 the Soviet leadership adopted 'Basic Guidelines for
Economic and Social Development' up to the year 2000.[65] Many
Western economists are very skeptical about the likelihood of
fulfilling the long-term targets of the 'Basic Guidelines' without
radical structural reform. Thus Hewett, having analysed the
plan targets against the past performance of the Soviet
economy, has found them over-ambitious and probably un-
achievable. As Hewett concludes, 'during 1987–88, as the
unattainability of the major targets in the 12th five-year plan
becomes increasingly evident, the debate over economic reform
is likely to once again gather speed. And if Gorbachev is still
General Secretary, and if he is as willing to learn from experience (as he seems to be), then in the 1990s, a truly interesting and
far-reaching reform is not out of the question.'[66]

The Soviet leadership's perception of the situation is quite different, as indicated by its obvious self-confidence and conviction
of the realisability of the plan. Moreover, in 1986, when the first
half year of the five-year plan period has already passed, the
final figures of the Soviet five-year plan of 1986–90 have been
presented to the population.[67] They show a remarkable increase

on the previous five years. According to Prime Minister Ryzhkov, the plan aims to achieve the upper level of the Basic Guidelines' targets, while industrial growth rates should exceed them. Statistics for industrial output in the first several months of 1986 showed a growth of more than 4 per cent, which is higher than planned and noticeably exceeds the growth rate achieved in 1985.

The Soviet population has already learned from the post-Stalin experience that the effects of various administrative campaigns against labour turnover or violations of discipline are usually short-lived and all these campaigns have petered out after a relatively brief period of time.[68] Nevertheless, the present labour discipline campaign, which is combined with a large-scale replacement of administrators and with a major effort to rationalise and streamline the ossified economy, may produce more than short-term improvements. Gorbachev's approach to reforms typically stresses pressure from the centre and political mobilisation, but it sharply differs from that of his predecessors in attempting to direct all administrative activity towards moving the economy to the stage of intensive development. Soviet leaders are searching for a program of action which would permit Soviet society to regain its dynamism while simultaneously preserving such of its basic characteristics as the domination of state property, the one-party state, central planning, firm political control over the population, closed borders, etc. They may be at least partially successful. The decline in Soviet growth rates of national income, industrial production and consumption is not irreversible. As Hanson justifiably remarks, 'the power of the new Soviet leaders to improve economic performance without radically changing the system should not be underestimated'.[69] There are no theoretical reasons to assert that centrally planned economies will be unable to move from extensive economic growth based on increased use of labour, capital and raw material imputs to intensive growth based on the improved use of inputs. It is not unlikely that the major targets of the 12th five-year plan will be attained. But there are reasons to expect that the Soviet-type economy will continue losing out in direct competition with Western economies. And the possibility that the Soviet economy will improve its performance and reach the intensive growth while preserving its particular character and internal stability should not be ruled out.

156

The Soviet socio-economic system at the stage of intensive development will be organised quite differently from its present organisation, even if its structural principles may be the same or remain fully compatible with those which determine today the essential features of Soviet institutions. In a recent article the prominent Soviet political scientist and columnist, Fedor Burlatskii, referred to the five existing, or historical models of the Soviet-type economy, among which he mentions the Yugoslav model, the Hungarian model and three successive Soviet models: the economy of War Communism, the still existing Stalinist model and a new economic model which is now taking shape in Soviet society.[70] In the same vein Leonid Abalkin, the new director of the Economics Institute of the Academy of Sciences, calls for a 'striking break with the past asserting that Soviet society needs a change in the existing mechanism in comparison with the previous one that is as deep, as radical and as principled as NEP was in relation to War Communism'.[71]

Only time will tell whether the cumulative effect of changes in the Soviet economy will amount to the emergence of a really new economic model. We are now witnessing the very beginning of the process of introducing and implementing a series of ongoing rationalising reforms which, taken together, may amount to a within-the-system reform of a magnitude unheard of in Soviet history since the 1930s when the Stalinist socio-economic system was born.

NOTES

1. *Literaturnaia gazeta*, 4 June 1986, p. 3; *Literaturnaia gazeta*, 6 August 1986, p. 8.

2. Boris Rumer, 'Realities of Gorbachev's Economic Program', *Problems of Communism*, May–June 1986, p. 20.

3. M. Feshbach, 'Population and Labor Force', in A. Bergson and H. Levine (eds), *The Soviet Economy: Toward the Year 2000* (London: Allen & Unwin, 1983), pp. 94–5.

4. E. Hewett, 'Gorbachev's Economic Strategy: A Preliminary Assessment', *Soviet Economy*, 4, 1985, p. 290.

5. V. Seliunin, 'Eksperiment', *Novyi mir*, 8, 1985, p. 187; J. Winiecki, 'Are Soviet-type Economies Entering an Era of Long-term Decline?'. *Soviet Studies*, 38:3 (July 1986), pp. 327–36.

6. *Pravda*, 17 June 1986.

7. See V. Zaslavsky, *The Neo-Stalinist State. Class, Ethnicity and Consensus in Soviet Soviety* (Armonk, NY: Sharpe, 1982), pp. 22–43,

139–55; V. Zaslavsky, 'Civil-military Relations and the System of Closed Enterprises in the USSR' (forthcoming).

8. The complaints of managers and economists that workers 'dictate' their conditions to factory administrators have become commonplace in the Soviet publications. See, for example, L. Markin, 'Sprosit' za distsiplinu polnoi meroi', *EKO*, 5, 1983, pp. 81–90; *EKO*, 2, 1985, pp. 92–9; *Voprosy ekonomiki*, 8, 1986, p. 110.

9. S. Bialer, J. Afferica, 'The Genesis of Gorbachev's World', *Foreign Affairs*, 63:4, 1986, p. 607.

10. R. Ryvkina, *Obraz zhizni sel'skogo naseleniia* (Novosibirsk: Nauka, 1979), p. 186.

11. T. Dzhafarli, Sh. Kistauri, B. Kurashvili, V. Rassokhin, 'Nekotorye aspekty uskoreniia naucho-teknicheskogo progressa', *Sotsiologicheskie issledovaniia*, 2, 1983, pp. 58–63.

12. T. Gustafson, *Reform in Soviet Politics. Lessons of Recent Policies on Land and Water* (Cambridge: Cambridge University Press, 1981), p. 95.

13. *Literaturnaia gazeta*, 14 May 1986, p. 3.

14. S. Bialer, J. Afferica, 'Genesis of Gorbachev's World', pp. 609–10.

15. A. Butenko, 'Protivorechiia razvitiia sotsializma kak obshchestvennogo stroia', *Voprosy filosofii*, 10, 1982, pp. 16–29; A. Butenko, 'Eshche raz o protivorechiiakh sotsializma', *Voprosy filosofii*, 2, 1984, pp. 124–29.

16. 'The Novosibirsk Report', *Survey*, 28:1, 1984, p. 96.

17. 'The Novosibirsk Report', p. 98.

18. T. Gustafson, 'Reform in Soviet Politics'; S. Bialer, J. Afferica, 'Genesis of Gorbachev's World'; J. Prybyla, 'The Chinese Economy: Adjustment of the System or Systemic Reform', *Asian Survey*, May 1985, pp. 553–86.

19. G. Popov, 'Total Cost Accounting in the Economy's Basic Link', *Problems of Economics*, August 1985, pp. 3–18; G. Popov, 'O sovershenstvovanii tsentralizovannogo khoziaistvennogo rukovodstva', *Voprosy ekonomiki*, 5, 1985.

20. G. Popov, 'Total Cost . . .', p. 4.

21. G. Popov, ibid., p. 5.

22. A. Levikov, 'Veriu — ne veriu', *Literaturnaia gazeta*, 22 October 1986, p. 10.

23. See *Pravda*, 19, 20 June 1986; E. Hewett, 'Gorbachev's Economic Strategy', pp. 286–7.

24. Iu. Sukhotin, 'Khoziaistvennyi mekhanizm v usloviiakh intensivnogo sotsial'no-ekonomicheskogo razvitiia', *Sotsiologicheskie issledovaniia*, 4, 1985.

25. N. Fedorenko, 'Planning and Management: What Should They Be Like?', *Problems of Economics*, December 1985, pp. 45–7.

26. 'The Novosibirsk Report', p. 90.

27. G. Popov, 'Total Cost . . .', p. 5.

28. K. Ulybin, 'Defitsit i vzaimodeistvie partnerov', *EKO*, 12, 1984, pp. 25–6.

29. 'The Novosibirsk Report', p. 98.

30. A. Tsipko, 'Vozmozhnosti i rezervy kooperatsii', *Sotsiologicheskie issledovaniia*, 2, 1986.

31. G. Shmelev, 'Obshchestvennoe proizvodstvo i lichnoe podsobnoe khoziaistvo', *Voprosy ekonomiki*, 5, 1981; A. Tsipko, 'Vozmozhnosti . . .'

32. For example, E. Konovalov, 'Inzhenernaia artel', *Izvestiia*, 13 March 1986.

33. A. Tsipko, *Nekotorye filosofskie aspekty teorii sotsializma* (Moscow: Nauka, 1983); A. Kolesnichenko, 'Iskusstvo tochnogo rascheta. K. 65-letiiu doklada Lenina ''O novoi ekonomicheskoi politike'' ', *Pravda*, 28 October 1986, p. 2.

34. E. Iasin, 'Obshchestvennaia sobstvennost', economicheskie stimuly i khozraschet', *EKO*, 12, 1984.

35. *Izvestiia*, 1 June 1985.

36. G. Popov, 'Total Cost . . .', pp. 8–9.

37. G. Popov, 'O sovershenstvovanii tsentralizovannogo khoziaistvennogo rukovodstva', *Voprosy ekonomiki*, 5, 1985, pp. 90–2; B. Kurashvili, 'Kontury vozmozhnoi perestroiki', *EKO*, 5, 1985, pp. 59–79.

38. N. Fedorenko, 'Planning and Management', p. 43.

39. B. Kurashvili, 'Kontury . . .'

40. *Sovetskaia kul'tura*, 4 January 1986; D. Kazakevich, 'K sovershenstvovaniiu potrebitel'skikh tsen', *EKO*, 1, 1986, pp. 33–43; W. Connor, 'Social Policy Under Gorbachev', *Problems of Communism*, July–August 1986, pp. 39–41.

41. E. Iasin, 'Obshchestvennaia . . .'

42. See Medvedev's interview in *L'Espresso*, 2 March 1986, p. 101.

43. N. Vainonen, 'Tovarno-denezhnye otnosheniia: iskusstvenno nasazhdat' ili umelo ispol'zovat'?', *Sotsiologicheskie issledovaniia*, 2, 1985; A. Eremin, 'Ratsional'nye li stoimostnye pokazateli planirovaniia?', *Sotsiologicheskie issledovaniia*, 1, 1985; M. Langshstein, 'Prioritet obshchenarodnykh interesov — osnova khozrascheta', *Sotsiologicheskie issledovaniia* 1, 1985.

44. V. Iakushev, 'Demokraticheskii tsentralizm v upravlenii narodnym khoziaistvom', *Sotsiologicheskie issledovaniia*, 2, 1984, p. 60; A. Eremin, 'Ratsional'nye . . .', p. 38; M. Langshtein, 'Prioritet . . .', p. 35.

45. *Ekonomicheskie nauki*, 10, 1974.

46. D. Valovoi, 'Pokazateli sotsialisticheskogo khoziaistvovaniia: razmyshleniia ekonomista', *Kommunist*, 15, 1984.

47. V. Iakushev, 'Raspredelenie po trudu: vzaimosviaz' khoziaistvennogo mekhanizma i sorevnovaniia', *Sotsiologicheskie issledovaniia*, 3, 1982; V. Iakushev, 'Demokraticheskii . . .'.

48. V. Iakushev, 'Demokraticheskii . . .', p. 55.

49. V. Iakushev, 'Raspredelenie . . .'; V. Iakushev, 'Demokraticheskii . . .'; N. Vainonen, 'Tovarno . . .'.

50. N. Fedorenko, 'Planning and Management', p. 52.

51. 'The Novosibirsk Report', p. 106.

52. N. Chernina, 'Direktora o sotsial'nykh faktorakh effektivnosti proizvodstva', *EKO*, 2, 1985, pp. 89–102.

53. *Voprosy ekonomiki*, 1, 1986, pp. 19–20.

54. P. Hanson, 'Soviet Directors' Views on Enterprise Autonomy', *RL Research*, 7 February 1985, p. 3.

55. *EKO*, 12, 1984, p. 69.

56. S. Bialer, J. Afferica, 'Genesis of Gorbachev's World', p. 610.

57. *Pravda*, 19 June 1986.

58. V. Medvedev, *Upravlenie sotsialisticheskim proizvodstvom: problemy teorii i praktiki* (Moscow: Politizdat, 1984), p. 177; see also V. Medvedev, 'Voprosy razvitiia obshchestvennykh nauk na sovremennom etape', in *Sovershenstvovanie razvitogo sotsializma i ideologicheskaia rabota partii* (Moscow: Politizdat, 1985), p. 112.

59. G. Weickhardt, 'Gorbachev's Record on Economic Reform', *Soviet Union*, 12:3, 1985, p. 276.

60. *Pravda*, 26 March 1986.

61. *Izvestiia*, 3 March 1986, p. 3.

62. See the new legislation on individual labour activity, to take effect in May 1987, which allows 29 types of individual labour, including automobile and housing repairs, opening a restaurant, private taxi service and the tilling of land plots. *Pravda*, 20 November 1986.

63. A. Aganbegian, 'Strategiia uskoreniia sotsial'no-ekonomicheskogo razvitiia', *Problemy mira i sotsializma*, 9, 1985.

64. See 'Prava, ogranicheniia, perspektivy', *EKO*, 11, 1985, pp. 58–78; A. Levikov, 'Veriu . . .'.

65. *Pravda*, 9 November 1985.

66. E. Hewett, 'Gorbachev's Economic Strategy', p. 304.

67. *Pravda*, 19, 20 June 1986.

68. T. Baranenkova, 'Puti ukrepleniia trudovoi distsipliny', *Voprosy ekonomiki*, 5, 1986, p. 60.

69. P. Hanson, 'Gorbachev's Economic Strategy: A Comment', *Soviet Economy*, I: 1985, p. 308.

70. F. Burlatskii, 'Besedy o kitaiskoi ekonomicheskoi reforme', *Literaturnaia gazeta*, 11 June 1986.

71. See 'Soviet Economist Urges Changes As Sweeping as Lenin's Program', *Glove and Mail*, 1 November 1986, p. A8.

7

Agricultural Reform, the Food Program and the 27th Party Congress

Stephen G. Wheatcroft

For the USSR agriculture has always been a major political problem. But the nature of the problem and the government's attitude to it have changed significantly since Stalin's time, and have been changing further in recent years. Stalin's neglect and abuse of the economic interests of the peasantry were replaced by Khrushchev's administrative reorganisations and then by Brezhnev's economic indulgence, as capital investment and other expenditures on agriculture reached an unjustifiable level. Since the war and until the late 1970s the share of capital investment going to agriculture had consistently been increasing, despite the fact that the agricultural share in Soviet GNP had been consistently declining. Low consumer prices for food were only maintained through the use of a large and growing level of subsidies. Since 1972 the Soviet Union has also been relying increasingly on the importation of agricultural produce and agricultural raw materials (especially grain for livestock feed), in order to maintain even this decreasing share of GNP (see Table 7.1). Such a situation could not continue indefinitely.

Agricultural reform has been on the political agenda in the USSR since the March 1965 Plenum. Following the Politburo resolution of May 1976 great emphasis was placed on the extension and development of inter-farm and agro-industrial complexes with the avowed intention of increasing agricultural productivity.[1] At the same time, but with much less publicity the first steps appear to have been taken gently to reduce the share of capital investment allocated to agriculture. However, before much was achieved the system underwent the political shock of the US grain embargo of the 1980–1 period, and although the

Table 7.1: The rising levels of net grain imports, agricultural subsidies and the imbalance between agriculture's share in national income and total capital investment

	Grain imports as % of production	Agricultural subsidies in % of GVO of agriculture	Agriculture's national income (%)	Share in capital investment (%)
Pre-war			25–30	11.3
1955–60	− 4.5		22.2	13.9
1961–65	− 1.2	3	21.6	15.2
1966–70	− 2.9	8.7	21.8	16.7
1971–75	+ 5.9	15.4	19.0	19.8
1976–80	+ 9.9	26.1	(16.0)	20.0
1980	+ 18.1	37.7	14.9	19.7
1981	+ 28.4		14.6	19.6

Sources: Grain imports, see Appendix 1 to this chapter. Agricultural Subsidies Calculated from V. G. Treml, *Agricultural Subsidies in the Soviet Union*, USDC, Foreign Economic Report, No. 15, December 1978, p. 8. And V. G. Treml, 'Subsidies in Soviet Agriculture: Record and Prospects', in *Soviet Economy in the 1980s: Problems and Prospects*, Part 2, Joint Economic Committee, Congress of the United States, Washington, 1983, pp. 177–8. GVO (Gross Value of Agriculture) from *Narodnoe Khoziaistvo, SSSR, 1984*, Moscow 1985, p. 224. Agriculture's share in National Income calculated from *Narodnoe Khoziaistvo, SSSR, 1922–1982gg.*, Moscow 1982, p. 417. Agriculture's share in capital investment, see Appendix 4 to this chapter.

embargo did not remain in force for long, it does appear to have provided the impulse for the launching of a new initiative at the May 1982 Plenum which incorporated the earlier attempts at agricultural reform into the Food Program.[2] Although the relative share of investment allocated to agriculture has continued to decline in subsequent years, there was, nevertheless, a substantial increase in the level of subsidies paid to agriculture and consequently a worsening of the burden of inefficient agriculture on the rest of the economy.

Gorbachev has been in charge of the party's agricultural department since 1978 and was probably involved in the Food Program from its inception.[3] It is natural to assume that the food problem is one that is of great concern to him. So what is he doing about it? What is happening to the agricultural reforms? Is there any real attempt to increase agricultural productivity, to lower the subsidies being paid to agriculture and to bring the level of investment devoted to the agricultural sector more into line with its current importance? Is the Food Program just rhetoric, as many claim, or does it cover a real attempt to reform agriculture? How has the Food Program changed since Gorbachev took over and what had been achieved by the time of the 27th Party Congress? These are some of the main questions that are addressed in this chapter. We will begin with a very brief consideration of the Food Program and the May 1982 Plenum.

THE FOOD PROGRAM AND THE COMPROMISE OF THE MAY 1982 PLENUM

The origins of the Food Program

The first real sign that the Politburo was making an urgent assessment of the food problem and of ways of dealing with it came after the introduction of the US grain embargo in January 1980. In October 1980 at a Plenum of the Central Committee it was first announced that the Politburo had authorised work to be carried out on the Food Program aimed at making the USSR self-sufficient in its food and fodder requirements.

As we now know the US grain embargo served little economic or strategic purpose and was abandoned in April 1981 by Reagan under pressure from US farmers.[4] However, it undoubtedly had great internal political consequences in the USSR, placing Brezhnev's agrarian policy on the political agenda in no uncertain terms.

The embargo must have raised very serious doubts about one of the important features of Brezhnev's agricultural policy as it had developed since March 1965. And these doubts did not go away once the Americans had withdrawn the embargo. The lifting of the embargo must have removed some of the urgency behind the Food Program but the program was, nevertheless, allowed to develop. This was partly presumably to guard against any subsequent US pressure, partly perhaps out of inertia, but partly also because once such an important item had been placed on the Politburo's agenda something had to be done; and there were undoubtedly many members of the Politburo who welcomed an opportunity to improve agricultural productivity, to lower the burden that the rest of the economy bore in subsidising the food bill and possibly to reform agriculture. Many must have felt that a change was needed and the embargo may well have contributed to an internal political atmosphere in the USSR that was at last making such a change possible.

In a speech in November 1981 Brezhnev had placed considerable emphasis on the need to include within the program a reform of the economic mechanism and to give more autonomy to individual farms:

> In drawing up the Food Program an important place should be assigned to such major problems as the improvement of the economic mechanism and the system of management, the management of the Agro-Industrial Complex as a whole. And of course local management. The collective farms and state farms themselves should have final say in deciding what should be sown on each hectare and when one job or another should begin.[5]

It is unclear (as it always is with Soviet politicians) whether this was Brezhnev's genuine feelings or whether he was acting as a spokesman in voicing an opinion that had come to prominence at a time when his earlier policies were being attacked. What is clear, however, is that four months later, when the Food Program did eventually emerge in May 1982, it was considerably more cautious and less radical than the above speech would have suggested. The analysis of the problem was rather obscure, and the policies advocated tended to rely more on changes in administration than any radical change in the economic mechanism.[6] A large increase in procurement prices and the writing off or rescheduling of debts certainly added to the problem of subsidies which many felt to be the main hindrance to real economic reform in agriculture. From an analysis of subsequent investment figures (see below) it looks as though the major and politically highly sensitive decision to reduce the share of capital investment going to agriculture was being continued, but this was certainly not at all visible from the rhetoric about the urgency of solving the food problem. In many ways Brezhnev's Food Program can be seen as a cheap ideological substitute and a few final concessions made to agriculture at a time when a growing proportion of scarce investment resources were beginning to be directed in a different direction.

The analysis of the food problem in the Food Program

In his speech introducing the Food Program at the May 1982 Plenum Brezhnev compared agricultural production in the five-year planning period preceding the historic March 1965 Plenum (i.e. 1961–65) with the level of agricultural production in the five-year planning period preceding the current 1982 Plenum (i.e. 1976–80). Brezhnev was able to show a growth in gross agricultural production in these years by 50 per cent which was well in advance of the growth in population and was sufficient to enable *per capita* agricultural production to rise by 28 per cent (see Tables 7.2 and 7.3).

Table 7.2: Growth in agricultural production, 1961–65 to 1976–80

	1961–65	1976–80	% growth
Indices			
Gross agricultural production	100	150	+50
Gross arable production	100	146	+46
Gross production of livestock produce	100	153	+53
Physical units			
Grain in mln tons	130.3	205	+57
Meat in mln tons	9.3	14.8	+59
Eggs in blns	28.7	63.1	+110
Vegetables in mln tons	16.9	26.3	+56
Fruit in mln tons	6.5	15.2	+134
Sugar beet in mln tons	59.2	88.7	+50

Source: L. I. Brezhnev, speech to May 1982 Plenum, *Prod. Prog.*, Moscow 1982, p. 7, for physical units. Indices from *Nar. Khoz. SSSR, 1922–1982*, Moscow 1982, p. 230.

The tone of the initial review of these results was therefore highly self-congratulatory. Brezhnev only slightly pierced this self-satisfactory tone with the following comments on the food program which appear to belong to two (or three) separate and distinctly different discourses. The first was in terms of the physiological problem:

But all the same we cannot be satisfied with the situation. We must see that the food problem is far from being removed from the agenda. If the general calorific value of the Soviet diet corresponds with the physiological norm, there is still a need to improve its structure. The demand for meat and milk produce is not satisfied, there are not enough fruit and vegetables.[7]

The basic problem is presented here as a scientific physiological one. Brezhnev did, however, go on to offer a second comment that belonged to a distinctly separate and more sophisticated discourse on the fundamental economic and political problems:

What is the matter here? The problem is primarily that the demand for foodstuffs is still exceeding food production — although it is increasing year by year. This is caused by a growth in the money incomes of the population, which together with stable state retail prices for the basic foodstuffs leads to an increase in demand. An additional factor is the decrease in the number of people directly employed in the agricultural sector of the economy and the growth in urban population. There is also an increase in the volume of purchases of foodstuffs from the state trading network by the rural population and finally there is an insufficiently rapid growth in the effectiveness of agriculture and of all the agro-industrial complex.[8]

The argument belonging to this second discourse had several important omissions. It failed to point out that the stable state retail prices had been achieved by very large subsidies that were a burden to other branches of the economy and were threatening the rational allocation of resources. By emphasising the long-term growth of agriculture in the first part of his speech, Brezhnev had concealed the existence of a declining trend in growth rates as can be seen from Table 7.3.

Table 7.3: Average annual agricultural growth rates

	Gross agricultural production %	Arable production %	Livestock production %
1966/70–1961/65	3.9	4.1	3.7
1971/75–1966/70	2.5	1.7	3.3
1976/80–1971/75	1.7	1.9	1.6

Source: Calculated from Appendix 3 to this chapter.

It also ignored the fact that the growth in livestock products was becoming less rather than more intensive (see Table 7.5) and that in any case it was becoming highly dependent upon a large increase in grain imports which were themselves costly and, as the Americans had kindly pointed out, vulnerable. The existence of the grain imports problem was alluded to later in Brezhnev's speech and was probably, as I have argued above, the main reason that the Food Program had initially been placed on the agenda. It may therefore be described as an unacknowledged (or only partially acknowledged) third discourse:

The project [Food Program SGW] is based on the need to diminish the imports of foodstuffs from capitalist countries. The interests of our country require that we set aside sufficient of our own foodstuffs and forage resources to guarantee us against any occurrence. Especially, as you know, the leadership of some states are attempting to turn a normal commercial operation, like for instance the sale of grain, into a means of putting political pressure on our country. We cannot put up with this and we will not put up with this. (Applause) I think that the members of the Central Committee will support such a question (Continuous applause).[9]

The main body of the program has a curious fascination with the elements of the physiological problem, and a total neglect of the economic and political problems. There is an attempt to treat the problem as a purely administrative and scientific one, as if it could be abstracted from economics and politics. The production targets were set not in relation to market demand, assessments of production possibilities or any form of economic factors, but simply to provide sufficient domestic production to ensure the provision from domestic resources of (or close to) levels that were described as physiological norms of consumption for the main food products, meat, fish, milk, eggs, sugar, butter, vegetables and fruit, by the year 1990 (the end of the 12th five-year plan) (see Table 7.4).

The main problem with Brezhnev's approach was his reluctance to face up to the major political and economic problems. The Russian population had grown used to low food costs, and, following the Polish experience, the Soviet government was naturally a little worried about the political unpopularity of greatly raising food prices. Brezhnev was undoubtedly aware

Table 7.4: Consumption of basic foodstuffs (in kgms per head of population per year)

	1980	1990	Norm
Meat and meat products	58	70	70
Fish and fish products	17.6	19.0	
Milk and milk products	314	330–340	360
Eggs (no.)	239	260–266	256
Sugar	44.4	45.5	35.2
Vegetable oil	8.8	13.2	
Vegetables and melons	97	126–135	165
Fruit and berries	38	66–70	80

Sources: L. I. Brezhnev, speech at May 1982 Plenum, see *Prod. Prog.*, Moscow 1982, p. 9. For norm see *Plan. Khoz.*, No. 11, 1982, cited here from K. Severin, ibid., p. 100.

of the economic nature of the problem, as his account of the disequilibrium between supply and demand indicates, and his November 1981 speech indicates that he, or the group he was speaking for at that time, had wanted to do something about it. But Brezhnev's position was awkward, because he more than anyone else was associated with the introduction of these subsidies and the increased investment in agriculture.

The March 1982 Food Program, as it finally appeared, failed to tackle the problem of reforming the economic mechanism and of introducing economically meaningful prices. The Plenum recommended the pursuit of much higher production targets, and in order to achieve these the following measures were to be taken: (i) administrative changes — the creation of a mechanism to administer the entire agro-industrial complex; (ii) a drive to increase agricultural productivity through more sensitive methods; (iii) a drive to reduce losses throughout the production, processing and distribution channels; (iv) an attempt to keep more of the population in the countryside and fed directly in-kind from the farms; (v) more use of ancillary farms and plots; (vi) better wages for agronomists; and (vii) increased procurement prices, in general, and additional subsidies for low-profit farms.

Many commentators have argued that there was really little new in this package. There was much rhetoric, but basically it appeared to be a continuation of the policies launched in the 1970s, and although there had been talk of increasing local initiative, all that really happened was the introduction of a new super commission for Agro-Industrial Problems under deputy chairman of the USSR Council of Ministers Z. L. Nuriev. If anything, the prospects for real reform appeared to have been made worse, because one of the decrees accompanying the program, entitled 'On measures to improve the economic mechanism and strengthen the economy of kolkhozes and sov-khozes', caused agricultural subsidies to rise substantially. Procurement prices were to be raised by 16 billion roubles from January 1983, 3.3 billion roubles a year were to be added by the state for an insurance fund, debts of 9.7 billion roubles incurred by low-profit farms were to be written off, and their debts of a further 11.1 billion roubles were to be rescheduled over the next ten years.[10] However, as we shall see below, behind the scenes with little publicity several factors appeared to be moving in the opposite direction.

DEVELOPMENTS SINCE THE MAY 1982 PLENUM

It was only four years since May 1982, but the political framework had changed considerably. The external complications were much less threatening than earlier. The Polish situation must have appeared to the Soviets to be under control. And the collapse of the US grain embargo must have increased the Soviet feeling of security on the food front. Although lip-service was still paid to the importance of solving the targets of the Food Program and achieving self-sufficiency in food production, the level of grain imports remained high, the level of grain sown has decreased, the share of investment devoted to the agricultural sector continued to decrease and there were ample signs that a serious reform of agriculture and a serious attack on the large subsidies paid to it were now being contemplated. Internally there have been great changes in the most senior party and state agencies, and these must have improved the chances of a serious reform of the agricultural system coming about. However perhaps the most crucial personnel changes took place only in October 1985 a mere four months before the party congress and far too recently to have allowed a serious reform of the system to have been worked out before the congress met. Consequently the fate of the economic system is still not obvious, although the writing appears to be on the wall. In this section we will briefly review a) the recent results of agricultural development and

169

the food supply situation, b) the continuing reduction in the share of capital investment being allocated to agriculture, c) some recent policy discussions and d) some of the major administrative changes on the eve of the party congress.

Recent results in agricultural production and food supply

There are currently few signs that the deceleration in growth rates for agricultural production have been decisively reversed

The 1981−85 (or 84) production figures show a continued decline in growth rates: from 1.7 per cent per year for gross agricultural production in 1976−80 to 1.1 per cent per year in 1981−84 (or 85) with a reduction from 1.9 to 0.5 per cent per year for arable production and 1.6 to 1.1 per cent for livestock products (see Appendix 3 to this chapter). For individual years we see that gross agricultural production rose by 6 per cent in 1983 and has remained at about the same level in 1984 and 1985. The same pattern holds for both arable and livestock production. The similarity between all these figures is rather suspicious. This kind of stability is unusual for the USSR and may indicate a reluctance to admit a further decline on the eve of the party congress. These figures may well be revised downwards in the future. But even from these figures it is clear that the earlier observed trend for growth rates to decelerate has continued from 3.9 to 2.5 per cent to 1.7 per cent and now to 1.1 per cent on average per year in four successive five-year periods.

The call for and repeated emphasis on the need for 'acceleration' first made at the March 1985 Plenum but re-emphasised at the recent party congress is needed more than ever if an average growth of 2.7 to 3 per cent per year is to be achieved in 1986−90 as planned.

In terms of individual crops, we still had the amazing situation of the failure, until the Autumn of 1986, to report the most important grain production figures.[11] Using odd references in speeches and the USDA estimates, we can see a 5.5 per cent increase in 1983 and then two very disappointing harvests in 1984 and 1985. According to my calculations this results in the lowest average five-year production level since the late 1960s (see Appendix 1 to this chapter) and at least 27 per cent below plan. Grain imports have consequently remained high with a record level of over 18 million tons or 26.5 per cent of production in

1984. The growth in produce of animal husbandry, however, is reported to be doing quite well, and this is reflected in the improvement in meat, milk and egg consumption listed in Appendix 2 to this chapter.

Some improvement in productive factors

As regards productive factors there have been some important improvements directed towards the intensification of the rural economy. There has been a quite remarkable increase in the area of clean fallow in recent years and a dramatic decrease in grain sowings. In the past five years the area of clean fallow has increased by 6.2 million hectares and the area sown to grain has decreased by 7 million hectares (see Table 7.5).

Table 7.5: Sown and fallow area in the USSR (in mln hectare)

	All sowings	All grains	Clean fallow
1975	217.7	127.9	11.2
1980	217.3	126.6	13.8
1981	214.9	125.5	16.4
1982	214.3	123.0	17.4
1983	213.0	120.8	19.5
1984	212.6	119.6	20.1
1985	209.8	118.1	—

Sources: *Nar. Khoz. SSSR, 1984*, Moscow 1985, p. 247; *Pravda*, 20 July 1986.

These are sobering figures for anyone who really believes that the Soviets are seriously worried about their immediate grain supplies. Gorbachev obviously feels confident enough to alter drastically the cropping system to increase the clean fallow area even at the expense of grain sowings! Western experts believe that such a policy is likely to have considerable effect in improving crop rotations and yields in drought areas.[12] Given the fact that grain is relatively abundant and cheap on the international market, this is a perfectly rational policy and is not necessarily a policy of despair, as it is sometimes presented in the West.

There also does appear to have been a substantial improvement in livestock intensification and a reversal of the trend towards declining milk yields and slaughter weights of the pre-1982 period, as can be seen from Table 7.6.

This brief review indicates that there are grounds for believing that some progress has been made in the move towards improving

Table 7.6: Livestock productivity indices

	Average milk yield per cow in kg/year	(% growth)	Average weight of meat per head of cattle sold to state in kgms	(% growth)
1975	2204		330	
1980	2149	− 0.5	350	+ 1.2
1985	2345	+ 2.3	362	+ 0.7
1981	2095	+ 2.5	345	− 1.3
1982	2134	+ 1.9	340	− 1.4
1983	2258	+ 5.8	350	+ 2.9
1984	2293	+ 1.6	355	+ 1.4
1985	2345	+ 2.3	(362)	+ 2

Sources: *Narodnoe Khoziaistvo SSSR, 1984*, Moscow 1985, p. 290; 1985 from TsSU plan fulfilment report *Pravda*, 26 January 1986.

the intensification of Soviet agriculture, and that there is plenty of scope for further improvements which could be carried out without greatly increasing the level of capital investment in agriculture.

Retail overhang on the food market remains but is probably being reduced

Although the increase in state retail turnover in 1983 was less than the increase in the wage fund, this inflationary trend has been reversed in subsequent years, and according to the plan fulfilment reports there have been quite substantial increases in the state retail turnover of meat, fish, butter and milk (see Table 7.7).

Despite these healthy figures there have remained reports of goods shortages, and until mid-1986 the TsSU plan fulfilment reports have repeatedly included the formulae 'despite the increase in trade turnover the population's demand for some foodstuffs and manufactured goods was still not completely satisfied' and stated that 'the annual plan for retail trade was underfulfilled'. The formula used for the July 1986 half plan fulfilment report is marginally better:

The plan of retail turnover, as a whole, for the country was

Table 7.7: Retail overhang indicators

	Wage fund %	State retail turnover All %	Meat %	Fish %	Butter %	Milk %
		Average annual change in				
1983/82	+3.5	+2.6	+5	−2	+10	+5
1984/83	+2.1	+4.2	+7	+4	+ 8	+3
1985/84	+3.3	+4.2	+4	+4	+ 6	+4
1st 1/2 1986 1st 1/2 1985		+6.9	+3	+7	+ 4	+5

Sources: Average wage fund calculated from wage rates and numbers of workers, employees and collective farm workers as given in TsSU Plan fulfilment reports. The rest of the data were taken directly from these reports. 1982 plan fulfilment, *Pravda*, 23 January 1983, 1983 plan fulfilment, *Pravda*, 29 January 1984, 1984 plan fulfilment, *Pravda*, 26 January 1985, 1985 plan fulfilment, *Pravda*, 26 January 1986, 1st 1/2 year 1986 plan fulfilment, *Pravda*, 20 July 1986.

fulfilled. The plan for the trade organisation for Belorussia SSR, Georgia SSR, Azerbaidzhan SSR, Armenia SSR and Turkmenia SSR was not fulfilled. There was some improvement in the supply to the population of foodstuffs and many non-food goods.[13]

The continuing reduction in the share of capital investment allocated to agriculture

The trend for a decreasing share of capital investment to be allocated to agriculture appears to be continuing. The politicians (including Ryzhkov) seem to be keen to emphasise that one-third of the country's capital investment is being allocated to the agro-industrial complex. This appears to be something of an exaggeration. Roughly one-third of all capital investment was allocated to the agro-industrial complexes in the 1976–80 period, but since then the share going to this enlarged agricultural concept[14] has continued to fall in a similar manner in which the share of investment going to the narrower concept of agriculture has also been falling, and according to my calculations the share planned for the AIK in 1986–90 will be roughly 27.6 per cent. See Table 7.8 and Appendix 4 to this chapter.

Table 7.8: The share of capital investment allocated to agriculture, agricultural complexes and agro-industrial complexes

	Agriculture %	Agricultural complexes %	Agro-industrial complexes %
1976–80	20.0	27.0	33.4
1981	19.6	26.7	
1982	19.1	26.6	32.5
1983	18.7	26.7	
1984	17.8	25.8	31.6
1985		25.5	30.7
1986–90 plan			27.6

Note: Agricultural complexes include pure agriculture and the construction and food processing industry related to it. Agro-industrial complexes also include industry processing equipment and supplies for agriculture.

Sources: See Appendix 4 to this chapter.

Agricultural and food policy discussions in the first months of the Gorbachev period, March 1985 to Tselinograd, September 1985

On 8 April 1985 there was an important meeting in the Central Committee on the work of the agro-industrial complexes, where several speakers complained that the work of the RAPO (District Agro-Industrial Association) was being hindered, that it had not become 'the independent object of planning and management, as was planned'. A. I. Dubko, the chairman of the collective farm 'Progress' in Grodno oblast, stated bluntly that:

> many organisations have been thought up, but they are not a help, rather a hindrance to the rural toilers in their pursuit of intensification. The land needs a single master who will be able to resolve the problem of increasing the efficiency of agricultural production without reference to departmental interests.[15]

In his summing up of the meeting Gorbachev picked up many of the criticisms of the hindrance to autonomous planning and management in the RAPO but seemed to go further by arguing that the Agro-Industrial Complex also needed financial autonomy:

The speeches have shown that we must carry through the improvement of management in this important sphere of the national economy to its logical end. The Agro-Industrial Complex as defined in the May 1982 Plenum should be planned, financed and managed as a single whole. We have not yet managed to achieve this, and as a result we are incurring extensive losses.[16]

The day after this meeting took place, but the day before it was reported, *Izvestiia* published the text of an interview with M. M. Lomach, the head of the Kuban Agro-Industrial Combine, who gave a description of what such autonomous management, planning and financing meant. The interview rather provocatively pointed out that there was a fine assortment of meat products (including as many as eight different types of sausage!) and that they were selling well to contented customers, but were the prices not somewhat higher than current state retailing prices? Lomach replied:

That's true. We set them with consideration for existing standards, the cost of raw materials and all other outlays. Our selling prices are higher than the state's. Why? Perhaps not all readers know that retail prices for meat items in state stores are kept low by a sizeable subsidy from the state budget.

But under the conditions of our experiment we are supposed to operate on a self-supporting basis. The Council of the combine has to consider our costs when it sets the price. And it should be clear even to a non-specialist that expanded reproduction would be impossible without a profit margin. We have been set the task of systematically reducing outlays at all stages of production, processing and sale of output. This will ultimately make it possible to systematically lower the selling prices. The logical conclusion of the experiment should be the production of food products at a unit cost that will allow them to be sold at prices close to the state's but without one rouble in subsidy from the budget.[17]

This is an important development for the political as well as the economic problem. Increasing local autonomy is not only likely to improve economic efficiency, but it may also allow the state to avoid the political blame for increasing retail prices. It would clearly be much more acceptable to the population at large to have the gradual introduction of new local (experimental) state combines selling produce at higher prices than to attempt to increase the prices in the current state retail networks. Of course the logical conclusion is presented as the reduction of prices to the level of the fixed state price while making a profit. But the really important thing is that subsidies are removed immediately, and the long-term logical conclusion can look after itself.[18]

In May the Politburo passed a resolution which drew attention to some of the serious losses caused by subsidising the sale of food products:

> The resolution notes that, as a result of lax oversight by party bodies, Soviet agencies, ministries and departments, there has been an increase in violations of the rules governing the use of food resources and the buying up of bread and other products from the trade network by collective farms, state farms and the public for use as livestock feed.[19]

Of course this kind of thing was not new. There was much concern about it in the late 1920s and has been, ever since. It is an almost inevitable consequence of rationing and subsidising foodstuffs, and it is often raised by critics who wish to point out the absurdity of the pricing system.

In September 1985, Gorbachev turned directly to the food problem in a major speech at a Central Committee-organised AIK conference in Tselinograd entitled 'Provide intensive development for agro-industrial production'. The title indicates nothing new, and the *Current Digest of the Soviet Press* ran their translation of the text of this speech under the heading 'Gorbachev restates food program's aims'. They were right in as much as the abandonment of the aims of the food program is simply a political non-starter at the moment, so Gorbachev is bound to restate them, but what I think was more important in this speech was Gorbachev's frank discussion of the subsidies problem, his placing it on the political agenda, even though he continued (for the moment) the traditional line that the main direction in solving the problem is to increase production:

> All the same, the problem of providing the population with foodstuffs has still not been completely solved. The demand for some products exceeds the supply. This is connected with

the fact that cash incomes in our country have grown faster than food production. At the same time, the state prices for basic products have remained virtually unchanged for two decades, although outlays on their production are growing. For instance, meat is sold in our stores at prices that are only one-third to one-half the outlays on its production. *At present* [my emphasis, SGW] this disparity is covered by state subsidies which in the case of meat amount to almost 20 billion roubles a year. An impressive total as you can see.

He then went on in a far more ominous tone to suggest that the party leadership were under considerable popular pressure to do something about this:

The fact that in our country basic food products are accessible to all strata of the population is a great achievement of ours. But, while noting this, one cannot fail to mention something that disturbs many Soviet people. The Central Committee is receiving more and more letters from working people that raise the question of a disrespectful attitude toward the labour of workers and peasants, labour that they put into the production of bread and other agricultural products . . .

There are many such letters Comrades, apparently there is food for thought here for both labour collectives and central agencies. And to put it bluntly for every family. Decisively changing the attitude toward bread and other foodstuffs is our common concern.[20]

So the scene is almost set. Recently policy discussions have shown an increased thrust in the argument to give local farms and RAPOs more autonomy in the field of management, planning and finance. In certain experiments this does involve removing subsidies and selling produce at much higher prices. The Politburo is expressing increasing concern over wastage caused by the irrational pricing policy (i.e. subsidies), and Gorbachev has begun to discuss frankly the problem of the subsidies and is claiming that the Central Committee is being inundated with letters advocating a change (presumably the removal of the subsidies). Gorbachev has clearly placed this question on the political agenda. A critical point appeared to have been reached when the Politburo sat down to discuss the results of the Tselinograd conference at its regular meeting of 12 September 1985.

177

Major administrative changes on the eve of the party congress, September to December 1985

There were two major decisions concerning agriculture and food policy which were made after September 1985 and before the party congress. One was a major change in administrative personnel and organisations. The second was the decision to continue with agricultural subsidies for 1986 at least, i.e. to avoid any major reform of agriculture for at least a year.

On 27 September N. A. Tikhonov was removed from the chairmanship of the USSR Council of Ministers and was replaced by N. I. Ryzhkov one of the most recent Gorbachev appointees to the Politburo (April 1985), who had been in charge of the Central Committee Economics Department since November 1982 and had earlier been a first deputy chairman of Gosplan. On 15 October Nikolai Baibakov was relieved of the chairmanship of Gosplan and placed on pension. He was replaced by Nikolai Talyzin who has subsequently been elected to be a candidate member of the Politburo. On 15 November there were important changes in the leadership of the State Committee for Material and Technical Supplies, as L. Voronin replaced N. Martynov and became another of Ryzhkov's deputies. A week later on 22 November a major reorganisation of top level (All Union) agricultural administration was announced which involved the absorption of the Ministry of Agriculture, the Ministry of Fruit and Vegetable Farming, the Ministry of Meat and Dairy Farming, the Ministry of Food Industry, the Ministry of Rural Construction, the State Committee for Production and Technical Provisioning of Agriculture into a new super committee, the USSR State Agro-Industrial Committee. This replaced the Nuriev Commission that had been set up after the May 1982 Plenum, and Nuriev was retired. The question of who would be the new Agroprom chief was clearly an important one that was likely to affect the consequences of future policy. V. K. Mesiats, the former minister who lost his ministry, was not given the post, but he appears to have been transferred to an equally important position as the 1st Secretary of Moscow Obkom. The new Agroprom chief is Vsevolod Serafimovich Murakhovskii, who appears to have been a long-time associate of Gorbachev's from Stavropol and Gorbachev's successor as 1st secretary of the Stavropol Kraikom.[21]

According to its terms of reference Gosagroprom (USSR) is

the central body for the state management of the agro-industrial complexes of the country and along with the Council of Ministers of the union republics is fully responsible for boosting production, for implementing plans for the purchase of farm products, for ensuring their complete preservation, and for the qualitative processing and for a considerable extension of the range of food products. Significantly enough the Ministry of Agriculture Procurements is not included in Gosagroprom but is transformed into a Union Republic Ministry of Bread Products, which is described as part of the system of the country's agro-industrial complex together with the organs of Gosagroprom,[22] the Ministry of Land Reclamation and Water Resources, the Ministry of Fisheries, and the State Committee for Forestry as well as Tsentrosoiuz (The Central Council of Consumer Co-operatives). According to the report all of the agencies in the agro-industrial complex system with the exception of Centrosoiuz will be planned and financed as an integral whole.[23]

It was a Politburo decision of 14 November 1985 that apparently took the decision 'to proceed with planning, financing and managing the agro-industrial sector as a single entity at all levels' which preceded the setting up of Gosagroprom.

On 7 December 1985, at an important conference of agricultural chiefs at the Central Committee, V. Nikonov (Secretary in charge of Agriculture) announced:

> In 1986 all enterprises in the processing branches of the Agro-Industrial Complex will change over to new methods and conditions of management, which proved successful during the economic experiments held recently. This work should be given a purposeful and well organised character without delay.[24]

This instruction seems to have raised some uncertainty as to what exactly was being proposed. Since autonomy and self-financing had been key elements in the economic experiments, the instructions could have been interpreted to mean that agricultural subsidies were going to be removed immediately, i.e. that all enterprises in the food processing branches were to operate on a self-supporting basis as had the experimental Kuban Agro-Industrial Combine. This would have resulted in immediate price increases right across the board, which would have undoubtedly caused enormous immediate problems. The

179

party leadership were clearly not in a position to take on such a major reform immediately and, as I have suggested above, the best strategy would have been gently to ease in the new experimental high-price combines and let the customers decide for themselves if they wanted to queue for deficit inferior goods or pay a little more in an 'experimental' combine. Nikonov's statement seems to have been both premature and possibly dangerous.

In order to allay concern on this matter Gorbachev used the opportunity of a speech in the USSR Supreme Soviet a few days later to assure his listeners that subsidies were to remain on staple products for the year 1986. Such a curious confirmation of a matter not normally discussed is, I think, indicative of the great uncertainty that had been generated on this topic. According to the TASS report:

> Gorbachev noted that the 1986 plan for agriculture is concerned with economic methods that proved their worth in previous large-scale experiments. These included cost accounting, self-financing and self-recoupment which are to be introduced in all collective farms and state farms. The fulfilment of this task will be facilitated by the organisational reform to finance and run agriculture as one whole. The farms will be given more autonomy . . . *As in previous years, the state will subsidise the output of staple products (primarily meat and milk and supplies of agricultural machinery and fertilizers). It means the inevitably growing costs will be met by the state rather than by a farm or an individual consumer.*[25] [my emphasis, SGW]

For the moment, apparently, the subsidies will remain, but the very fact that Gorbachev has stated that the subsidies will remain for 1986 must indicate that their removal is no longer unthinkable.

AGRICULTURAL REFORMS AND THE FOOD PROGRAM AT THE 27TH PARTY CONGRESS

Finally we come to the 27th Party Congress itself and especially to the main speeches by Gorbachev and Ryzhkov. There were no major surprises at the congress. The main materials had been distributed and publicly debated well in advance, and the main immediate changes had been carefully carried out at least three months earlier. However, the congress was important. It had clearly acted as a major deadline by which the calendar for reforms and new policy initiatives were set, and it also provided some indication of future changes. The tone of the speeches, the way they handled (or ignored), the major problems and the way in which they were received were all very interesting.

In Ryzhkov's report on 'the basic directions of economic and social development of the USSR for 1986–1990 and for the period up to 2000' the new Chairman of the Council of Ministers suggested that a third of capital investment would continue to be allocated to the Agro-Industrial Complex. But since he also suggested that the level of capital investment in this sector will only grow by 22 per cent while total capital investment will grow by 36 per cent, it can be calculated that this face-saving 'almost a third' actually refers to 27.6 per cent and would indicate a quite substantial shift in resource allocation out of this formerly privileged sector. From this it would appear that there are still political problems involved in squarely facing up to the food and agricultural problems.

Gorbachev, however, was repeatedly emphasising that 'we must face up to the real problems',[26] and indicating that the time for Brezhnev-like self-congratulation has passed. While not wishing to place too much confidence in the official reports of the applause, they do not appear to have been supportive of the suggestion that the truth needed to be told and that a less indulgent attitude was needed for agriculture.

Concerning agriculture the targets of the May 1982 Plenum were to remain, despite the poor results of the intervening years. A further development in agriculture was the expressed intention to establish fixed purchase plans for agricultural products and to give the farms the opportunity to use, as they see fit, all the produce harvested over and above the plan. They will have the choice of selling it, either to the state, or on the collective farm market or through the co-operative trade network in a fresh or processed state, or they could use it for their subsidiary holdings.[27] The audience was reported to have made no response to this announcement.

Gorbachev also stated that 'there is to be a transition to improved planning methods based on progressive norms. The role of cost accounting will be substantially increased'. Again

181

there was no reported response from the audience.

The only two responses that the audience was reported to have made in the part of Gorbachev's speech dealing with 'solving the food problem' was when he ended the section and when he stated:

> A reliable barrier must be erected in the way of mismanagement and sponging, and an end must be put to excuses such as 'objective cicumstances' . . . The farms will have to use chiefly their own funds to expand production, increase profits and incomes and provide incentives. (Applause).[28]

From this it would appear that the audience was somewhat enthusiastic about the suggestion that agriculture should pay its own way more, i.e. that agriculture should not be as liberally provided with subsidies and with central capital investment allocation as earlier. It remains unclear, however, how exactly the more autonomously managed, planned and financed units in the agro-industrial complexes will in the short run operate and whether Gorbachev will be able to make agriculture more self-sufficient and less dependent on subsidies.

As a postscript we should note that when the detailed party-state decree 'On further completing the economic mechanism of economic management (khoziaistvovaniia) in the agro-industrial complex of the country' was published at the end of March, it was explicitly stated that the supplementary payments to unprofitable farms that had been introduced in November 1982 as part of the Food Program subsidies were to be extended for 1987–90.[29]

NOTES

1. From the early 1970s attempts had been made to combine the activities of kolkhozes and sovkhozes in association with related industrial processing, construction, and equipment and raw material supplying enterprises into the MKP (*Mezhkhoziaistvennoe predpriiatie* — the inter-farm enterprise), the MKO (*Mezhkhoziaistvennoe ob"edinenie* — the inter-farm association) and the APK (*Agrarno-promyshlennyi kompleks* — the Agro-industrial complex). Following the May 1976 Politburo Resolution attempts were made to regroup them into the more centralised RAPO (*Raionnoe Agrarno-Promyshlennyi Ob"edinenie* — Regional Agro-Industrial Association). The statutes of RAPO were published in February 1979, before the May 1982 Plenum

(see *Izvestiia*, 7 February 1979). For an account of the administrative reforms associated with these new animals see V. Litvin, 'Agro-Industrial Complexes: Recent Structural Reform in the Rural Economy of the USSR', and Everett Jacobs, 'Soviet Agricultural Management and Planning and the 1982 Administrative Reforms', in R. C. Stuart (ed.), *The Soviet Rural Economy*, 1984.

2. Keith Severin, 'An assessment of the Soviet Food Programme', in *The Soviet Economy after Brezhnev*, NATO Colloquium, Brussels, 1984, p. 87, appears to accept at face value the claims of an official of the International Section of the Central Committee who stated in a press interview in early May 1982 that 'it was in 1979 that Brezhnev first raised the alarm over the food situation'.

3. After more than 20 years working in the Young Communist League and Party Organisations in Stavropol, Gorbachev, a qualified agronomist-economist, took charge of the Agricultural Department of the Central Committee in 1978 and was quickly promoted to candidate membership of the Politburo in 1979 and to full membership in October 1980. For biographical data see *Pravda*, 12 March 1985. Gorbachev's responsibilities in the Central Committee were described by K. Zeimitz and R. Koopman in 'Gorbachev and agricultural reform', in *USSR Outlook and Situation Report*, USDA, ERS-85-4, April 1985, p. 29.

4. For an assessment of the politics of the grain embargo see John C. Roney, 'Grain Embargo as Diplomatic Lever: A Case Study of the US-Soviet Embargo of 1980–81', in *Soviet Economy in the 1980s: Problems and Prospects*, Part 2, Joint Economic Committee Congress of the US, 1983, pp. 124–40.

5. *Pravda*, 17 November 1981, pp. 1–2.

6. See D. Gale Johnson for an evaluation of the food program in these terms. D. Gale Johnson and K. McConnell Brooks, *Prospects for Soviet Agriculture in the 1980s* (Bloomington: Indiana University Press, 1983), p. 93.

7. L. I. Brezhnev, speech to May 1982 Plenum of Central Committee cited here from *Prodovol'stvennaia programma SSSR na period do 1990 goda i mery po ee realizatsii: Materialy maiskogo Plenuma TsK KPSS 1982 goda*, Moscow 1982, p. 7.

8. L. I. Brezhnev, speech to May 1982 Plenum, *Prod. Programma*, Moscow 1982, p. 7.

9. L. I. Brezhnev, *Prod. Program.*, Moscow 1982, p. 11.

10. *Prod. Program.*, Moscow 1982, pp. 59–60.

11. Grain production figures have not been included in plan fulfilment reports since 1980 or in statistical handbooks since 1982!

12. See D. Gale Johnson in D. Gale Johnson and K. McConnell Brooks, *Prospects for Soviet Agriculture in the 1980s*, pp. 37–41.

13. See TsSU Plan fulfilment reports *Pravda*, 29 January 1985, 26 January 1986 and 20 July 1986.

14. See note to Table 7.8.

15. *Pravda*, 12 April 1985.

16. Ibid.

17. *Izvestiia*, 11 April 1985. The interviewer continues by asking whether this obligation wasn't burdensome. Lomach replied that it

was but that they were selling their produce.

18. The Kuban Agro-Industrial Combine Experiment was clearly considered of very great importance. The commencement of its economic experiments was even recorded in the TsSU plan fulfilment report for the first half of 1985. See *Pravda*, 27 July 1985.

19. *Pravda*, 7 May 1985, p. 1.

20. M. S. Gorbachev, speech in Tselinograd 7 September 1985, *Pravda*, 11 September 1985.

21. For biographical details see *Pravda*, 2 November 1985.

22. The new Minister of Bakery products is to be the old Minister of Procurements G. S. Zolotukhin, *Pravda*, 4 December 1985.

23. Reported here from *Soviet News*, 4 December 1985.

24. *Pravda*, 5 December 1985.

25. *Soviet News*, 18 December 1985, p. 470.

26. See especially Gorbachev's closing speech to the congress, *Pravda*, 7 March 1986.

27. A subsequent decree of the Central Committee and the Council of Ministers, published three weeks after the party congress, explained the details of this new scheme in more detail. The 1986 grain purchase targets are to remain in operation for 5 years. Sales to the state above the targets are to be rewarded with a 100 per cent bonus, provided that their annual production plan has been fulfilled and that their volume of production exceeds their 11th Five-Year Plan average. Above target producers will also be given priority in the purchase of scarce cars, tractors, machines and others resources (*Pravda*, 29 March 1986).

28. M. S. Gorbachev, Political Report to 27th Party Congress.

29. *Pravda*, 29 March 1986. (I am grateful to Bob Miller for drawing my attention to this point.)

Appendix 1: Grain production and net imports (in mln tons)

	Year	Production	Net imports	All grain	Imports from US	Net imports as % of production
Domestic						
	1970	186.8	− 7.2	180	0	0
	1971	181.2	1.4	182	2.9	0.8
	1972	168.2	21.0	189	13.7	12.5
	1973	222.5	5.2	227	7.9	2.3
	1974	195.7	0.4	196	2.3	0.2
	1975	140.1	25.4	165	13.9	18.1
	1976	223.8	7.7	230	7.4	3.4
	1977	195.7	16.8	213	12.5	8.6
	1978	237.4	12.8	250	11.2	5.4
	1979	179.2	30.2	209	15.2	16.9
	1980	189.2	34.3	224	8.0	18.1
	1981	160.0	45.5	206	15.4	28.4
	1982	180	40.3	220	6.2[a]	22.4
	1983	190	33.9	224	14.1[a]	17.8
	1984	170	45	215	18.3[a]	26.5
	1985	178				

Note: a. Wheat and maize only and for accounting year October to September.

Sources: 1970–81, J. C. Roney, 'Grain Embargo', p. 216. 1982–4, *USSR Outlook and Situation Report*, USDA, April 1985, pp. 19, 24. 1985, Food Outlook, FAO, December 1985.

Appendix 2: Per capita food consumption in the USSR

	Meat	Milk	Eggs	Fish	Sugar	Veg. oil	Pot.	Veg.	Fruit	Grain
1960	39.5	240	118	9.9	28	5.3	143	70	22	164
1965	41.0	251	124		34.2		142	72	28	156
1970	47.5	307	159	15.4	38.8	6.8	130	82	35	149
1975	56.7	316	216	16.8	40.9	7.6	120	89	39	141
1980	57.6	314	239	17.6	44.4	8.8	109	97	38	138
1981	57	305	245		43.9		105	98	40	138
1982	57	295	249		44.5		110	101	42	137
1983	58.4	309	253	17.6	44.2	9.6	110	101	44	136
1984	60.4	317	256	17.5	44.3	9.6	110	103	45	135
1985 plan	62	318	253		44.9		115	110	49	137
1985 prel.	60.3	318	260	17.7	45		110	106	46	134
1990 plan	70	330 – 340	260 – 266	19	45.5	13.2	110	126 – 135	66 – 70	135
Norm	70	360	256		35.2		110	165	80	110

Sources: *Nar. Khoz. SSSR*, various years, exp. 1982, p. 447, 1983, p. 441, 1984, p. 459. Preliminary figures for 1985 from M. S. Gorbachev, *Pravda*, 11 September 1985 (speech at Tselinograd). 1990 plan as given at 1982 May Plenum and confirmed at 27th Party Congress. Norm see *Plan. Khoz.*, No. 11, 1982.

Appendix 3: Gross agricultural production

	Average gross agricultural production per year in mlrd r. (1973 prices)			Arable production		Livestock production	
1956–60	73.7						
1961–65	82.8	100	(+2.4%)	100		100	
1966–70	100.4	121	(+3.9%)	122	(+4.1%)	120	(+3.7%)
1971–75	113.7	137	(+2.5%)	133	(+1.7%)	141	(+3.3%)
1976–80	123.9	150	(+1.7%)	146	(+1.9%)	153	(+1.6%)
1981–84	129.6	157	(+1.1%)	150	(+0.5%)	162	(+1.1%)
1981–85[a]	130.7	158	(+1.1%)				
1986–1990 plan			(+2.7%)				
1980	122.0	100		100		100	
1981	120.7	99	(–1.1%)	98	(–1.0%)	103	(+3.0%)
1982	127.4	104	(+5.6%)	104	(+6.1%)	106	(+2.9%)
1983	135.2	111	(+6.1%)	111	(+6.7%)	110	(+3.8%)
1984	135.0	111	(–0.1%)	111	(0%)	110	(0%)
1985[a]	135.0	111?	(0%)				

Note: Figures in brackets refer to annual average growth rates. The reported stability in the last three years is extremely dubious.

Sources: For all except ([a]) *Nar. Khoz. SSSR, 1984*, Moscow 1984, pp. 224, and pp. 228–9. For 1985 ([a]) see TsSU Report on the results of the fulfilment of the state plan of economic and social development in 1985, *Pravda*, 26 January 1986. 1986–90 plan, *Pravda*, 9 March 1986.

Appendix 4: Capital investment in agriculture, agricultural complexes and agro-industrial complexes

	All mln r.	Agric. mln r.	in % to all	Agric. complexes mln r.	in % to all	Agro-industrial complexes mln r.	in % to all
1918–40	61.7	7.0	11.3				
1956–60	192.5	26.7	13.9				
1961–65	279.3	42.3	15.2	54.6	19.5		
1966–70	398.4	66.7	16.7	92.4	23.2		
1971–75	562.8	111.2	19.8	147.9	26.3		
1976–80	717.7	143.2	20.0	193.9	27.0	240	33.4
1981–84	663.7	124.6	18.8	175.5	26.4	213	32.1
1981	156.5	30.6	19.6	41.8	26.7		
1982	161.9	31.0	19.1	43.1	26.6	+ 52.3	+ 32.5
1983	171.0	32.0	18.7	45.6	26.7		
1984	174.3	31.0	17.8	45.0	25.8	55	31.6
1985	179			45.6	25.5	55	30.7
1986–90 plan[a]							27.6?

Note: a. Ryzhkov's statements in the Report on the basic directions of economic and social development of the USSR for 1986–90 and for the period up to 2000 (*Pravda*, 4 March 1986) suggests that a third of capital investment will continue to go to the Agro-industrial Complex. But since he suggests that the level of capital investment in this sector will only grow by 22% while total capital investment will grow by 36% it is clear that a third is a very rough approximation for something like 27.6%, i.e. $55 \times 1.22 = 67.1 / 179 \times 1.36 = 243.4$.

Sources:

All capital investment
1918–40–1976–80, from *Nar. Khoz. SSSR v 1984g.*, Moscow 1985, pp. 378–9, 1981–4 ibid., p. 377.
1985 TsSU, 1985 plan fulfilment report, *Pravda*, 26 January 1986.

All productive capital investment in agriculture
1918–40–1976–80 from *Nar. Khoz. SSSR v 1984g.*, Moscow 1985, pp. 378–9. 1981–1984, ibid., p. 383.

All capital investment in agricultural complexes including construction, food processing industry, etc.
1961–65–1984 from *Nar. Khoz. SSSR v 1984g.*, Moscow 1985, p. 382, table.
1985 TsSU, 1985 plan fulfilment report, *Pravda*, 26 January 1986.

All capital investment in agro-industrial complexes including production of equipment for agricultural complexes, etc.
1976–80–1984 from *Nar. Khoz. SSSR v 1984g.*, Moscow 1985, p. 382 text.
1985 TsSU, 1985 plan fulfilment report, *Pravda*, 26 January 1986.

All percentages calculated by myself. The statistical handbook calculations are rounded in a way which avoids the indication of the decline in percentage of investment going to the different concepts of agriculture.

8

Foreign Policy and Defence

G. Jukes

If Brezhnev was the most popular (or least unpopular) General Secretary among the party faithful, it was because of a greater willingness to let people alone than had been displayed by his predecessors. However welcome this may have been to officials, it was in his later years to result in the institutionalisation of existing inefficiences. The rare intervention, such as the appointment of Ustinov as Defence Minister in 1976, resulted merely in stabilising military expenditure after that year at its existing proportion of Gross National Product rather than the reduction which would probably have been economically wise, as well as more consistent with the spirit of the *détente* which Brezhnev had ardently pursued. References to inefficiency and poor performance were not lacking from Brezhnev's speeches, but action seldom followed. The consequences in diminishing growth rates internally and immobilism in foreign policy were becoming obvious long before Brezhnev's death in November 1982. His immediate successor. Iuurii Andropov, a mere week after Brezhnev's funeral, devoted most of his speech at a Central Committee Plenum[1] to severe criticisms of underfulfilment of the 11th Five Year Plan, and said that what mattered most was to improve management, planning and the economic mechanism. Stating that it was 'mandatory' to create conditions in which good management would be rewarded and bad penalised, he foreshadowed drastic changes. Although the collapse in his health occurred before any real action took place, signs of opposition from entrenched interests had already begun to be observed, and do-nothingism received a further lease of life under the next transitional leader, Konstantin Chernenko. On coming to office in March 1985, Gorbachev therefore faced a situation already recognised as serious by at least some sections within the leadership for several years, and his election must therefore have reflected, as had that of Andropov before him, a majority view within the Politburo of the need for thorough-going changes rather than for mere tinkering with the existing system. Much of his first year in office was taken up in advancing like-minded protégés to leading positions, and the 27th Party Congress of February–March 1986 represented his first opportunity to lay down the new 'general line' to the party as a whole, amplifying what he had already said to the Central Committee Plenum in April 1985,[2] soon after he took up his post.

It has been traditional ever since Lenin's day for the party leader to take special responsibility for foreign relations, including the military balance, and for the Political Report of the Central Committee, which he delivers to the party congress, to open with an extended discussion of the world situation. In adhering to that format, Gorbachev's report to the 27th Congress,[3] followed tradition. There were however, significant differences in the way the subject-matter was treated compared, for example, to the counterpart report delivered by Brezhnev to the 25th Congress in 1976,[4] and that read for him to the 26th Congress in 1981.[5]

In all these speeches the discussion of international relations has followed a 'protocol' order in dealing with relations first with the other socialist countries, secondly with the non-aligned world and international communist movement, and thirdly with the leading capitalist states.

That was where the resemblance ended. In both the previous reports, the first two sections were relatively long, in the Gorbachev report they were short and almost cursory, as shown by the number of paragraphs in each section of the three reports (see Table 8.1).

Perhaps even more striking than the change in relative

Table 8.1: CPSU Congresses, number of paragraphs in each report

Section	25th	26th	27th
Socialist countries	30	29	5
Third World and international communist movements	27	38	2
Capitalist countries	49	54	63

emphasis was the change in the nature of presentation. The reports to the 25th and 26th Congresses consisted mostly of brief reviews of relations on a country-by-country basis, whereas the Gorbachev report was fundamentally issue-oriented. No socialist or Third World country was mentioned by name, and the capitalist world was discussed in terms of three 'main centres of present-day imperialism', the United States, Western Europe and Japan: two of these are, of course, single countries; they are the only individual countries mentioned by name in the entire first section, and only the policies of the United States are discussed.

The report substitutes for the Brezhnevian country catalogue a discussion of issues, beginning with a quotation from Marx on progress in exploitative society ('that hideous pagan idol who would not drink the nectar but from the skulls of the slain. Even the pure light of science seems unable to shine but on the dark background of ignorance. All our invention and progress seem to result in endowing material forces with intellectual life, and in stultifying human life into a material force'). Gorbachev glosses this with the statements that 'ignorance and obscurantism go hand in hand in the capitalist world with outstanding achievements of science and culture. This is the society we are compelled to be neighbours of, and we must look for ways of co-operation and mutual understanding. Such is the command of history'.

Having restated the customary 'peaceful coexistence' formula in new and somewhat warmer terms than usual, the report first discusses the scientific and technological revolution, pointing to increased unemployment, concentration of power in fewer hands, and militarism as problems it creates for capitalist countries, and the way it highlights unresolved socio-economic problems in developing countries. While claiming superiority for socialism in diffusing the benefits of modern science and technology, the report emphasises that it 'not only opens up prospects, but also sets higher demands domestically and in international relations, a change of mentality, the forging of a new psychology, and the acceptance of dynamism as a way and a rule of life'.

The state of the present-day world is described in terms which combine old clichés about capitalism with rather fresher and more lively formulations. The world is seen as 'full of hope, because people have never before been so amply equipped for the further development of civilisation', but also as over-burdened with dangers and contradictions 'which prompts the thought that this is perhaps the most alarming period in history'.

The contradictions described are:

(i) Relations between countries of the two systems. Capitalist hostility is described in familiarly polemical terms, but alleged American military confrontationism is described as a 'flight into the past, which is no answer to the challenges of the future'. It is rather an act of despair, which, however, does not make this posture any less dangerous.

The Soviet Union is said to be 'dealing with a society whose ruling circles refuse to assess the realities of the world in sober terms . . .', 'an indication of the wear and tear suffered by its internal system of immunity, of its social senility . . .'

(ii) The intrinsic contradictions within the capitalist world itself:
    a. Between labour and capital.
    b. Inter-imperialist contradictions.
    c. Transitional monopolies.
    d. Between imperialism and developing countries.

These are interlinked within the familiar concept of a deepening general crisis of capitalism, but are dealt with in a more integrated fashion than in the past. Thus proliferating economic crises and technological advances from the mid-1970s onwards are described as having facilitated a general capitalist 'counteroffensive', in which the workers have been deprived of much of what they had gained in the preceding 15 years, as well as making more acute the rivalries between individual capitalist countries. And the discussion of labour-capital contradictions ends with a warning that any substantial further *internal* right-ward shift in some (unspecified) capitalist countries poses a 'serious danger' to *international* relations.

Inter-imperialist contradictions are summarised as intensi-fying under the impact of science and technology, and in turn intensifying the power of national state-monopoly capitalisms, 'with the role of the bourgeois state becoming increasingly aggressive and egoistic' (in respect to what is not stated speci-fically, but the context would seem to indicate generalised aggressiveness toward other capitalist states as well as the non-capitalist world).

Transnational corporations did not readily lend themselves to the Brezhnevian country-by-country approach, but in the Gorbachev speech are dealt with at greater length than other inter-imperialist contradictions. Points made in respect of them are: that by the 1980s they accounted for more than one-third of capitalist world production, more than half its foreign trade, and nearly 80 per cent of its innovation (patents); that they are mostly American and constitute a second US economy which, with a labour force 50 per cent of that of US manufacturing industry and a gross output nearly 40 per cent that of the United States, was larger than any other capitalist economy except Japan, the largest transnationals' output being comparable to the GNP of a country. They were undermining the sovereignty of both developed and developing countries, exploiting or opposing state-monopoly regulation as they saw fit, and were overall 'active conductors' of US state hegemonism and the imperial ambitions of its ruling circles.

In dealing with relations between the USA, Western Europe and Japan, 'the three main centres of present-day imperialism', attention is drawn to the erosion since the late 1960s of US economic, financial and technological superiority over the other two centres, to American manipulation of exchange and interest rates and to the use of pressure and dictation to co-ordinate the positions of the 'three imperialist centres'.

Western European reservations about 'whether present US policy coincides with Western Europe's notions about its own security' were mentioned, but no easily optimistic conclusions are drawn; listeners were told that 'Washington should not expect unquestioning obedience to US dictation from its allies and competitors', but also that 'the existing complex of economic, politico-military and other common interests of the "three centres of power" can hardly be expected to break up in the prevailing conditions of the present-day world'. The coming decades, it was also noted, could see the rise of 'new capitalist centres of power'. Although this would 'doubtless lead to a further growth of the bulk of contradictions', the overall message conveyed by this section of the report is that capitalism is not in decline but expanding, and that it is this growth which threatens US capacity to manipulate it, not any absolute decline in US power.

While the Third World had been mentioned only briefly in its own right, its relations with imperialism were dealt with at length and, like the preceding section on the capitalist 'centres of power', in sober (from a Soviet point of view, even pessimistic) terms. Most of the section described how 'by political manoeuvring, blandishment and blackmail, military threats and intimidation, and all too often by direct interference in the internal affairs of newly free countries, capitalism has in many ways managed to sustain the earlier relationships of economic dependence'. Discussion of the effects of debt, the increased North-South income disparities, and alleged causal connections between the growth of Third World debt and of US military expenditure over the last decade are not accompanied by any suggestions that the Third World countries themselves, or the Soviet Union, can do much to alter the situation, a striking contrast with the claims made in previous reports for the efficacy of Soviet help. This section of the report concludes rather fatalistically that 'sooner or later, in this area too, capitalism will have to choose between the policy of force and shameless plunder, on the one hand, and the opportunity for co-operation on an equitable basis, on the other. The solutions must be radical — in the interests of the people of the developing states'. But there is no suggestion that capitalism can be *forced* to choose these solutions.

The final contradictions considered are ecological-environmental pollution and depletion of natural resources. It is stated that they can be dealt with only by co-operation on a world scale, and that 'effective international procedures and mechanisms' must be developed to this end.

Capitalism is blamed for causing an 'impoverishment of cultures', 'under the onslaught of unbridled commercialism and the cult of force, the propaganda of racism, of lowly (*sic*) instincts, the ways of the criminal world and the ''lower depths'' of Society'. But beyond saying this impoverishment 'must be, and certainly will be, rejected by mankind' no prescriptions are offered for dealing with this situation.

The peroration of the foreign relations section of the report argues that it is imperative to reduce the time of search for political accords and 'to secure the swiftest possible constructive action', denigrates imperialism's attempts to 'stay in the saddle of history' in terms of costs to the entire world, and reiterates as a historical demand the need for 'constructive and creative interaction between states and peoples on the scale of the entire world'. It further justifies this dialectically by a claim that 'the prevailing dialectics of present-day development consists in a combination of competition and confrontation of the two systems and of a growing tendency to interdependence of the states of the world community', describing this as the way in which 'a contradictory but interdependent and in many ways integrated world is being built'.

At the 25th Party Congress in 1976 Brezhnev, then lauding the apparent triumph of *détente*, agreed presumably for the benefit of party conservative forces, that it meant only abstention from using or threatening force to settle disputes *between* states, but had no relation to the class struggle, i.e. disputes *within* states, such as civil wars, insurgencies or *coup d'état*, and therefore did not adversely affect the world revolutionary process.[6] In other words, he was concerned to indicate the limits to interaction and the continuing distinction between the two systems. The emphasis in the Gorbachev speech, on the other hand, is on interdependence, which implies co-operation *as well as* competition; and while no ideological passes are obviously sold, the 'dialectics' reference may be more significant than it appears. Dialectically, Brezhnev's formulation was fully orthodox: the thesis, capitalism, and antithesis, socialism, giving rise to a synthesis in which socialism, prevailing through class struggle within capitalist countries, would at some undefined future date become communism on a world scale. The Gorbachev formulation, on the other hand, has struggle between capitalism and socialism as thesis, growing interdependence as antithesis, and a world which is 'contradictory' in that both systems survive, but one which is in many respects 'integrated', as the synthesis. This corresponds in dialectical terms to the *realpolitik* view which the report presents of capitalism as still strong and expanding, even if ultimately doomed to disappear, and shifts the time of its putative disappearance even further into the indefinite future.

The final paragraph of the section reinforces the impression of a desire to play down ideological differences by defining the 'main trend of struggle' not merely as to 'fight for peace' as did Brezhnev in 1976, but to create 'worthy, truly human material and spiritual conditions of life for all nations, ensuring that our planet should be habitable, and in cultivating a caring attitude towards its riches'. The very last sentence of all is reminiscent of Malenkov's utterances in his brief period as leader (for example 'the fact that our social and economic system differs from that of some of our neighbours cannot be an obstacle to the furtherance of friendly relations with them'[7]) rather even than Khrushchev's proclamations of peaceful coexistence. It merely invites capitalism 'to compete with us under the conditions of a durable peace', without claiming any predestined outcome for such competition.

The cardinal features of the first section are therefore emphasis on globalism and interdependence. While following past practice placing the blame for international problems on capitalism in general and the United States in particular, it differs from recent predecessors in virtually ignoring the strictly military factor in the Soviet response. This is mentioned once in the preamble, with the flat statement 'we have secured military strategic parity and have therefore substantially restricted imperialism's aggressive plans and capabilities to start a nuclear war', and never referred to again. The stress throughout is on the alleged outdatedness of militaristic responses and the need for (and feasibility of) 'constructive and creative interaction between states and peoples in the scale of the entire world'. It harks back to Khrushchev[8] in its invitation to the capitalist system 'to compete with us', but goes further than him in inviting it to do so 'under the conditions of a durable peace' rather than under the formula of 'peaceful coexistence'.

Also notable for its omission is any reference to continued ideological struggle, such as was emphasised at various times by both Khrushchev and Brezhnev under the rubric 'there can be no peaceful coexistence of ideas'.[9] The concept is present, but under descriptions which emphasise co-operation and interaction despite ideological differences. There are undoubtedly many self-serving elements in the report — the continued attribution of world problems to capitalism, especially the United States is the most obvious — and it would be easy to dismiss its approach as cosmetic. However, the primary target of the report is not the outside world, but the Soviet communist party itself, and the significance of the view which is being presented to it should not be understated.

The second and third sections of the report deal with internal economic and social matters. They do, however, contain the only specific reference to the needs of the Soviet military. It comes rather oddly at the end of the third section (entitled 'Further Democratisations of Society and Promotion of the People's Socialist Self-government'), contains no suggestion that they should have increased resources devoted to them, and includes an implicitly critical statement, not noted in previous reports, that among the objects of 'unflagging attention' by the

Central Committee and Politburo is 'the tightening of military discipline'. Whether this refers to misconduct among troops (e.g. the widely rumoured excess in black marketing and drug addiction on the part of Soviet troops in Afghanistan) or to abuse of power by senior officers (such as a four star general, Nikolay Shchelokov, who was stripped of his rank in 1984 for corruption[10]) is entirely a matter for conjecture. It is nevertheless highly unusual for such a basic shortcoming to be mentioned at all in a speech of this kind.

The linkage between domestic and foreign policy is an axiom of Marxism-Leninism, and the dramatic innovations proposed in the domestic sphere are parallelled in the fourth section of the report,[11] 'Basic Aims and Directions of the Party's Foreign Policy Strategy', which is essentially the leadership's proposed course of action in response to the world situation described in the first section.

This clearly implies a reduction of Soviet as well as US forces. 'Lastly, this means realising that in the present situation there is no alternative to co-operation and interaction between all countries . . . co-operation between capitalism and socialism can proceed only and exclusively in forms of peaceful competition and peaceful contest.'

In the military sphere 'we intend to act in such a way as to give nobody grounds for fears, even imagined ones, about their security. But to an equal extent we and our allies want to be rid of the feeling that we are threatened . . . the Soviet Union lays no claim to more security, but it will not settle for less'.

The section concludes with a detailed list of 'Fundamental Principles' for an 'all-embracing system of international security'. These are striking in their comprehensiveness — undoubtedly calculated for dramatic effect, like Khrushchev's proposal of 1959 for General and Complete Disarmament. They go beyond that proposal by including political, economic and human rights measures as well as military ones. They may be summarised as follows:

1. *Military.* Renunciation by the nuclear powers of nuclear or conventional war against each other or third parties.
   Prevention of an arms race in outer space.
   Cessation of nuclear weapons tests, destruction of all nuclear and chemical weapons, renunciation of development of other means of mass annihilation.

Reduction of conventional forces to 'limits of reasonable adequacy'.

Renunciation of formation of new military alliances and of enlargement of existing ones, pending their disbandment.

Reduction of military budgets.

2. *Political*. Non-interference in 'the right of each people to choose the ways and forms of its development inter-dependency'.

Just political settlement of international crises and regional conflicts.

Confidence-building measures; guarantees against external attack, and of frontiers.

Anti-terrorist measures.

3. *Economic*. Renunciation of discrimination and of economic blockades and sanctions 'if not directly envisaged in the recommendation of the world community'.

Joint quests for just debt settlement.

A new world economic order guaranteeing equal economic security to all countries.

Utilisation of funds saved by reduction of military budgets, primarily for developing nations.

Pooling of efforts in space and in resolving global problems.

4. *Human rights*. Co-operation in disseminating ideas of peace, disarmament and international security.

Greater flow of information and broader contact between peoples.

Extirpation of all forms of racial, national or religious exclusiveness, including genocide, apartheid and advocacy of fascism.

Greater international co-operation to implement personal, political and social rights 'while respecting the law of each country'.

Humane and positive decisions on marriage, family reunion and promotion of contacts between people and between organisations.

Increased co-operation in culture, art, science, education and medicine.

It is suggested that the principles 'could become the point of departure and a sort of guideline for a direct and systematic dialogue' among world leaders, especially of the five nuclear powers. Finally, a 'World Congress on Problems of Economic Security' is proposed.

There is obvious propagandist content in some of the proposals, and many of them have been put forward on a number
of previous occasions, especially those in the military field.
There are also vaguenesses which could prove the source of end-
less negotiating difficulty (for example, how are 'limits of
reasonably adequacy' of conventional forces to be defined? Or
how is co-operation 'while respecting the laws of each country'
to be effected in implementing personal, political and social
rights?). However, as a basis for discussion, the principles
constitute a credible agenda; undoubtedly they have been put
forward for their eye-catching potential and because it is hardly
feasible to refuse to discuss them without exposure to domestic
and international embarrassment. From the presentational point
of view, they are probably intended as a counterpart in the
'dramatic initiative' field to the proposals for rejuvenating the
Soviet economy. At the same time, their globalistic flavour is
consistent with the analysis presented in the first section of the
report, itself a considerable departure from the style of such
reports at previous congresses of the Brezhnev era. And while
the role of the report as a signal to the outside world is apparent,
its main function is as a message to the party faithful and Soviet
society as a whole. It is therefore appropriate to consider what
the essence of that message is.

In brief, the party and society are being told that the Soviet
relationship with the outside world is not solely nor primarily
adversarial; that while there is a danger of war, and the United
States in particular remains hostile, there are also scope and
need for co-operation with the major centres of capitalism, and
purely military solutions to security problems are no longer possible for any country. Parity has been achieved; the Soviet
Union does not need more security than it now has, and would
be safer with fewer armaments than with more, provided its
adversaries also reduce their levels. This implies that the Soviet
military effort is as large as it needs to be, and that there is scope
for reducing it by seeking agreement with potential adversaries.
It is therefore aimed at the military, as are the passages on
'acceleration' of the economy in the second section of the report
which state unequivocally that 'top priority will be given to the
development of light industry and other industries that directly
meet consumer demand' and emphasise the need for 'a more
energetic orientation of science towards the need of the national
economy', while referring to heavy industry mostly in terms of

the need for greater efficiency and innovation rather than increased production. It has been classic in the past for heavy industry to be identified with military needs and light industry with consumerism;[12] and while this is an oversimplification, light industry including electronics, having obvious military applicability, the passage quoted above clearly reiterates the identification with consumer goods; while the reference to the role of scientific research in economic development will not be lost on those elements of the audience, military or industrial managers, who are aware of the demands military-oriented research makes on relatively scarce resources of highly trained scientific manpower. Here, too, comparisons may be drawn with a previous congress, the 20th, of February 1956.

At that congress Khrushchev enunciated three innovative propositions,[13] first, that major war with capitalism was no longer inevitable; second, that economic competition was more likely than war, peaceful coexistence being a long-duration matter not a short-term tactic; and third, that there were increased chances that a number of states would make a peaceful, rather than a violent, transition to socialism.

All three propositions derived from a claimed strategic parity achieved by the introduction of two types of manned bomber (Bear and Bison), credited in the West[14] with the capacity to reach US territory. The doctrine of non-inevitability of war derived from the presumption that the United States had become as vulnerable to a nuclear attack as the Soviet Union had ever been since 1945, and could therefore no longer contemplate initiating it with any hope of impunity. The argument for the elevation of peaceful coexistence to a long-term strategy rather than a time-gaining tactic was a consequence of the previous postulate that capitalism would not cease to compete with socialism, but would have to do so by peaceful means because of the risks the United States' new-found vulnerability entailed for attempts to resort to military solutions. The argument about possibilities for peaceful transition to socialism rested on the proposition that henceforth the United States would be more inhibited in resisting 'progressive' forces such as anti-Western popular insurrection in the Third World.

All three propositions were suspect at the time they were made, because the central pillar upon which they rested was shaky — the two bomber types provided no more than a possibility, since one of them (Bison) lacked the range to attack US territory except on a one-way mission and the other (Bear) was too slow to stand much chance of eluding US air defences.[15] Although the lack of effective parity was subsequently remedied, this did not occur until the late 1960s. The second proposition has proved over-optimistic, because weaknesses in the Soviet economy, largely linked to the economic and technological efforts required to maintain military parity, has rendered the Soviet Union somewhat ineffective in economic competition, not merely with the United States but with several other non-communist industrial powers, except in the limited field of arms exports. Thirdly, the proposition that deterrence achieved in the nuclear field would spread over into non-nuclear situations has proved unfounded.

Apart from shortcomings inherent in the reasoning, the concepts evoked opposition within the Soviet Union and the international communist movement. Military reservations, unstated at the time, became manifest from January 1960[16] onwards; apart from general military tendencies to lavishness, and concern to maintain the widest possible range of options, much of the hostility of senior military officers must have derived from the knowledge that the claimed strategic parity did not yet exist, and that even when it did, it would rest upon missile systems never tried in war.[17] Hard-liners within the party itself would have been dubious about the implied degree of co-operation within capitalism and about the ability to test it in peaceful economic competition. As for the thesis on peaceful transition to socialism, it was very soon to be proved over-optimistic, the inclination in that direction of countries such as Ghana, Guinea, Mali and Indonesia all having changed by the mid-1960s, and the possibility of peaceful Viet Minh takeover in South Vietnam resulting from parliamentary elections, due under the 1954 Geneva agreements to be held in 1956, vanishing when the South Vietnamese government refused to hold them.

The situation now is difficult in several ways. The existence of military parity in 1956 was dubious, and remained so for another ten years. It is now conceded to the extent that the Reagan administration justified large increases by claims that the Soviets were even 'ahead', and accepted to the extent that both in the United States and among its allies there is disquiet at the possibility of its being upset by the Strategic Defence Initiative, thereby leading to a new arms race in a Soviet effort to restore it. Peaceful competition, though acrimonious at times, has endured

201

for 30 more years, proving that peaceful coexistence is feasible as a long-term proposition. But the third possibility, that several countries would adopt Soviet-style socialism by non-violent means, has not been borne out; only one, Chile, did so, and the result was reversed by a military *coup d'état*. And in peaceful economic competition the Soviet Union has not fared especially well except in exports of armaments, largely because stabilisation of defence spending after 1976 at an injudiciously high level has left it ill-equipped to compete with anything else.

The situation faced by Stalin's successors at his death in 1953 was also one of a command economy sorely stretched by heavy defence spending. A succession crisis was resolved in Khrushchev's favour at least partly by his espousal of continued priority for heavy industry, which ensured him military support. But in 1955 a massive program of cuts in forces manpower was initiated, and re-evaluation carried out in 1955–57 brought the Stalin naval program almost to a halt; the program which replaced it, devised under the aegis of the new naval Commander-in-Chief, Admiral Gorshkov, ultimately produced a smaller but considerably more modern navy than Stalin had endorsed, and the key word is 'ultimately', because under the new program ships and submarines were introduced at a much lower rate compared to Stalin's crash program.[18]

The key role played by Marshal Zhukov in the immediate post-Stalin period has tended to be highlighted only in terms of his actions in saving Khrushchev from defeat during the anti-party group crisis of 1957, and his own removal from office in November of that year. What was probably of greater importance, and is certainly of greater prominence in Khrushchev's own memoirs,[19] was that his enormous prestige as the greatest Soviet general and Stalin's Deputy Supreme Commander was clearly influential in the great reshaping of the Armed Forces. He was appointed Minister for Defence in February 1955, and held that office until November 1957. In that period cuts in manpower and the naval program were initiated, the Bear and Bison intercontinental bombers came into service (and decisions not to produce them in large numbers were taken, Bear for its slowness and Bison because it lacked intercontinental range), and restructuring of the Armed Forces towards less manpower and more modern equipment and doctrines began. This is not to claim that Zhukov was responsible for every facet of the rethinking, but had he not endorsed the changes, they could not have taken place without military unrest. After his departure a third stage reduction, announced by Khrushchev in January 1960,[20] was greeted with considerable qualifications even by those who endorsed it, and Khrushchev may have come to regret that Zhukov's authority was no longer there to be involved. The point of similarity between Khrushchev's situation in 1955 and Gorbachev's now is that economic development requires a reduction in the financial and manpower demands of defence; the difference is that there is no senior military leader obviously prepared to trade size for modernity, not one with the authority to call his profession to heel. In short, Gorbachev has no Zhukov; the present Minister of Defence, Marshal Sokolov, derives his status from peacetime competence and preventing the war in Afghanistan from becoming a débâcle. Such a record fits a marshal to represent his profession and articulate its needs; it does not confer the wherewithal for forcing it to accept unpalatable cuts without protest.

The most dynamic of the senior military is not Sokolov, but the former Chief of General Staff, Marshal Ogarkov. The commonly-held view that he was 'disgraced' by removal from that post is probably wrong, because the post to which he was transferred, Commander of the Western TVD (theatre of military operations) is the largest of the fieldforce super-commands created in a reorganisation planned while he was Chief of General Staff and implemented shortly after his removal from that post. While the new post involves a step down in the hierarchy, and the loss of his First Deputy Ministership, it is the largest field command in Soviet peacetime history, and the centrepiece of a new structure for whose creation he was primarily responsible. There are two aspects to the appointment worth noting: one is that as an officer who began his career in the Engineering Troops, never commanded anything larger than a division, and rising meteorically entirely within the General Staff, Ogarkov has been the subject of envious disparagement by passed-over officers for his lack of experience of field command.[21] To allocate the largest of the new commands to himself might well appeal to him, as well as filling the largest gap in his career pattern.

The second aspect of the appointment is that it may well have suited senior political figures to have him out of Moscow.[22] In 1967 some elements of the political leadership had favoured the outstanding 'defence civilian', Dimitri Ustinov, to succeed the ailing Marshal Malinovskii as Defence Minister, and had been sufficiently confident of success to leak the news to the Moscow diplomatic circuit. But Malinovskii's prolonged terminal illness had given the senior military time to rally in support of his replacement by another professional soldier and the eventual appointment of Marshal Grechko had apparent elements of compromise, Brezhnev having served in World War II as chief political officer of an army commanded by Grechko. In 1976 Grechko died very suddenly, giving the senior military no opportunity to rally behind one of their number, and Ustinov was quickly appointed in his place. But by 1984 his own health was failing, and the political leadership may have felt that Ogarkov, who ranked directly below Ustinov in the defence hierarchy, would be the subject of a military lobby to succeed him. Ogarkov has on a number of occasions argued for even higher priority for defence,[23] and has shown himself a polished performer in public. So there may have been a fear of an 'overmighty subject' which led the political leadership at least to encourage his aspirations to be a field commander. Both these aspects of the appointment are largely speculative, but so is the contention that he was disgraced; and either or both is more consistent with the few known facts than the idea of a disgraced senior officer being given the largest peacetime field command ever, in a new armed forces structure devised under his own aegis. The Minister, Marshal Sokolov, is unlikely to hold his post for very long (because of his age — he is 75 years old); his appointment is clearly transitional compared to Malinovskii, Grechko or Ustinov, who were 59, 64 and 68, respectively, when appointed, or Admiral Gorshkov, who became Commander-in-Chief of the Navy at the age of 46, and held the post for 29 years.

Whether a military lobby would arise behind Ogarkov is, however, a moot point. He has not the stature of a Zhukov, and many of the senior military clearly resent his appointment over their heads. It is also worth noting that he had not suggested military manpower should be larger — what he has argued for is a higher level of war preparation of the economy in peacetime, and higher levels of readiness in the existing forces (which may carry an implication that more of the existing divisions should be kept at or near full strength, but does not necessarily do so). The present Minister, Marshal Sokolov, and Chief of General Staff, Marshal Akhromeev, are both clearly transitional appointments, given their ages and past career patterns. How matters will eventuate remains to be seen; but what can be said is that unlike the other bureaucracy concerned with the outside world, the Ministry of Foreign Affairs, and a number of ministries devoted to the economy, the Defence hierarchy is still headed by appointees of pre-Gorbachev days, and whether or not Ogarkov is a Minister manqué, the most dynamic and innovative of the senior military has been noted for utterances which call for greater, not lesser, priority for defence needs, though not necessarily for indefinite retention of present manning levels.

A further factor which makes Gorbachev's situation more difficult than that of Khrushchev is the attitude of the United States. The President from 1953 to 1960, Dwight D. Eisenhower, was one of the very small number of generals in the United States to have been accorded five-star rank. As Supreme Commander both of Allied forces during World War II and of NATO after it, he was one of very few US presidents whose status and experience outranked those of his main military advisers, the Chiefs of Staff. During his presidencies, his unique status was deployed in resisting demands for major increases in military expenditures, a process not unlike that going on at the same time in the Soviet Union, but with Eisenhower capable of being his own Zhukov as well as his own Khrushchev. Enough evidence survives of Eisenhower-Khrushchev exchanges to indicate that each was influenced by the actions of the other,[24] so that post-Korean War reduction in the manpower of the US armed forces was parallelled in the Soviet Union. It is perhaps significant that the increase in US defence spending which followed almost immediately on the accession of President Kennedy saw an abandonment of the third stage of manpower reductions announced by Khrushchev in January 1960, the total failure to materialise of another reduction mentioned by Khrushchev to a Western journalist in 1963,[25] and complete indifference at the time of his overthrow in 1964 by a Defence hierarchy which had thrown its weight behind him in the 'anti-party group' crisis of 1957.

By contrast with the Eisenhower years, Gorbachev faces a US administration which has made enormous increases in defence spending compared to its predecessor, and is actively pursuing, in the Strategic Defence Initiative, a course of action about which there is more agreement that it will cost a great deal than there is about whether it will work. And by contrast with

Eisenhower, who conceded as early as 1958 that the Soviet Union had acquired military parity for all practical purposes, the present administration explicitly proclaimed restoration of military superiority as a goal.

So in pursuit of military expenditure reductions, Gorbachev cannot under present conditions rely on tacit arms control co-operation from the other superpower. The Reagan administration, while not actually declining to participate in arms reduction, has cast doubt on the value of past measures and rejected the notions of parity or sufficiency.

However, there is some possibility that manpower reductions can be pursued within the context of Soviet-European and Soviet-Chinese relations. Military manpower is less central to the superpower balance than levels of nuclear armament, and Soviet armed forces manpower is a function of several factors, of which US forces manpower is the least important. It derives in part from the notion of universal liability to serve which, notwithstanding the flexibility conferred by ability to confer exemption for educational, physical or socio-economic reasons, relates the size of the armed forces more to the number of young men reaching military age than to the actual need for manpower at any given time.

More importantly, it relates to the small size of the Soviet alliance system relative to that of the United States. Apart from the limited French and British nuclear arsenals, the allies of each superpower contribute and equip conventional forces, and the shortfall arising from the Soviet Union's relative lack of allies is made up by Soviet forces. The burden this entails has been increased since the late 1960s by the decision, taken in 1969, after armed clashes along the Ussuri River frontier, to increase forces along the Sino-Soviet border, without reducing those in or adjacent to Central and Eastern Europe. Since the end of the 1960s the Soviet military has become accustomed to the larger force levels this decision entailed, and the rest of the economy has learned to live with them. But their contribution to relative economic stagnation (which includes not merely expenditure on maintaining the forces, but tying up of manpower needed elsewhere, including scientific manpower) must have been considerable. Increases in capacity both of military air transport and of Aeroflot have greatly increased capacity to move troops and at least some of their heavy equipment compared to 1969, when the west-east movement to the Chinese border was conducted mostly by rail; but the classic Soviet military nightmare[26] is of simultaneous conflict on the European and Far Eastern borders, requiring each to be reinforced from the other. It is in this context that proposals for troop reductions in Europe, and negotiations for an improved relationship with China, need to be viewed but Japan and the United States are also involved, because an aspect of the Soviet military nightmare is Chinese manpower equipped by Japanese and American resources. Gorbachev's laudatory references to the Soviet Union's 'great neighbour, Socialist China' and to the 'enormous' potentialities for Sino-Soviet co-operation continue a policy line embarked upon by Brezhnev in his speech at Tashkent in March 1982.[27] One aspect of improved Sino-Soviet relations is likely to be mutual reductions of forces along the border. That may prove easier to negotiate, because no third parties are directly involved, than two other issues declared by China to be obstacles to normal relations, namely the Soviet presence in Afghanistan and the Soviet-backed Vietnamese presence in Kampuchea. That this is likely to be a factor in Soviet thinking is confirmed by a specific statement about China: 'The distinctions in attitude, in particular to a number of international problems, remain. But we also note something else — that in many cases we can work jointly, co-operate on an equal and principal basis, *without prejudice to third countries*' (my emphasis). And it could also have a spin-off effect in the relationship with Japan which, bound to China by cultural and actual or potential trading links and apprehensive of the proximity of large Soviet forces, would be likely to welcome any agreement which reduced the Soviet military presence in its vicinity; especially as a more benign Chinese attitude to Japanese high-technology trade with the Soviet Union would probably result, and any reduced Chinese defence expenditure resulting from *détente* along the Sino-Soviet border could be expected to lead to high non-military purchases from Japan.

Even granted the element of search for propagandist effect, the totality of the report does not indicate the 'mixture as before' in Soviet conduct of international relations. The emphasis on interaction and interdependence goes far beyond mere coexistence as formulated by Brezhnev or even Khrushchev; and the customary criticism directed specifically at the United States is accompanied by less adversarial comment: that the two countries 'coincide on quite a few points', that there is a divergence between the interest and aims of the military-industrial complex and the 'actual national interests of that great country', and that 'one cannot confine oneself to relations with only one, even a very important, country'. The reference to a world in a 'process of swift changes' and consisting of 'many dozens of countries, each having *perfectly legitimate* interests' (my emphasis) is unusual in conceding legitimate interest to exploitative societies (which most of these countries are in Marxist-Leninist terms); and the further statement that all 'without exception' have 'to master the science and art of restraint and circumspection' implies not merely of capitalist but also of socialist-country support for movements which might interfere with 'civil international discourse and co-operation'. Taken in conjunction with the emphasis on European-American differences and the need to 'end the schism of Europe', the indications are of a move towards greater rapprochement with the non-communist world in general, Western Europe in particular and with China. The references to the need for 'international economic security that would in equal measure protect every nation against discrimination, sanctions and other attitudes of imperialist, neocolonialist policy' indicate a further rationale; some of the European-American differences have resulted from American attempts to force on the Europeans more stringent measures of anti-Soviet economic discrimination, especially in regard to export of advanced technology, than the European countries consider reasonable.[28] And the instruments of 'neonationalism' given greatest prominence in the report are the transnational corporations, most of which are American. In brief, the report appears to outline an approach to the West which attempts to avoid excessive dependence on the Soviet-American relationship.

This makes sense both historically and economically. Granted that the 'acceleration' of the Soviet economy requires inputs from the West, the only remaining question is to which countries the Soviet Union should turn. As the report notes Western Europe and Japan managed to outdo their American patrons in some things and are also challenging the United States in such a traditional sphere of US hegemony as that of the latest technology; few of the inputs the Soviet needs are likely to be a US monopoly. Furthermore, Western Europe has a long tradition of trade with the Russian Empire and the Soviet Union, which frequently runs a favourable Soviet balance. In 1977,[29] for example, Soviet exports to 16 Western European countries totalled 7316.4 million roubles, and Soviet imports from them 6671.0 million roubles; in the same year exports to Japan were 853.4 million, imports from it 1527.1 million, exports to US 271.6 million, imports from it 1261.5 million. Five of the top seven non-communist trading partners were in Western or Northern Europe (Federal Germany, 1st, Finland, 3rd, Italy, 4th, France, 5th, Britain, 7th). Their trade was in approximate balance, whereas Japan's 2nd position and America's 6th resulted from the large excess of Soviet imports over exports, the Japanese exports being mostly machinery; the American, cereals. In 1977 Western Europe accounted for 22 per cent of Soviet imports. There are therefore complementarities in Soviet-West European trade, with Soviet forestry products, minerals, oil and natural gas being exchanged for European manufactures. These complementarities exist in trade with Japan also, but to a lesser extent, and do not exist at all in Soviet-American trade. The direction which the report implies is therefore that of building on an already established pattern.

While Western European countries (and Japan, to a lesser but significant extent) are likely to welcome increased trading opportunities, they would be unlikely to do so without wishing to extract some political price, and it is here that strategic considerations may prove relevant. The likelihood of general nuclear war is regarded as low, that of nuclear war limited to Europe as also low but somewhat higher, but the most comprehensive threat is that of conventional invasion, in which nuclear weapons fail to deter and are not used for fear of the consequences. There is therefore considerable scope for 'wooing' Western Europe with proposals for conventional force reductions, an issue of less direct concern to the United States than the central nuclear balance. NATO planning envisages a considerable post-outbreak American reinforcement, but nevertheless the bulk of the NATO conventional force would be supplied by the European members, and while the United States looks carefully at the nuclear, missile, air and naval balances, there has never been any question of the peacetime US Army attempting to match the size of the Soviet ground forces. It may therefore be significant that apart from a brief mention in the 'General Principles' for disarmament, the only specific reference to reduction of conventional as well as nuclear weapons is in connection with Europe.

There are also good internal reasons for reduction in Soviet conventional forces, especially the army. While they contribute little to the image of the Soviet Union as an advanced power militarily the equal of the United States, they consume manpower and resources on a large scale. There are some similarities here with the past, but also some differences, concerning the likely military reaction to manpower cuts. The military is highly respected in Soviet society, but its great wartime figures are now dead, and its ability to compete for scarce resources may be damaged by relative loss of stature, as well as by its inability to bring the war in Afghanistan to a quick and triumphant conclusion. (Although Gorbachev blamed 'counter-revolution and imperialism' for turning Afghanistan into 'a bleeding wound',[30] he indicated readiness to withdraw 'as soon as a political settlement is reached', making no reference to military history or even uttering routine words of praise for Soviet military performance there.)

The playing down of support for Third World revolutionary movements and for ideological struggle in general, when compared to the emphasis on interaction and interdependence, points to increased trade, mostly with countries other than the United States. There is a limit to the extent of Soviet ability to pay for high technology imports with raw materials, oil and gas; there must therefore be an expectation of increased Soviet medium and high technology imports, probably from Third World countries and Eastern Europe for the most part. (See Chapter 9 below.)

The references to (unspecified) points at which the Soviet Union and United States 'coincide' indicate an intention to alleviate conflict with it if possible; but the confining of attacks on 'imperialism' essentially to denunciation of the United States indicates an intention to downgrade the US-Soviet relationship overall, while building relations with Western Europe, China and to some extent Japan. This is not likely to reflect mere pique with the Reagan administration, which has little time left to it; it must therefore be based on a longer-term, rather pessimistic view of the relationship under Reagan's successors. Growth in American manifestations of nationalism has undoubtedly caused strains with US allies, especially in Europe, and the report duly notes these, though it cautions against drawing excessively hopeful conclusions from them. There is a marked shift away from the politics pursued by Khrushchev and Brezhnev of attempting to enlist the United States' interest in joint 'world management', of the sort that prompted the Chinese to accuse the Soviet Union of 'collusion' with the United States'[31] and the French to develop their own nuclear weapons. This could result in part from the generational change of leadership; the older generation inclined towards fear of Germany and Japanese revenge-seeking leading to cataclysmic war into which the United States could be dragged against its will, while the newer leaders, having risen to the top in an era which has seen Germany and Japan became the Soviet Union's two largest non-communist trading partners (a parallel may exist in the way Australia's attitude to Japan has developed), and having seen agreements reached with one US president nullified or repudiated by his successors, simply regard the United States as too unpredictable for a close relationship, as well as of declining importance within the capitalist world in every sense except the military. But it is likely also to reflect perceptions of a changing world in other respects: the switch from country-oriented to issue-oriented analysis in the first section of the report, the acknowledgment of the vigour of capitalism and the need not merely to coexist but to co-operate and interact, which clearly reflects much more than a mere downgrading of some countries and upgrading of others. It is a changed view of the total system and of the way the Soviet Union must 'fit' within the world. How this view will translate into action remains to be seen, but it would be unwise to under-rate its significance, bearing in mind that its primary audience was not Western Kremlinologists, but the Soviet party and Soviet society as a whole.

The new party statute (*Ustav*) adopted by the congress incor-porates two changes in wording which suggest an intention to control party work in the Armed Forces more closely. The first describes the Central Committee as controlling such work through 'the political organs' rather than 'through the Chief Political Directorate', implying that where necessary the Direc-torate can be bypassed and instructions issued directly to the political apparatus in Military Districts, Fleets, or lower for-mations. This change was described in the leading article of *Armed Forces Communist* No. 12 of 1986 as 'a material altera-tion' which 'raised the authority of political organs of all levels'.

The second alteration increases from three to five the years of previous party membership required of appointees to leadership of the Political Department of an Army or a Naval squadron, and indicates a perceived need for more evidence than hitherto of capacity and of commitment to party objectives, rather than mere party membership as a career-serving formality.

The 12th issue of *Armed Forces Communist* (cleared for press on 4 June), in addition to the leading article already mentioned, carried a higher than usual number of articles attacking short-comings in performance by officers. They included an article by the Chief Inspector, Army General and Deputy Defence Minister V. Govorov, in which officers criticised and named included a major-general and several colonels. Denigration of the self-image of the Armed Forces is not to be lightly undertaken in a society where the impact of World War II is still heavily felt and frequently celebrated as a major achievement of the Soviet order. But an attack upon inefficiency and waste is consistent with the approach being taken to the economy as a whole, and also consistent with an attempt to reduce the burden which defence expenditure, at the levels which had become institutionalised under Brezhnev, represented for that economy.

NOTES

1. Speech at Plenary Meeting of the CPSU Central Committee, 22 November 1982. Y. V. Andropov, *Speeches and Writings* (Oxford: Pergamon Press, 1983), pp. 7–19.

2. 'Report on the convening and tasks of the 27th Party Congress', in *Pravda*, 24 April 1985.

3. Mikhail Gorbachev, *Political Report of the CPSU Central Committee to the 27th Congress of the Communist Party of the Soviet Union, 25 February 1986* (Moscow: Novosti Press Agency Publishing House, 1986, in English). Russian text, *Pravda*, 26 February 1986, pp. 2–10.

4. In *Documents and Resolutions, XXVth Congress of the CPSU* (Moscow: Novosti, 1976), pp. 5–107.

5. Report of the CPSU Central Committee and tasks of the Party in the field of foreign and internal policy, 23 February 1981. *Pravda*, 24 February 1981.

6. *Documents and Resolutions* (see note 4), p. 39.

7. Malenkov, Speech to USSR Supreme Soviet, 8 August 1953. *Pravda*, 9 August 1953.

8. E.g., Khrushchev, 'A practical solution must be found for catching up with and outstripping the most developed capitalist countries in per capita output', Political Report to 21st Party Congress of the CPSU, *Pravda*, 28 January 1959.

9. E.g., World Communist Declaration, *Pravda*, 6 December 1960, and Brezhnev, *Pravda*, 27 July 1973.

10. *Krasnaia zvezda*, 10 November 1984; *Times*, London, 17 December 1984.

11. Gorbachev, *Political Report* (see note 3), pp. 78–94.

12. E.g., Khrushchev, *Pravda*, 2 October 1964, and *Khrushchev Remembers: The Last Testament* (London: André Deutsch, 1974), pp. 142–7, and *Khrushchev Remembers: Vol. I* (Harmondsworth: Penguin, 1977), pp. 547–8.

13. Report of the Central Committee to the 20th Congress of the CPSU, 14 February 1956. *Pravda*, 15 February 1956.

14. E.g., *The Military Balance 1964–65* (London Institute for Strategic Studies, 1964), p. 3.

15. *Khrushchev Remembers: The Last Testament*, pp. 39–40.

16. E.g., speech by Defence Minister, Marshal of the Soviet Union R. Ia. Malinovskii, *Pravda*, 16 January 1960; article by Marshal Konev, *Sovetskaia Rossiia*, 23 February 1960, and Soviet Ministry of Defence pamphlet *Vigilantly Stand Guard in Defence of Peace* (Moscow: Voenizdat, 1962).

17. P. Rotmistrov, *Krasnaia zvezda*, 25 April 1964.

18. Discussed in M. MccGwire, 'The Turning Point in Soviet Naval Policy', Ch. 16 of M. MccGwire (ed.), *Soviet Naval Developments: Capability and Context* (New York: Praeger, 1973).

19. *Khrushchev Remembers: The Last Testament*, pp. 13–14.

20. *Pravda*, 15 January 1960.

21. Ogarkov's highest field command was a division, in Germany 1959–61. *Voennyi Entsiklopedicheskii Slovar'* (Moscow: Voenizdat, 1983), p. 507.

22. Discussed, e.g., by R. A. Wolff in 'Soviet Command Changes and Policy Implications: A new chapter in the History of the Soviet High Command', *Defence Studies* (University of Edinburgh, May 1985), pp. 10–11.

23. In *Kommunist*, October 1981, p. 82.

24. *Khrushchev Remembers: Volume I*, pp. 548–9.

25. *Izvestiia*, 15 December 1963.

26. Ogarkov (see note 23).

27. Brezhnev, speech in Tashkent on 24 March 1982, *Pravda*, 25 March 1982.

28. E.g. US sanctions on the export of gas and oil technology to the USSR, imposed on 19 December 1981, were the subject of protest by the European Commission and the governments in France, Italy, West Germany and UK. They related to exports for the USSR's Urengoi natural gas pipeline of components manufactured in Europe which included US-licensed technology. The governments insisted on deliveries proceeding, and protested that US action was 'an impermissible attempt to enforce US law in foreign countries'. The sanctions were lifted in November 1982. *Keesing's Contemporary Archives*, pp. 31458–9 and 31965–7.

29. *Vneshniaia Torgovlia SSSR v 1977g.* (Moscow: Statistika, 1978), Table IV, pp. 9–14, and V, p. 15.

30. Gorbachev, *Political Report* (see note 3), p. 86.

31. E.g., 'US Imperialism's counter-revolutionary global strategy has active support of the Soviet leaders', editorial, *Renmin Ribao* (Peoples Daily), 2 February 1966.

9

The Soviet Union and
Eastern Europe:
Genuine Integration at Last?

Robert F. Miller

INTRODUCTION

The Soviet–East European relationship has been the focus of considerable activity since Gorbachev's accession to power as General Secretary. There was not much evidence of its importance at the 27th Congress itself, to be sure. Nevertheless, much of the business of the congress was more or less directly linked to developments in the evolving relationship between Moscow and the East European capitals. In addressing the need for accelerated economic development to raise the prestige of socialism in the world, Gorbachev made it clear that he was not referring to the Soviet Union alone. The East European countries would be expected to bear a share of the burden.

In the area of military relations little seems to have changed.[1] Despite rumours of Romanian opposition to the long-term extension of the Warsaw Pact, Ceausescu ultimately went along with his bloc colleagues and agreed to precisely that when confronted by determined Soviet insistence. Gorbachev's subsequent avalanche of disarmament proposals, aimed as they ostensibly were to reduce defence expenditures, had undoubtedly struck a responsive chord among his Warsaw Treaty Organisation (WTO) partners. All of the East European economies, like their Soviet counterpart, would certainly benefit from a reduction in such spending. As a recent study for the US Congress shows, the East European countries do not spend as great a share of GNP on defence as the Soviets do (and it is very difficult to calculate just how much any of them do spend). Nevertheless, the amount is still quite substantial — on the order

214

of 3 per cent of GNP per annum by official calculation that certainly understates the actual level of expenditures. Moreover, with the collapse of *détente* in the early 1980s, the rate of growth of military spending climbed steeply (by almost twice the rate of growth of GNP for the region as a whole).[2]

The more directly political aspects of the Soviet–East European relationship are perhaps intrinsically more interesting and complex. It is clear that some bloc leaders are more enthusiastic than others over the advent of the new team in the Kremlin. All of them must feel a certain amount of ambivalence toward Gorbachev and his policies. On the one hand, as responsible communist politicians, they must be relieved to have a healthy, dynamic and authoritative figure once again at the head of the bloc, confronting the assertive leader of the rival superpower camp. The obvious incapacity of the three previous Soviet leaders was undoubtedly an embarrassment. On the other hand, the very weakness and lack of direction in Moscow gave the local satraps a good deal of additional leeway in managing their own societies. As long as they made the expected genuflections to Soviet leadership in international affairs and kept their reformist strivings within accepted structural and ideological bounds, they could anticipate relative toleration of their domestic activities. That Ceausescu, well known as a maverick among East European leaders, was able to get by with the barest minimum of compliance was largely due to the Soviet leaders' unwillingness to exert the effort necessary to bring him into line.

Under Gorbachev the nuances of the Soviet–East European political relationship appear to be subtly changing, and not entirely to the liking of some of the bloc leaders. On the whole, most of them seem to be accepting the logic of the need for a change as presented by Gorbachev. Their domestic problems are generally similar. But their acceptance is also partly due to a shared perspective on the nature of the international climate in the Reagan era, although, again, some evidently take the deterioration in East–West relations more seriously than others, just as some are more sanguine than others over the possibilities of playing Western Europe off against the United States. The Polish and Czechoslovakian leaders, having most recently experienced the baleful consequences of a radical opening up to the West, now seem most reluctant to get involved in the Soviet version of the West's 'differentiation' game, that is, trying to split the respective opposing alliance by playing individual countries off against the others.

In one way or another all of these considerations are related to the new economic strategy being promoted by Gorbachev. His emphasis on acceleration of economic growth through reliance on scientific and technological innovation as the key to closing the economic gap between East and West and, hence, to refurbishing the image of 'real socialism' is directed at Eastern Europe as well as at the domestic Soviet economy. Furthermore, Gorbachev evidently regards the participation of the East Europeans in the process of technology-based economic expansion as a major force for political integration as well. Khrushchev had a similar vision but lacked the economic and technical sophistication — and the time — to bring it about.[3]

The watchword of the Gorbachev approach to relations with Eastern Europe, as it was under Khrushchev, and to a lesser extent under Brezhnev, too, is integration. The question is to what extent Gorbachev 'really means business' this time. It is no secret, not even in Eastern Europe itself, that past efforts at co-ordinated planning and a viable 'international socialist division of labour' have been largely stillborn. For a number of reasons connected with the basic model of development foisted upon the satellite economies by Stalin and tacitly maintained under his successors, the individual economies have been structurally incapable of genuine co-ordination, let alone integration. For one thing, following the Soviet model, the various currencies of the bloc countries are mutually non-convertible. For another, the underlying autarchic structure of the economies and the basically political determination of internal prices associated with it, have meant that the costs of production of individual items destined for intra-bloc exchange bear at best a very tenuous relationship to real exchange values. The implications of this price indeterminacy are several. In recent decades the Soviets have become mainly suppliers of raw materials and energy to the East European economies. In return, the latter have become suppliers of manufactured consumer and producer goods, as well as agricultural products. While the value of Soviet deliveries is generally known, since it is basically linked to world market prices (e.g. the five-year rolling average for petroleum products), the same thing cannot be said of most of the manufactured goods shipped to the USSR by the East European partners. That has been especially true in respect to quality standards. Much of what the East Europeans ship to the Soviet

Union simply could not be sold elsewhere. To what extent the Soviet economy has been subsidising the East Europeans or vice versa is a moot question.

In addition to these problems of intransitivity of prices and costs, the initial impulse toward autarchy in each country during the period of 'High Stalinism' and its central role in the development and maintenance of the *nomenklatura* system of party dominance have continued to operate with remarkably little change up to the present time. Taut planning and careful control over access to scarce consumer goods have, as in the Soviet Union, remained an important factor in the ability of the party leadership to maintain the loyalty of the lower ranks of the party apparatus and, hence, their command over the system as a whole. What is left over and is of sufficiently high quality has tended to be preferentially directed toward the world capitalist market as a source of hard currencies. Other than in military production, where they have never been able to resist Soviet pressures to contribute to the 'common defence', the East Europeans have up to now been remarkably successful in parrying Soviet requests for economic integration, perhaps because the logic of the political stability argument — that total control over resources is the key to maintenance of the solidarity of the various *apparats* — has been so persuasive to their Soviet masters.[4]

Gorbachev intends to change this pattern and is now demanding full value for whatever the Soviets deliver to their bloc partners. He is seeking to ensure that the mutual economic dependence that has developed so fitfully over the years becomes structurally so organised that the individual East European economic policy-makers can no longer shift between East and West in plotting their short-term developmental priorities. The success or failure of this exercise in structural integration will have a major impact on the future character of political as well as economic relations between the Soviet Union and Eastern Europe.

SOME COMMON PROBLEMS

By the standards of the developed capitalist countries at least some of the countries of Eastern Europe have not been doing too badly in recent years on certain general measures of economic performance (see Tables 9.1 and 9.2). The marked decline in growth rates noted for the Soviet Union in Chapter 6 and visible in Table 9.1 was clearly parallelled in the East European economies. From the data in Table 9.2 it would appear that the reputation for success enjoyed in the West by Hungary, the GDR and to some extent Bulgaria and Czechoslovakia is not really warranted. Much of that reputation is based on the superficial impression of relatively high living standards by

Table 9.1: Growth of produced national income in Eastern Europe and the USSR, 1971–83 (average annual growth in real terms, %)

	1971–75	1976–80	1981	1982	1983
Eastern Europe	7.6	3.6	− 1.3	0.1	3.3
USSR	5.6	4.2	3.3	4.2	3.6

Source: Jan Vanous, 'Macroeconomic Adjustment in Eastern Europe in 1981–1983: Response to Western Credit Squeeze and Deteriorating Terms of Trade With the Soviet Union', in Joint Economic Committee, US Congress, *East European Economies: Slow Growth in the 1980s* (Washington, DC, 28 October 1985), p. 38.

Table 9.2: Annual rates of growth of GNP in Eastern Europe, 1970–84 (in constant prices, %)

Country	1970–75	1975–80	1980	1981	1982	1983	1984
Bulgaria	4.5	1.2	− 2.8	3.0	3.1	− 1.7	3.1
Czechoslovakia	3.4	2.2	1.7	− 0.5	1.4	1.0	2.2
GDR	3.5	2.4	2.4	2.0	0.0	1.6	3.0
Hungary	3.4	2.3	0.5	− 0.1	1.5	− 1.2	1.3
Poland	6.6	0.9	− 3.2	− 5.3	− 0.6	4.6	3.4
Romania	6.2	3.9	− 1.7	0.5	2.3	0.3	4.3

Source: John P. Hardt and Richard Kaufman, 'Policy Highlights: A Regional Economic Assessment of Eastern Europe', in Joint Economic Committee, 28 October 1985, p. VIII.

casual Western tourists and uncritical journalists. An inspection of the shares of national income going to consumption and accumulation during the early eighties shows that the maintenance of living standards was achieved by a sharp drop in the accumulation share — in most countries it declined from the customary level of about 25 per cent of national income to around 20 per cent, and even less than that in Czechoslovakia and the GDR. Romania was forced to cut its accumulation from its usual insane rate of almost 35 per cent to 27.8 per cent from

from 1980 to 1982.[5] This cutback in investment could not be maintained for long without serious consequences for economic growth. Moreover, the evidence throughout the bloc indicates that the rate of return on investment was also declining. Larger quantities of increasingly scarce and costly supplies of labour, energy and raw materials were required to sustain the modest rates of growth achieved in the region. Even the reputedly successful economies, such as the Hungarian and East German, were failing to match the standards of quality or productivity of the OECD economies with which they should be compared. The improvement recorded in 1983 and 1984 reflected a reversal of the trend toward decreasing allocations to investment, but given the increasing capital/output ratios, this renewed growth was being purchased at a very high cost, and consumption was bound to suffer.

Although there are some relatively bright spots in the overall picture, especially the performance of the GDR, the general tendencies are similar. That suggests basic structural causes for the pattern of decline. In view of the fact that these countries perforce still generally follow the Stalinist model of economic organisation and administration, it is not surprising that they have been experiencing the same generic problems that are responsible for the slowdown in the Soviet economy. The relatively smaller size and lesser complexity of their economies have at times permitted the East Europeans to avoid some of the more serious obstacles to innovation and adaptation commonly noted in the Soviet economy.[6] On the other hand, the relatively poor resource endowments of these countries make them that much more susceptible to the systemic weaknesses of extensive development under the prevailing Soviet model. Accordingly, Gorbachev's diagnoses and prescriptions, to the extent that they are appropriate for the Soviet economy, are relevant to the East European situation as well. In any case, their heavy dependence on the USSR for energy and raw materials gives Moscow a good deal of leverage in influencing their production plans and priorities.

In some respects their internal socio-political situation is indeed substantially more precarious than that in the USSR. Despite the fact that perhaps a majority of the population in most of these countries considers the regimes as an alien implant, the latter had managed to acquire a modicum of legitimacy by promising, and usually delivering, a steady improvement in living standards. That is why they found it necessary, in the early eighties, to take the uncharacteristic step of increasing the share of national income going to consumption at the expense of accumulation. The experience of Poland during the Solidarity period undoubtedly heightened anxieties throughout the bloc, including the Soviet Union, that a violation of the implicit bargain with the working class — political quiesence in return for a rising standard of living — could have dire political consequences. But the general economic slowdown made it increasingly difficult to maintain the bargain. The need for reform was evident.

The question was what kind of reform and how far it could be allowed to go before disrupting the existing structure of political, social and economic relations on which communist party rule rested. Most of the leaders were long-term veterans of the Leninist power-maintenance game. Indeed, only Poland's Wojciech Jaruzelski could be considered a 'new boy' in the party-political arena, but his was surely a special case. The others mainly represented the same category of unimaginative, self-satisfied bureaucrats with whom Gorbachev was forced to contend in his struggle to reform the Soviet economic system, with the same kind of 'psychological barriers' to change. To be sure, Honecker in East Germany and Kadar in Hungary were somewhat different. They had managed, in different ways, to make their respective economies perform reasonably well. Mere loyalty to the Soviet Union would no longer be sufficient, as Todor Zhikov, the super-loyalist and longest serving satrap of Moscow, painfully learned in July 1985, when Soviet Ambassador Leonid Grekov publicly complained of the poor quality of Bulgarian goods shipped to the USSR and of the slack performance of the Bulgarian economy in general.[7] Ceausescu's blustery independence was equally coolly received by the leadership, especially since the Romanian leader was now more dependent than before on Soviet trade and economic assistance. By the time of the 27th Congress, it was clear that his room for manoeuvre in foreign as well as domestic policy had been substantially reduced.[8] On the eve of the congress there was speculation that the Soviet leaders would force through some important changes in the leadership lineup of certain East European regimes.[9] As things turned out, no such changes took place. Nevertheless, the respective East European leaders were forced to go to considerable lengths to accommodate Gorbachev's demands for change in the criteria of bloc economic relations.

GORBACHEV'S PROPOSED SOLUTIONS

A major plank in Gorbachev's foreign policy is clearly to confront the West with a solid phalanx of COMECON countries, firmly and purposefully directed from Moscow. No longer would the West be given the opportunity to play one East European country off against the others by the strategy of 'differentiation', which has underpinned the Western policy of *détente* and the FRG's *Ostpolitik* since the early 1970s. Underlying Gorbachev's policy is the implicit ideologically-based conviction that economic integration is the key to the co-ordinated political action that this strategy requires. It represents a tacit repudiation of the encouragement given by Brezhnev to the individual bloc countries to make their own commercial and investment deals with the West to accelerate economic development. As the saying goes, it is no accident that the Romanians, who were among the most aggressive in defending their freedom to deal with the West, have been the most vociferous critics of the new insistence on economic integration and interdependence. Recent evidence of Ceausescu's capitulation to Moscow's demands is an indication of the vigour with which Gorbachev is pursuing the new line.[10]

Actually, the origins of the current integrative impulse can be traced to the COMECON summit meeting in Moscow in June 1984 under Chernenko (Gorbachev was not even a member of the Soviet delegation). Some of the provisions of the December 1985 Complex Program were foreshadowed in the Declaration of that meeting, for example, the emphasis on production co-operation and the creation of joint transnational firms. The Declaration also contained a call for the formulation of a more concrete program of co-ordinated action by the time of the drafting of the next set of five-year plans (that is, by the end of 1985). But the emphasis was still on voluntary participation and vague statements of good intentions.[11]

Gorbachev indicated his special interest in the process in his keynote speech at the April (1985) Plenum of the CPSU Central Committee a month after taking over the party leadership. Continual reference to this Plenum at the 27th Party Congress and ever since suggests a decision to portray it as the beginning of the Gorbachev era and a 'turning point' in Soviet history. In his speech Gorbachev referred to the 1984 COMECON summit and the need to fulfil its decisions in the light of the complicated international situation:

> It has become an ever more important task to improve and enrich co-operation in all ways, to develop all-round links with the fraternal countries of socialism, to secure their close mutual actions in political, economic, ideological, defence and other areas, to care for the organic combination of the national and international interests of all the participants of the great commonwealth.[12]

Most of these phrases sounded conventional enough, but in the ensuing months the drive for a binding program of integration gained momentum. It reached a crescendo on 18 December 1985 with the signing of the 'Complex Program of Scientific and Technical Progress of the Member Countries of the Council of Mutual Economic Assistance up to the Year 2000'.[13] Gorbachev's speech at the 41st (Extraordinary) Session of COMECON, at which the Complex Program was adopted, has not been published, but reports indicate that it was extremely forceful and demanded an end to foot-dragging on integration by individual East European leaders.[14] Some idea of the atmosphere of the December session can be guessed from the fact that Ceausescu is reported to have complained at a Romanian Communist Party Political Executive Committee meeting nine days later that the Complex Program violated the spirit of the Declaration of the 1984 COMECON summit. Significantly, Romania was the last to sign a bilateral agreement on scientific and technical co-operation with the Soviet Union in connection with the Complex Program.[15]

The integrative impulse behind the Complex Program can also be seen in the virtual identity of its developmental priorities with those set forth for the Soviet economy in the 12th Five-Year Plan and beyond. The five sectors singled out for accelerated development on a co-operative basis throughout the bloc are the 'electronisation' of the economy, comprehensive automation of production processes, the development of nuclear power (along with other energy sources), the creation of new materials, and biotechnology. Whether or not these priorities accord with the real needs of the respective economies as perceived by experts or even by their party leaders, the latter are committed to implementing them and thus contributing to the development of the Soviet, as well as of the overall bloc economy. Furthermore, by endorsing the principle of 'gradual equalisation of the level of . . . economic development', the Complex Program commits them to assisting the industrialisation of the Third World economies of Mongolia, Cuba and Vietnam.[16]

Some time before the 27th Party Congress a new note began to be introduced in the promotion of socialist economic integration, an idea that was implicit in the formulations of the Complex Program, if not openly stated. In the words of a Soviet specialist on COMECON, the objective of integration was 'the strengthening of the technical and economic invulnerability (*neuiazvimost'*) [of the COMECON states] to hostile actions by the imperialists'.[17] This defensive rationale for integration has apparently evoked a positive response among ruling circles throughout the bloc. It evidently serves the interests, not only of the Soviet Union, but also of the party elites in most of the East European countries, who have never been entirely comfortable with the effects of Western economic penetration.

Up to now the main form of production co-operation between the Soviet economy and the individual East European economies have been government-to-government linkages. Agreements on the delivery of commodities and the transfer of technology are arranged by the central agencies of the respective countries and are included in the plans of individual enterprises by the national planning organs. There have also been a number of joint production endeavours involving several countries under the aegis of specialised functional agencies of COMECON, such as Intermetal and Interatom. Part of the financing of these joint ventures comes directly from the participating countries and part through COMECON's International Investment Bank. There is also a commercial credit bank, the International Bank for Economic Co-operation, which, like the IIB, operates on the basis of so-called 'transferable roubles'.[18]

Now, under the Complex Program, the emphasis is on direct, contractual agreements between enterprises, institutes or intermediate-level bodies in two or more countries. A principal vehicle for such agreements are the 'Inter-Branch Scientific and Technological Complexes' (MNTKs), mentioned in Chapter 5 as a prominent feature in the new scheme for the management of science and technology in the USSR announced at the 27th Party

Congress. It will be recalled that the centrepiece of the MNTKs is the so-called 'head organisation' (*golovnaia organizatsiia*), which is usually a scientific research institute of the USSR Academy of Sciences. Currently the MNTKs are being given the power to conclude co-operation contracts with East European scientific and production organisations.[19] At the 41st Session of COMECON in December 1985 Soviet Premier N. I. Ryzhkov also mentioned other, smaller-scale forms of structural integration between Soviet and East European institutes and enterprises, including so-called 'science and production associations', where the transnational partners are working under a unified plan. A. K. Antonov, a Deputy Chairman of the USSR Council of Ministers and the permanent representative of the USSR in COMECON, noted in mid-February 1986 the existence of 93 major developmental projects in which Soviet and East European scientific, technological and production organisations were already jointly engaged.[20] It is important to point out that in all 93 cases a Soviet R&D institution was operating as the 'head organisation'.

This type of grass-roots integration is evidently now favoured as a more certain way to bring about positive Soviet control over the bloc economy than the traditional 'top-down' methods practised through COMECON and its various centralised agencies. Indeed, in his address to the 11th Congress of the East German Socialist Unity Party (SED), Gorbachev, in supporting the idea of direct, lower-level production and R&D contracts, stated his opinion that the central organs of COMECON should be removed from the business of operational involvement and limited to broad questions of technological co-operation and development strategy.[21]

As was noted in the Introduction, remarkably little was said about Eastern Europe by Gorbachev or the other Soviet speakers at the 27th Party Congress. Perhaps this relative silence was due to the absence of any major crisis in intra-bloc relations, unlike the concern over Solidarity in Poland during the last Soviet party congress in 1981. In any event, the main issues of the management of economic relations had already been discussed in connection with the Complex Program the previous December. The new Soviet leaders had shown their intention to take command of the military and political aspects of the relationship before the congress as well. Nevertheless, the congress was important for signs that the Gorbachev team was fully in command at home. Once assured of this, the East European delegation leaders quickly fell into line to endorse the new policies. As usual, the only thing of particular interest in their speeches were the nuances of difference in their handling of important issues of the relationship and in their attitudes to current Soviet policies. A useful point of discrimination is the use of the word 'integration' and its associated implications. Erich Honecker avoided using the word altogether. He rather smugly recounted the recent economic achievements of the GDR and pledged continued loyalty to the USSR and the camp in maintaining a united front for peace and against imperialism. The closest he would come to 'integration' was to endorse the 'close unification of our spiritual and material potentials'.[22] Not surprisingly, Nicolae Ceausescu made no mention of the term either. He chose to interpret the Complex Program as a vehicle for ensuring the 'socio-economic development of each country', adding, 'it is necessary to do everything to make the co-operation of the member countries of COMECON a model of new relations of complete equality and mutual benefit'. Romania, he added defiantly, would continue to trade with all countries, East or West.[23] The faithful Gustav Husak pledged that his country, Czechoslovakia, would link the further development of socialism at home with intensified co-operation with the USSR and the other fraternal countries. 'We completely support the process of acceleration of international socialist integration and the realisation of the Complex Program . . .'[24] Janos Kadar, by contrast, managed to avoid any mention of integration or the Complex Program, although he was full of praise for Gorbachev's domestic and foreign policy initiatives.[25] Todor Zhivkov, despite neglecting to use the word integration, made it clear that that was the objective of his country's economic policy.

> In recent times the course of our party to draw the People's Republic of Bulgaria ever closer to the fraternal Soviet land is going over to a new stage — the creation of joint science-production associations, ever closer co-operation in the realm of science, education and in other spheres. This is for us today socialist internationalism in action.[26]

(Zhivkov evidently succeeded in erasing the stigma of his country's poor economic performance in dealing with the Soviet Union by this demonstration of vigorous support for

Gorbachev's policies, because he was given the honour of replying as spokesman for the foreign delegates to a speech by Gorbachev at a reception in the closing moments of the congress on March 6th.[27])

Wojciech Jaruzelski's address proved to be particularly fulsome, not only in its praise of Soviet domestic and foreign initiatives, but also in the enthusiasm of his commitment to integration:

> The future of People's Poland depends first of all on the daily labour of our people, who love their motherland. Participation in the broadly conceived international division of labour has great significance. Its main direction is all-sided co-operation with the Soviet Union, the deepening of socialist integration, the unification of the intellectual and material potentials of the member countries of COMECON, with special reliance on the acceleration of scientific and technical progress. This relates as well to the sphere of the superstructure — the constant drawing together of our peoples, the further expansion of contacts between workers, peasants, the scientific and technical intelligentsia, cultural figures, and the youth of our countries.[28]

As in the Soviet domestic arena, so in Eastern Europe, too, the thrust of Gorbachev's policy in the aftermath of the congress was to maintain the momentum of his initiatives for economic integration and closer co-ordination of political activity. A month and a half after the Soviet party congress he attended the 11th Congress of the SED in East Berlin. There he kept up the propaganda for integration and massaged the egos of his German hosts by praising not only their performance in the key areas of scientific and technological development, but also their commitment to using the tried and true methods of central planning and administration.[29] His colleagues M. S. Solomentsev and N. I. Ryzhkov conveyed a similar message at the party congresses in Czechoslovakia and Bulgaria in late March and early April, respectively. And Gorbachev used the occasion of the meeting of the Political Consultative Committee of the Warsaw Pact in Budapest in the second week of June to keep up the pressure, spending a few days after the meeting to confer with Janos Kadar on economic relations. Ryzhkov carried on similar conversations with his Hungarian opposite number Gyorgy Lazar.[30]

These latter meetings undoubtedly required a good deal of nerve on the part of Gorbachev and Ryzhkov. The Chernobyl' disaster inevitably drew a cloud over the prospect of linking the East European economies to Soviet technology, especially since nuclear power was one of the five specific areas singled out for accelerated development under the Complex Program. In Poland and Romania measures for a review of their nuclear programs and associated safety provisions were officially announced.[31] Nevertheless, in Budapest Gorbachev did not hesitate to refer to the Chernobyl' accident, but he managed to turn it to his advantage by using it to issue an appeal for trans-European co-operation in the framework of the International Atomic Energy Agency. Thus even if the East European leaders were embarrassed by the Soviet handling of the disaster, they took pains to conceal their feelings and greeted Gorbachev's long-awaited 'explanation' on 18 May as fully adequate.

At the 10th Congress of the Polish United Workers' Party at the end of June, Gorbachev delivered a notably forthright and thoughtful speech enunciating his views on the foundations of Soviet–East European relations and their place in the further development of East–West economic contacts. His remarks are worth quoting here at length, because they reflect the essence of his approach to a number of important issues in East–West relations.

Before our parties stands a task of historical significance — to combine social justice, characteristic of socialism, with a high level of economic effectiveness. We should, we are simply obligated, to make socialism stronger, developing more dynamically, more successfully competing with capitalist society in all parameters. And this demands, first of all, the full and effective utilisation of those really inexhaustible possibilities which are discovered by the scientific and technological revolution.

It is understandable that we must act together here, unifying our efforts. This is required by the national economic interests of our countries, the political situation in the world arena, and, last but not least, by considerations of economic security. It goes without saying, we took a long time to learn what traps are set out on the trade routes leading to the West. There was mention here of what great costs Poland has borne. And not only she alone. Harm has been done by the very idea that it is simpler to buy on the capitalist market than to produce for ourselves. Now we at home have decisively overcome such attitudes. Of course, it is not a question of winding up economic links with the West. It is a question of something else — of using them rationally, of eliminating distortions, of not allowing dependence.

And, of course, unconditional priority should be given to co-operative links with the fraternal countries, to acceleration of the process of socialist economic integration. On this plane the Complex Program of scientific and technical progress, adopted within the framework of COMECON, will have the greatest significance.[32]

It is, of course, too early to tell how successful Gorbachev's plans to unify the bloc on a new, technologically higher level will be. Many of the caveats that apply to the prospects for effective modernisation in the Soviet Union apply with equal force in Eastern Europe. One would expect that Gorbachev's reliance on the 'human factor' would have even less chance of success there than in the USSR, since the legitimacy of 'real socialism' among the popular masses is by now marginal at best. Gorbachev unquestionably seems to have a better idea of what it will take to make the socialist commonwealth a more effective competitor in the international arena than any Soviet leader since Khrushchev. He appears to have a more consistent view of the political and economic requirements for such a program. But as the experience of Chernobyl' shows, firm intentions may not be enough.

CONCLUSIONS

Gorbachev's early handling of the problem of relations with Eastern Europe offers some important insights into his ideas on the kind of world he considers propitious for the flourishing of 'real socialism'. It presents a useful vantage point for examining his perspectives on the three basic levels of Soviet policy at home and abroad — goals, strategy and tactics. His insistence on immediate, concrete steps toward economic integration suggests that he has no intention of abandoning Lenin's cherished goal of a unitary communist world system, capable, as the opportunity arises, of the piecemeal absorption of additional member countries. The strategy for attaining this fundamental goal envisages a substantially greater role than previously for the non-Soviet members of the existing socialist commonwealth, both in building the internal socio-economic foundations of the commonwealth and in advertising the achievements of 'real socialism' on the road to communism. For Gorbachev it is apparently no longer sufficient for the Soviet Union to possess ultimate political and military control over an East European buffer zone. The societies and economies of these countries must be fully enlisted in, and share responsibility for, building up the world socialist system and helping to make it as invulnerable as possible to the hostile activities of the opposing capitalist world system.

As far as dealing with the latter is concerned, Gorbachev's approach harks back not so much to the Khrushchev era, with which his policies obviously have so much in common, but to the era of Lenin himself. In Lenin's day, when the fledgling Soviet state was economically prostrate and exposed to the allegedly constant threat of 'hostile capitalist encirclement', the Soviet founding fathers devised the policy of NEP at home and Rapallo and the United Front abroad. At home Gorbachev has appropriated Lenin's idea of the *prodnalog* (tax in kind) to legitimise a major feature of his agricultural policy. In foreign affairs he has clearly adopted the Rapallo approach in endeavouring to split the Western alliance. Individual Western countries are being deluged with inducements of various kinds to take the first small steps toward *rapprochement* with the USSR in an effort to create material linkages and psychological predispositions ultimately comprising a structure of good relations with Moscow, to the necessary detriment of their solidarity with Washington.

Contrary to the common Western interpretation that Gorbachev is so firmly constrained by the magnitude of his domestic social and economic problems that he is limited in his capacity for foreign policy ventures, the evidence suggests that an active foreign policy along the lines indicated is an integral component of his overall strategy. Accordingly, arms reduction is regarded not only as desirable in itself to facilitate the transfer of resources to the civilian economy, but also as providing a favourable climate for the differentiated approach to the countries of the Western alliance. The replacement of Andrei Gromyko as Foreign Minister, the shift of Anatolii Dobrynin from Washington to Moscow to strengthen party direction of foreign policy and the apparent downgrading of the military in foreign policy decision-making can all be taken as evidence of this turn toward a new, more active, yet more flexibly 'Leninist' strategy in foreign relations.

A major element of this strategy is the tightening of control over the actions of the junior members of the bloc. As we have seen, economic integration is regarded as one of the principal foundations for ensuring Soviet dominance and effective co-ordination of bloc initiatives toward the outside world; An important corollary of the strategy is to maintain basic similarities in their structures and processes of economic planning and management. Initial expectations that a 'pragmatic' Gorbachev would be more tolerant of diversity in the bloc seem to have been disappointed. Barely five months into his reign he is reported to have warned a gathering of bloc party economic secretaries to abandon their fascination with market solutions.[33] His decision to maintain existing patterns of centralised decision-making for the Soviet domestic economy (albeit in combination with an appeal for greater local initiative in policy implementation) was clearly intended to apply beyond the borders of the USSR. Gorbachev's preference for the more orthodox centralised approach of the East Germans to the quasi-market experiments of the Hungarians has been made quite explicit. Indeed, Hungarian economists have been reported to be seriously discouraged by the Soviet leader's attitude toward their reforms.[34] The little publicised COMECON summit meeting in November 1986, at which Gorbachev is reported to have castigated his bloc colleagues for dragging their feet on integration, suggests that the course he has chosen is far from fully supported by all of his East European counterparts. It also indicates the inertial strength of the existing institutional structures, which, as we have argued, hardly foster genuine economic integration.

Thus although Gorbachev has gone to considerable lengths to assure the East Europeans publicly that effective economic and managerial innovations will be carefully studied with an eye to possible adoption by the USSR and others, it would appear that he is not inclined to countenance significant deviations from the Soviet centralised model in its present incarnation. Integration will logically require a high degree of structural uniformity, which is regarded, moreover, as an effective barrier to Western efforts at 'differentiation'. General Jaruzelski's enthusiastic endorsement of integration and of the overall inward orientation of the bloc's developmental policies suggests that those who nurture hopes of any substantial leverage on Poland's behaviour as a result of her resumption of membership in the IMF seem likely to be disappointed.

A number of Western observers have argued that Gorbachev's commitment to accelerated scientific and technological progress will require massive purchases of Western hi-tech products. Without such imports, they contend, the Soviet Union and its Eastern European partners are doomed to a perpetual lag in the development of those areas which comprise the most important elements of national power in the contemporary era, with unpredictable consequences for long-term social stability. Yet Gorbachev's integration strategy is designed precisely to avoid such dependence on the West for the maintenance of power and stability. He appears fully conscious of the inevitability of a high degree of interdependence in the modern world, but he is clearly determined to trade with the West only on his own terms, relying on technology generated within the bloc as the main source of innovation. Publicly at least, he seems confident that internal socialist forces are capable of meeting the challenge. Meanwhile, the lure of technological imports is a useful weapon for the Soviet counterpart of the differentiation strategy. There is little doubt that he will use it skilfully and, unfortunately, given the customary Western commercial appetites, with no small degree of success.

To assume that Soviet economic needs will give the West much tangible influence on Soviet behaviour, that the stability of the Soviet empire somehow depends on what the West is willing to sell it (admittedly these are two separate questions), is to misunderstand the nature of Gorbachev's predicament and exaggerate the vulnerability of the Soviet-type systems. Victor Zaslavsky has recently argued quite convincingly that these systems are highly stable and represent a viable alternative model of a modern socio-economic system.[35] This alternative model is uniquely well designed for system-maintenance and to preserve the power positions of the ruling party elites. Gorbachev undoubtedly understands this and shows every sign of willingness to uphold the essential features of 'real socialism' as they presently exist. There is no reason to expect that he will not continue to pay the economic price for doing so.

NOTES

1. See, for example, the article by A. Iakolev, 'Mezhdunarodnoe znachenie Varshavskogo Dogvara', *MEMO*, no. 7 (July 1985), pp. 14–25, where the basic continuities in the military and political role of the Pact are celebrated on the thirtieth anniversary of its origin, especially the formulation on p. 24: 'A visible demonstration of the concern of the CPSU and all the fraternal parties for the unity and the further strengthening of the positions of socialism in its struggle against the forces of aggression and war is the agreement on the extension of the Warsaw Pact. This agreement expresses the general understanding that the content of the historical document signed thirty years ago, its spirit and letter fully correspond to the interest of all socialist countries.'

2. For Poland it was six times as great; for Hungary, about the same as the rate of GNP growth. See Thad P. Alton, Gregor Lazarcik, Elizabeth M. Bass and Krzysztof Badach, 'East European Defense Expenditures, 1965–1982', in Congress of the United States, *East European Economies: Slow Growth in the 1980's* (Washington, DC, 28 October 1985), pp. 478, 481.

3. In fairness to Khrushchev it should be pointed out that in his day the centrality of state-of-the-art technology in economic growth and in the structural lag of the Soviet economy behind its main Western competitors was not fully understood; nor were the limits of further development based on the traditional 'extensive' methods of the Stalinist model as evident as they are today.

4. The theoretical principles behind the relationship between autarchy and the political economy of the bloc have been admirably set forth by a young Yugoslav economist, O. Golubovic, in *SEV — zajednica planskih privreda*, unpublished MA thesis (Belgrade: Economics Faculty, Belgrade University, 1983).

5. Vanous (see Table 9.1).

6. Note, for example, the case of the anti-friction metal depositing process allegedly invented in the USSR some 30 years ago, which was rapidly adopted in an East German engine plant, but has yet to be endorsed for industrial application in the USSR. N. Il'inskaia, 'Spros za iznos', *Sotsialisticheskaia industriia*, 5 March 1986, p. 4.

7. See Rada Nikolaev, 'Bulgaria on the Eve of the 13th Party Congress', *Radio Free Europe Research*, Bulgarian SR/4, 22 April 1986.

8. See Slobodan Stankovic, 'Newspaper Claims that Ceausescu Has Obstacles in Dealing with Moscow', *RFE Research*, Yugoslav SR/6, where an article in the Zagreb daily *Vjesnik* is cited to support the allegation that Soviet pressure is forcing the Romanian leader to curb his pretensions to an independent foreign policy stance.

9. The main candidates for retirement were Gustav Husak in Czechoslovakia, Todor Zhivkov in Bulgaria and Nicolae Ceausescu in Romania. See, for example, Rada Nikolaev, 'Bulgaria . . .'; and Vladimir Socor, 'Toward a Post-Ceausescu Leadership in Romania?', *RFE Research*, RAD Background Report/5 (Eastern Europe), 10 January 1986.

10. See, for example, the Long-Term Program of co-operation

between the USSR and Romania for economic and scientific and technical co-operation to the year 2000 signed in Moscow on 16 May 1986. *Ekonomicheskaia gazeta*, no. 24 (June 1986), pp. 19–21.

11. 'Zaiavlenie ob osnovnykh napravleniiakh dal'neishego razvitiia uglubleniia ekonomicheskogo i nauchno-tekhnicheskogo sotrudnichestva stran-chlenov SEV', *Ek. gaz.*, no. 26 (June 1984), pp. 4–5.

12. 'Plenum Tsentral'nogo Komiteta KPSS 23 aprelia 1985 goda', *Kommunist*, no. 7 (May 1985), pp. 17–18.

13. *Sots. ind.*, 19 December 1985, pp. 1–3.

14. See Vladimir Sobell, 'Mikhail Gorbachev Takes Charge of the CMEA', *RFE Research*, RAD Background Report/146 (Eastern Europe), 20 December 1985.

15. Anneli Maier, 'Ceausescu Criticizes CMEA Co-operation', *RFE Research*, Romanian SR/1, 10 January 1986. The Romania–Soviet 'Long-Term Program' was not signed until 16 May 1986. *Ek. gaz.*, no. 24 (June 1986), pp. 19–21.

16. 'Kompleksnaia programma', Section I.4, *Sots. ind.*, 19 December 1985, p. 3.

17. Iu. Shiriaev, 'Tribuna bratskogo sotrudnichestva', *Kommunist*, no. 2 (January), 1986, p. 112.

18. For recent accounts of the operations of these COMECON institutions see 'Deiatel'nost' MBES v 1985 godu', *Ek. gaz.*, no. 22 (May 1986), p. 20; and 'MIB: orientatsiia na uskorenie nauchno-tekhnicheskogo progressa', ibid., no. 23 (June 1986), p. 21. There are numerous anecdotes emanating from Eastern Europe which establish that the 'transferable rouble' is neither transferable nor even a rouble, but only a book-keeping convenience whose value is subject to arbitrary manipulation.

19. See the speech by Premier N. I. Ryzhkov at the 41st (Extraordinary) Session of COMECON on 17 December 1985, 'Kliuchevoe zveno ekonomiki', *Sots. ind.*, 18 December 1985, p. 3, where these arrangements are foreshadowed. Since then a number of legal impediments to transnational co-operation have been duly abolished. For example, the Five-Year Plan Directives issued at the 11th Party Congress of the SED in East Berlin on 20 April 1986 make provisions for such relations with the USSR. FBIS Daily Report, Eastern Europe, 21 May 1986.

20. A. Antonov, 'Sodruzhestvo umnozhaet sily', *Sots. ind.*, 13 February 1986, p. 2.

21. 'Vystuplenie tovarishcha Gorbacheva M.S.', *Sots. ind.*, 19 April 1986, p. 3.

22. *Izvestiia*, 28 February 1986, p. 6.

23. Ibid., 28 February 1986, p. 7.

24. Ibid., 28 February 1986, p. 6.

25. Ibid.

26. Ibid.

27. *Sots. ind.*, 7 March 1986, p. 2.

28. Ibid., 27 February 1986, p. 7.

29. 'Vystuplenie tovarishcha Gorbacheva M.S.', *Sots. ind.*, 19 April 1986, pp. 1, 3.

30. 'Vstrecha v Budapeshte', *Izvestiia*, 12 June 1986, p. 2.

31. See, for example, 'Ceausescu, Chernobyl, Cernavoda', *RFE Research*, Romanian SR/7, 2 July 1986. A DPA report from Hamburg on 20 June mentioned a petition by some 300 East Germans demanding a pause in the GDR's nuclear energy program as a result of Chernobyl'. FBIS-86-120, 23 June 1986, p. E 11. In general, East German reactions to the Chernobyl' disaster have been noticeably smug and condescending: such accidents, it is implied, could not occur with (East) German technology or technical thoroughness.

32. 'Vystuplenie tovarishcha Gorbacheva M.S.', *Sots. ind.*, 1 July 1986, pp.1, 3.

33. Elizabeth Teague, 'Gorbachev Addresses Hungarian Workers', *Radio Liberty Research*, RL 227/86, 10 June 1986, pp. 2–3.

34. Private communication to the author by a Western economist recently in contact with Hungarian reform economists.

35. Victor Zaslavsky, 'The Soviet World System: Origins, Evolution, Prospects for Reform', *Telos*, no. 65 (Fall 1985), pp. 3–22.

Conclusion

The Gorbachev Era Launched

T. H. Rigby

One might expect an incoming Soviet leadership to enjoy an extraordinary freedom of action, especially by contrast with a newly elected administration in the West, and the ability, if they so wish, to carry through smoothly and expeditiously a wide-ranging program of change. The absence of opposition parties, of a free press, independent trade unions and other interest organisations; the centralised, hierarchical structure of the ruling party itself, with its outlawing of 'factions' (and therefore of open opposition to the leadership and its policies), and the direction of all aspects of the life of society by official organisations run by party members and supervised by the party apparatus — all this combines to suggest that a new Soviet leadership should have a completely free hand in deciding its policies and every confidence that they would then be promptly implemented.

Of course, a new leadership might be broadly satisfied with things as they stand, and its desire for change limited to matters of detail. So far as the Gorbachev leadership is concerned, we have seen one area, namely the composition of the party membership itself, in which it has evidently resolved that a 'steady as she goes' policy is the appropriate one. It is abundantly clear, however, that this is untypical and that Gorbachev's rhetoric of radical change 'amounting to a revolution' reflects a genuine resolve to effect major modifications in the settled structures, procedures and policies of the Soviet system.

Why, then, did so little change in the first two years of Gorbachev's incumbency as General Secretary? Paradoxically, it is the very factors which concentrate so much power in the hands of the Soviet leadership, and potentially in those of the

General Secretary himself, that obstruct the speedy implementation of a reform program. One consequence of single-party rule is that when the General Secretary changes, the rest of the ruling oligarchy initially remains; the new chief executive does not *form* a government, he *inherits* one. Nor, as we have seen, does this weakly institutionalised power structure automatically confer effective formal powers on the top man which enable him quickly to assert his personal dominance over the policy-making process. Furthermore, the direct administrative authority which the political leadership enjoys over all areas of social activity, has given rise to a bureaucratic machine of awesome scale and complexity, individual parts of which cannot be speedily reorganised or redirected without serious disturbance to the others. Formal and informal groupings among party, government, military and police officials, with their intricate and changing pattern of interests, attitudes, affinities and rivalries, must be taken into account by a new leader if he wants this machine to facilitate his innovations and not frustrate them. He must therefore devote much attention to the Byzantine intricacies of bureaucratic politics at the same time as building up his alliances and authority step-by-step within the ruling oligarchy itself. And, finally, the very lack of legitimate channels for opposing or critising the leadership's policies means that if sections of the public are egregiously outraged by these they may have no recourse except to unlawful assembly or riot, the domestic and international repercussions of which could be very damaging to the regime. This acts as a further inhibitor of decisive action in important policy areas.

When these systemic factors are taken into account, both the build-up of Gorbachev's personal authority and the changes achieved in his first two years appears far more impressive. We should, to be sure, beware of viewing these two processes as simply two sides of the one coin. Some important changes that have come to fruition under Gorbachev were initiated long before he assumed the General Secretaryship. Nor can we assume that he was the sole, or even the prime mover in all the changes that have occurred since 1985, even if he figured as the most authoritative public advocate of them. Nevertheless, Gorbachev, far more than any Soviet leader since Stalin in the 1930s, has emphatically linked his authority with the cause of radical and many-sided change, and the two themes therefore constantly overlap.

Of all important developments since Gorbachev's takeover, the new party program and rules offer the best example of a measure initiated some years earlier and affording little clear evidence of his making a major input. True, as Graeme Gill points out, the program contains a passage tending to enhance the new party leader's authority by a coded denigration of his predecessors, Stalin, Khrushchev and Brezhnev, but this 'dialectical' Soviet version of legitimation by apostolic succession is now traditional at times of leadership change. The increased emphasis on the party as against the state in economic management and the transition to communism would suit the new party leader, but this shift in relative status was already apparent under Brezhnev. The same could be said for the greater realism and pragmatism of the revised program compared with Khrushchev's original 1961 version, and its avoidance of striking objectives or formulations intended to inspire but also inviting alarm (like the 'merging of nationalities') or derision (like the achievement of full communism by the 1980s). The references to 'openness', one of Gorbachev's favourite themes, may reflect his influence. On the other hand, the increased stress on collective leadership probably registered the limits of Gorbachev's power in these early months of his incumbency and the interest of powerful colleagues in maintaining these limits. As Gill points out, perhaps the best feature of the revised program from Gorbachev's viewpoint is its relative lack of specific objectives, the conspicuous exception being the economic targets set for the year 2000, which would manifestly require substantial changes in socio-economic arrangements and attitudes to have a chance of succeeding. At the same time it is important to realise that while the party program is now far less utopian in its specific goals, the document is *fundamentally* utopian in that it sets up an imagined ideal state of society as the end and justification of all organised social activity in the Soviet Union. However weak the inspirational force of this ideal may now be, its constant assertion remains indispensible to any Soviet regime, since without it the arguments for the communist party and its leaders to enjoy a monopoly of legitimate power immediately collapse.

Of all fields of policy, foreign relations potentially offer an incoming Soviet leadership the freest hand in launching striking new initiatives, relatively unconstrained by the vast inertia of the party-government bureaucracy, and it is noteworthy that Gorbachev assumed a central and highly visible role as *the*

237

Soviet foreign policy spokesman far more quickly than any of his predecessors. His activism and the freshness and seeming reasonableness of his thinking and style were not, however, rewarded by major foreign relations breakthroughs. One inhibiting factor, as Geoffrey Jukes's analysis reminds us, is the constant interplay between foreign affairs and defence, given the power of the military and defence industry lobbies and the intractability of technological factors. The new Soviet leadership of the mid-1980s, unlike that of the mid-1950s, did not inherit areas of major dispute or conflict (the Korean War, the first Vietnam War, the division of Austria, the Soviet-Yugoslav conflict), the relatively cost-free liquidation of which could win major reductions in global and regional tensions. Afghanistan is only a weak parallel here, for although some political advantage could accrue from a more conciliatory stance, any settlement that would satisfy the Afghan resistance and its international supporters seemed to carry the unacceptable price of a hostile regime arrayed along one of the USSR's most sensitive borders. Nor was Gorbachev blessed with an amenable US administration, as was Khrushchev at the highpoint of 'peaceful coexistence' and Brezhnev in the heyday of 'détente'. At the end of his first two years, in the wake of the abortive Reykjavik summit, the fruitfulness of the Gorbachev approach in foreign relations remained unproven.

This approach, however, clearly had a public relations dimension as well as its directly diplomatic one. Gorbachev, ably seconded by his Foreign Minister Eduard Shevardnadze, advised by experienced diplomat-become-Central Committee Secretary Anatolii Dobrynin, and probably with the blessing of veteran Andrej Gromyko, presented an urbane, frank, reasonable and conciliatory Soviet face to the world, which was intended to foster a climate of public opinion conducive to positive official responses to Soviet initiatives. This paralleled and complemented a striking public relations drive domestically, aimed at promoting trust and co-operation among the Soviet population, and particularly its more influential segments. Some measures appear to have been directed simultaneously (though in varying proportions) at both foreign and domestic publics, for example the ending of Academician Sakharov's Gorky exile, the release of other well-known dissidents and certain dramatic cases of permissiveness in the cultural sphere. Such measures certainly did not indicate any abdication of party control over culture and communications or a calling-off of the KGB drive against dissidents, which continued in ever more sophisicated forms.[1] Yet it would be misleading to dismiss them as purely propagandistic and hypocritical. Space is lacking for a detailed account of the Gorbachev regime's early record in the culture and communications area, but several overlapping aspects can be discerned.

While the regime continues to set — and patrol — the bounds of permitted public expression, those bounds have been widened considerably. The beginnings of this process were already apparent in the year preceding the 27th Congress, but it accelerated markedly in the middle and later months of 1986. In the arts the chief landmarks were the Cinema-workers Congress in May, the 8th Congress of the Union of Soviet Writers in late June, the 15th Congress of the All-Russian Theatrical Society in October, and the Foundation Congress of the Union of Theatre Workers of the USSR in December. Although there was evidence of formidable conservative resistance both within the party and government bureaucracies and among the intelligentsia themselves, the reformers were now making major gains. It was clear that Gorbachev was keen to enlist the support of the creative intelligentsia in his program of social renewal and was prepared to cede them greater autonomy and freedom of expression. Whether his No. 2 in the Central Committee Secretariat Egor Ligachev directly opposed him in this, as some observers believe, or whether there was something like an agreed division of labour between them, with Ligachev having the job of preventing the process from getting out of control, was still debatable.[2]

In the media, the declared policy of 'openness' (*glasnost'*), came into its own, after a hesitant start, in the wake of the Chernobyl' accident of 26 April 1986, and brought the substantial reporting of such negative aspects of Soviet life as organised crime, drug addiction, and man-made and natural disasters, public reference to which had generally been taboo for decades. The highpoint was the prompt reporting of the Alma-Ata demonstrations of 17 December 1986 against the appointment of the Russian Genadii Kolbin to head the party leadership in Kazakhstan, but the media handling of this incident, giving as it did a grossly misleading impression of its character, scale and motives, also epitomised the limitations of *glasnost'*.[3] There can be little doubt that it reflects in part a genuine conviction that the leadership will earn more credit and co-operation from the population by openly acknowledging setbacks and problems rather than trying to conceal them. On the other hand it is probably also motivated by the new leaders' realisation that the Soviet people will come to hear of these events anyway, and popular attitudes towards them may be largely determined by foreign radio accounts if they do not get in first with their own version. Thus if *glasnost'* brings more information, it also brings more disinformation.[4]

By contrast with the Gorbachev regime's fresh and innovative approach to the management of culture and public communications, its massive and many-sided campaign for greater order and discipline represents a continuation and intensification of measures initiated under General Secretary Andropov in 1983. These measures were doubtless triggered by a sharpening awareness of the great economic and social costs which alcohol abuse, corruption and slackness on the job had come to represent under Brezhnev's indulgent rule. Their salience during Gorbachev's first years in office may have reflected both the wider consensus attained on this issue within the new leadership and the relative straightforwardness of the attempted remedies, in contrast with the highly controversial and complex issues of structural reform.

How effectively Gorbachev deals with the latter, however, is likely to prove decisive for the success or failure of his regime. In the early 1980s there was near consensus among Western Sovietologists that the rapid decline and levelling off of Soviet economic growth, which made it no longer possible to maintain or expand simultaneously current consumption, capital investment and military capacities, and which opened up the prospect of widening technological and economic gaps *vis-à-vis* the West, could not be remedied without more or less radical changes in the way the Soviet economy was structured and operated. Since taking office Gorbachev has made it abundantly clear that he shares that view. At the same time, sharply divergent opinions are held by Western scholars both as to *how* radical the changes must be to have any chance of succeeding, and *how* radical are the remedies contemplated by Gorbachev himself.

Whether we see particular changes in the system as amounting to a change *of* the system, depends, of course, on what we think the essentials of the system are, and on this, too, opinions differ. No one, however, would seriously argue that the many and varied adjustments of administrative structures and procedures, incentive arrangements and investment priorities during

Gorbachev's first two years, described by Robert F. Miller in Chapter 5 and Stephen Wheatcroft in Chapter 7, in any way threaten those essentials. Yet the question remains, does Gorbachev intend to go very much further, and will he be obliged to do so if he is to succeed in revitalising the Soviet economy? As Victor Zaslavsky shows in Chapter 6, some of the proposals currently being aired by Soviet scholars and administrators would amount to a radical departure from the centralised command economy prevalent since the 1930s and the same could be said of some of the administrative changes already initiated or foreshadowed, if carried to their logical conclusions. True, if we follow Zaslavsky in identifying the essentials of the Soviet system with 'the dominance of state property, the one-party state, central planning, firm political control over the population, closed borders, etc.', such changes could still be characterised as 'within-system reform'. Nevertheless, they would have far-reaching ideological and political implications, and not least for the long-entrenched practices through which the communist party exercises its 'leading and directing role' in Soviet society. At the same time, they could bring major international as well as domestic benefits, not only by enhancing the system's standing and image abroad, but also by facilitating more effective interaction with the advanced Western economies and integration with the socialist economies of Eastern Europe, the promise and problems of which are analysed by Robert F. Miller in Chapter 9. After two years of Gorbachev's primacy, however, Sovietologists remained divided over whether he was aiming at such a radical within-system reform. Paradoxically, this argument may never be settled definitively, for if radical reforms do not eventuate, this may be attributed to the inertia of the system or to internal opposition, and if they do it may be argued that change developed a momentum of its own which took it much further than Gorbachev intended.

Beyond that, moreover, there lies a further question: what happens if a radical, within-system reform is attempted but fails, and economic and social problems assume even more critical proportions? Predicted responses to this contingency have ranged from a resurgence of full-blown Stalinism through radical liberalisation to a nationalistic military dictatorship. Such scenarios may seem bizarre, and they surely command a low probability, but we should not totally ignore them. Considerably greater probability, perhaps, should be accorded the fairly widely held view that change will fall considerably short of a 'radical within-system reform', being limited to adjustments to the centrally directed system combined with a small measure of individual enterprise in the personal consumption sector and a massive drive to inject greater conscientiousness, dynamism and purpose into the operation of the system. Nor can it be excluded that such modest measures could effect sufficient improvement in the system's performance, at least in the short to medium term, to sap the pressures for more radical change.[5]

Meanwhile, however, it is not through structural reforms but through its drive for order and discipline and through its massive changes of personnel that the Gorbachev regime has so far been making its greatest impact on Soviet society. *Perestroika*, it is constantly urged, begins with the individual, be he worker or leader, and those leaders who prove incapable of reforming themselves, of keeping 'in step with the times', cannot be allowed to remain in office. The greatly accelerated turnover of officials has extended to all levels and to all the vast structures of power through which the USSR is run. As J. H. Miller has shown in Chapter 3, by the time of the 27th Congress it had brought striking changes in the membership of the supreme ruling bodies of Party and state and in the wider circles of the Soviet political elite. There were no further changes at the summit until the January 1987 CC Plenum, which approved the retirement of Brezhnev-leftover D. A. Kunaev from the Politburo, the election of A. N. Iakovlev as a candidate member, the retirement of M. V. Zimianin from the Secretariat, and the addition to that body of N. N. Sliun'kov and A. I. Lukianov. These changes were generally seen as further strengthening Gorbachev's preponderant influence in the party executive (though Sliun'kov's primary association was evidently with Ryzhkov, but not dramatically so. Meanwhile turnover continued at a brisk, if reduced, rate among the 'top 500'. It was now greater among government than among party officials. Of the 104 members of the USSR Council of Ministers (excluding the *ex officio* republic premiers) 40 were changed in the eleven months preceding the congress in February 1986 and a further 23 in the eleven months that followed it. By contrast only 6 of the 72 RSFSR regional first party secretaries were changed in the latter period, compared with 25 in the former.[6] The different rhythms of change are probably due to Gorbachev's concern to effect as many as possible of the party replacements prior to the regional conferences that preceded the 27th Congress, and to the continuing impact of Ryzhkov's takeover of the Council of Ministers from the ancient Brezhnev crony Tikhonov in September 1985. At the same time, the substantially greater aggregate turnover since the accession of Gorbachev among members of the central government than among the regional party secretaries (60 per cent compared with 43 per cent) is probably acounted for largely by the considerably higher age profile of the former.

Some observers have suggested that Gorbachev's personal commitment to cadre-renewal and the rooting out of corruption, inefficiency and stagnation is liable to provoke resentment and non-co-operation among the bureaucracies which could frustrate his purposes and even threaten his authority. A measure of insecurity, resentment and passive resistance is indeed inevitable and may be widespread, but its political significance is surely overshadowed by the fact that more and more senior posts come to be occupied by officials who have benefited rather than suffered from the renewal drive, and who will therefore have a stake in the success of the leaders who sponsor it, in this case primarily Gorbachev.

In Chapter 1 we argued that Mikhail Gorbachev had achieved by the time of the 27th Congress far greater personal authority than had any previous General Secretary at a comparable stage of his incumbency.[7] The evidence strongly suggests that his authority grew further during his second year in office. The constant and prominent reporting of his activities by the press, radio and television, and the degree to which it already overshadowed the reports of the activities of senior Politburo colleagues, was enjoyed by Gorbachev's predecessors Khrushchev and Brezhnev only after they had been many years in the top job. He figured as constant spokesman for the regime both in foreign relations and across a broad spectrum of domestic affairs: from industry to ideology to internal party matters.[8] His words in encounters with various groups around the country began to be imbued with nationwide policy significance. Thus in August the Politburo considered and endorsed both his formal speeches and informal conversations in his visit to Vladivostok and Khabarovsk as possessing 'principled importance';[9] and a few weeks later it went a step further by adopting a formal resolution published in the press which proclaimed 'the principled importance of [his] propositions and conclusions expressed in meetings held with the *aktiv* and working people of the Krasnodar and Stavropol regions on 17–19 September', adding that 'the conclusions so formulated develop the guidelines of the 27th Congress'.[10] This amounted to according the *obiter dicta* of the General Secretary, endorsed by his Politburo colleagues, not in advance but *after* he saw fit to utter them, an authority on a par with the most important collective decisions of the party. It is hard to think of a parallel to this since Stalin's time.

From this one should not rush to the conclusion that the oligarchical structure of power was now effectively a facade and the Soviet Union had entered a new phase of personal rule. There is significant negative evidence to the contrary. In the year following the 27th Congress Gorbachev had acquired no new posts or titles, nor had there been a marked flow of his former associates into high positions: indeed the second-level officials linked with other Politburo members noted by J. H. Miller in Chapter 3 continued to outnumber those with earlier links to Gorbachev. Some observers also saw evidence of high-level opposition to the General Secretary in the fact that some of his more striking proposals at the January 1987 Plenum, notably those for a national party conference in 1988 and for elements of genuine competition in party and soviet elections, were not specifically endorsed in the Plenum resolutions. Nevertheless, the snowballing accumulation of authority around the person of the General Secretary which was discussed at the end of Chapter 1 was manifestly continuing. The evident setbacks at the time of the Chernobyl' accident and the abortive Reykjavik talks had only briefly slowed the process. By 1987 any newly-appointed minister or regional party secretary would understand very clearly who was likely to be the boss for many years ahead and adjust his own loyalties accordingly, whatever his earlier associations. The Gorbachev era was now well and truly launched. No one can confidently predict what it holds ultimately in store for the Soviet Union and for the rest of the world. We can at best follow developments as they unfold with a degree of understanding, and with any luck discern the most likely possibilities that lie immediately ahead. This book, we trust, will contribute in some measure to these vital purposes.

NOTES

1. In evaluating the record of the early Gorbachev regime in the area of 'human rights' it is important to bear in mind that the intensified campaign to crush active dissidence by a repertoire of measures ranging from psychological pressure through physical attacks by 'unknown persons' to sackings, job transfers, imprisonment, incarceration in 'special' mental hospitals, and exile, had been going on for some six years by the time Gorbachev took office, and had succeeded in gravely crippling the dissident movement. These methods continued to be used under Gorbachev, but attracted less international attention, largely because there were so few well-known persons left among the critically depleted ranks of dissenters from whom the new victims were drawn. Moreover, the greater permissiveness in cultural expression and in the criticism of certain types of social evil has narrowed the front of potential dissidence among the intelligentsia. On the other hand the suppression of unauthorised activity and criticism among religious and ethnic groups seems if anything to have intensified.

2. See Paul G. Ruehl, 'Die Kulturpolitik im Umfeld des XXVII. Parteitages der KPdSU', *Osteuropa* 8–9 (August–September), 1986, pp. 725–38, Iu. Vishnevskaia, 'Itogi s"ezda teatral'nykh deiatelei SSSR', Radio Liberty, *Issledovatel'skii biulleten'*, no. 52 (31 December) 1986.

3. See *Pravda*, 19 December 1986. Cf. Ann Sheehy, 'The Alma-Ata Riots and their Aftermath' (RL 3/87), *Radio Liberty Research Bulletin*, no. 1 (January 7), 1987.

4. Cf. Marshall Goldman, *USSR in Crisis* (New York-London: Norton), p. 129. For reviews of the development and limitations of greater media openness during this period, see Vera Tolz, '*Glasnost'* in the Soviet Media since the Twenty-Seventh Party Congress' (RL 391/86), *Radio Liberty Research Bulletin*, no. 43 (October 22), 1986, and Victor Yasmann, 'Drafting a Press Law: *Glasnost'*, as an Alternative to the Free Flow of Information' (RL 14/87), ibid., no. 2 (January 8), 1987.

5. We cannot cite here the numerous books and articles bearing on the matters discussed in the preceding paragraphs. For a penetrating discussion of the economic problems and alternatives and their wider implications, see the two articles by Jan Winiecki, 'Are Soviet-type economies entering an era of long-term decline?', *Soviet Studies*, XXXVIII, no. 3 (July 1986), pp. 325–48, and 'Soviet-type economies: considerations for the future?', ibid., no. 4 (October 1986), pp. 543–62. See also Hans-Herman Hohmann, 'Radikale Reform? Zum Kurs Sowjetischer Wirtschaftspolitik nach dem XXVII Parteitag der KPdSU', *Osteuropa*, no. 8–9 (August–September), 1986, pp. 620–30, and Helmut König, 'Ein Jahr Gorbatschow', ibid., no. 10 (October), 1986; pp. 836–63. For one view of the larger issues and prospects, see Seweryn Bialer, *The Soviet Paradox. External Expansion, Internal Decline* (New York: Knopf, 1986). Cf. Goldman, *USSR in Crisis*.

6. I am indebted to Professor Shugo Minagawa for drawing this contrast to my attention.

7. Cf. Thane Gustafson and Dawn Mann, 'Gorbachev's First Year. Building Power and Authority', *Problems of Communism*, May – June 1986, pp. 1 – 19.

8. See, for example, *Pravda*, 22 May 1986, 2 October 1986, 24 October 1986. It is characteristic that although Ligachev gave the main report at the Central Committee conference on the social sciences held at the beginning of October it was Gorbachev's relatively short speech on this occasion (*Pravda*, 2 October 1986) that received by far the greater publicly and was treated as providing the key guidelines for those concerned.

9. See *Pravda*, 16 August 1986.

10. Ibid., 1 October 1986.

Index

Academy of Sciences USSR 11,
14, 77, 79, 111, 128, 132,
224
acceleration (*uskorenie*) 45, 48,
50, 112, 120, 123, 170,
199, 208
Afghanistan 138, 197, 210, 238
Afonin, V. G. 65, 89n46
Aganbegian, A. G. 112, 154
Aliev, G. A. 15, 22, 24, 26, 28,
32, 68
Andropov, Iu. V. 17, 22–3,
32–3, 40, 42, 64, 66, 78,
82–3, 86n23, 89n48, 105,
189–90, 240
Antonov, A. K. 24, 224
Arkhipov, I. V. 24, 64
armed forces *see* military
Armenia, Armenian 68, 94,
104–5, 173
Azerbaidzhan, Azeri 68,
93–4, 104, 173

Baibakov, N. K. 78, 87n34, 178
Beliakov, O. S. 65
Belorussia, Belorussian 68, 74,
78, 86n21, 87n29, 88n37,
94, 104, 173
Biriukova, A. P. 24, 26, 67, 77,
85n11, 86n19
blue-collar workers *see* workers
Bodiul, I. I. 68
Bulgaria 147, 218, 220, 225–6,
232n7, 232n9

Ceausescu, N. 214–15, 220–2,
225, 232n8, 232n9
Central Asia 75, 93, 116–17,
137
Chebrikov, V. M. 15, 22, 24,
26, 68

Cheliabinsk (city and province)
87n30, 96
Chernenko, K. U. 23, 32–3,
40, 42–3, 65–6, 89n48,
90, 189, 221
Chernobyl' 88n25, 111, 129,
132n3, 133n18, 227–8,
234n31, 239, 244
Chervonenko, S. V. 65
China 54, 125, 206–8, 210–11
clerical workers *see* white-collar
workers
clientelism 79, 81–3
collective farmers *see* peasants
Committee of State Security
(KGB) 15, 24, 28, 38n17,
77–9, 92, 238
communism 42–4, 46, 48–9,
52, 57n8, 229, 237
Communist Party of the Soviet
Union (CPSU)
Central Auditing Commission
10, 21, 70–3, 86n21
Central Committee 7, 17, 21,
34, 55, 60n42, 63, 65,
69–75, 78, 81, 86n21,
110, 176–7, 183n3, 189,
197, 211
Departments 64–5, 82,
84–5nn9–11, 183n3,
211
Committee of Party Control
21, 65, 84n9
membership, personnel
policies 3, 17–21, 51–2,
68, 70–5, 81, 85n11,
90–108 *passim*, 242–3
party Program 3, 10, 40–55
passim, 237
party Rules 3, 6, 10, 40, 55,
60nn39–43, 88n41, 211
Politburo 10, 15, 23–36

passim, 62–3, 65, 67,
69, 73–4, 110, 122, 163,
176–7, 190, 243–4
Secretariat, Central
Committee, 21, 23–5,
28, 32, 63, 65, 238–9,
242
Constitution USSR 38n17, 50,
59n34
corruption 75, 81, 94, 105, 110,
136, 138, 154, 197
Council for Mutual Economic
Assistance (COMECON) 5,
221–6, 228, 230,
233nn14–15, 18–19
Council of Ministers USSR
10–11, 23–4, 31, 38n17,
67, 69, 82, 86n21, 87n30,
87n35, 126–7, 242
see also Presidium of Council
of Ministers
Czechoslovakia 136, 215, 218,
225–6, 232n9

Defence, Ministry of 24, 38n17,
62, 75
Demichev, P. N. 15, 24, 38n17,
69, 86n19
democratisation 45, 51–2
Dnepropetrovsk (city and
province) 66, 68, 81–3
Dobrynin, A. F. 24, 65, 85n11,
229, 238
Dolgikh, V. I. 15, 24, 28, 65,
85n11

East Germany (GDR) 28, 111,
131, 218–19, 224, 226,
230, 232n6, 234n31
Eastern Europe 5, 206, 210,
214–34 *passim*, 241
Economy
agriculture 4, 27, 32, 47,
58n19, 64, 101–2, 115,
117, 119, 122, 124–5,
139, 146, 151, 154,
161–88 *passim*
raion agro-industrial
association (RAPO)
174, 177, 182n1

USSR Food Program
162–9, 182
cost accounting, economic
accounting (*khozraschet*)
124, 155, 180
defence industry 67, 69,
85n16, 199, 200, 202
heavy industry, industry,
manufacturing 47,
102–3, 115, 117, 120–1,
123, 154, 199, 200
investment 114–15, 117–18,
120–3, 154, 164,
169–70, 173, 181, 188,
218–19, 223, 240
organisation 47, 115, 119–27
passim, 140, 142, 146–7,
150, 157, 169, 174–5,
178–9, 223–4, 230, 241
performance, productivity
44, 47–8, 109–11,
114–17, 122, 136–8,
144, 149, 156, 170–2
policy debates 4, 111–12,
139–57 *passim*
prices 118, 125, 130–1,
134n32, 141, 146, 149,
151, 161, 164, 166–7,
169, 175–7, 179, 216
quality 112–13, 116, 118
retail trade, consumer goods,
services 96, 102–3, 154,
166, 172–3
self-financing
(*samofinansirovanie*)
124–5, 153, 155, 180
self-recoupment
(*samookupaemost'*) 180
El'tsin, B. N. 15–16, 24, 36,
84–5n10, 89n45
employees *see* white-collar
workers
Epishev, A. A. 65
Estonia, Estonian 93–4, 104–5

Far East 117, 243
farmers *see* peasants
Fedorenko, N. P. 144, 159n38,
159n50
foreign affairs, relations 33, 50,

53–4, 59nn33–5, 75,
77–9, 87n30, 131, 138–9,
189–213 *passim*, 229,
237–8
foreign trade 118, 131, 162,
170, 193, 208–9, 213n27,
216–17, 219–21, 227–8,
231

generations, change of 66–7,
71–4, 79–80, 85n13,
85n15, 90, 97, 110
Georgia, Georgian 68, 93–4,
104–5, 173
glasnost' (openness) 239–40,
245n4
Gor'kii (city and province) 96
Gostev, B. I. 65, 85n11
Grishin, V. V. 16, 22, 25, 66,
86n19
Gromyko, A. A. 15, 22, 24, 26,
33, 229, 238
Grossu, S. K. 34

Honecker, E. 29, 220, 225
human factor 2–3, 61, 113,
129, 131, 135n41, 228
Hungary 67, 111, 147, 218–19,
226, 230
Husak, G. 225, 232n9

Iakovlev, A. N. 24, 83, 85n11,
242
Iakushev, V. M. 149, 159n44,
159nn47–9
Iastrebov, I. P. 65
intelligentsia 103, 226, 245n1
Internal Affairs, Ministry of
(MVD) 77, 79, 92

Jaruzelski, W. 220, 226, 230

Kadar, J. 220, 225–6
Kapitonov, I. V. 26, 65, 86n19
Karlov, V. A. 64–5
Katushev, K. F. 28
Kazakhstan, Kazakh 31, 36, 68,
86n21, 93–4, 104–5, 116,
239
Kemerovo (city and province) 96

Khrushchev, N. S. 2, 9, 17, 19,
25–7, 30–4, 36, 41–2, 44,
61, 64, 67–8, 71, 73, 80,
114, 124, 126, 136, 142,
154, 161, 195–7, 200,
202–3, 205, 207, 210, 216,
228–9, 237, 243
Kirghizia, Kirghiz 94, 104–5
Kolbin, G. V. 34, 89n45, 239
kolkhozniki see peasants
Komsomol (Communist Youth
League) 11, 13–14, 34, 55,
83, 97, 107n18
Kosygin, A. N. 11, 26, 28,
85n12, 148
Kruchina, N. E. 65, 89n46,
89n51
Kunaev, D. A. 15, 22, 24–7,
36, 94, 242

labour force *see* workers
Latvia, Latvian 68, 94, 104–5
Lenin, V. I. 9–10, 124, 190,
228–9
Leningrad (city and province)
36, 69, 86n20
Ligachev, E. K. 15, 22, 24, 26,
33, 35, 69, 82, 88n42, 96,
239, 246n8
Lithuania, Lithuanian 94, 104
Lizichev, A. D. 65–6, 89n51
Luk'ianov, A. I. 65, 242

manual workers *see* workers
Marchuk, G. I. 24, 68
Marxism-Leninism 46, 50–1,
54, 130, 197, 208
Masliukov, Iu. D. 24, 67,
89n45
Medvedev, V. A. 24, 65,
85n11, 153, 160n58
military 4, 13–14, 28, 51, 53,
59–60n25, 66, 75, 77–80,
88n38, 92, 94, 96, 99, 103,
107nn7–9, 108n31, 148,
189–213 *passim*, 214–15,
240
Great Fatherland War 66–7,
71, 212
see also Defence, Ministry of;

Economy, defence
  industry
Mishin, V. M. 34
Moldavia, Moldavian 31, 34,
  94, 104−5
Moscow (city) 36, 66, 68,
  86n19
Murakhovskii, V. S. 24, 32, 64,
  68, 89n46, 178

nationalism 49−50, 58n23, 68,
  74−6, 87n29, 104−5, 138,
  237, 241
nationality *see* nationalism
Nikonov, V. P. 24, 32, 89n46,
  179−80
nomenklatura 110, 217
non-manual workers *see* white-
  collar workers
Nuriev, Z. L. 66, 68, 86n18,
  169, 178

Ogarkov, N. V. 88n38, 203−5
ownership 145−6, 241

Pasternak, V. S. 65
peaceful coexistence 191,
  195−6, 200−1, 238
peasants 74−5, 77, 92, 98−9,
  101, 108n22, 124−5
Pel'she, A. Ia. 65, 67
pensioners 78, 103, 107n14,
  108n28
Poland 77, 138, 167, 169, 215,
  218, 220, 224, 226−7, 231
Ponomarev, B. N. 65, 67, 78
Popov, G. Kh. 141−2, 146
Presidium of Council of
  Ministers USSR 23−6, 32,
  38n17, 63−4, 85n12
  see also Council of Ministers
    USSR
Presidium of Supreme Soviet
  USSR 15, 24, 31−3, 127
property *see* ownership

rabochie see workers
Razumovskii, G. P. 24, 33, 65,
  85n11, 89n46

restructuring (*perestroika*) 47,
  61, 88n44, 112, 242
Riabov, Ia. P. 24, 89n45
Romania 138, 214, 218, 220,
  222, 225, 227, 232nn8−9,
  233n10, 233n15
Romanov, G. V. 23, 28, 32, 69,
  86n20
Rusakov, K. V. 65
Russian Soviet Federative
  Socialist Republic (RSFSR)
  77, 93−4, 96, 104, 107n16,
  242
Ryzhkov, N. I. 15, 22, 24, 26,
  28, 36, 39n20, 67, 69, 82,
  89n45, 96, 116, 120−1,
  128, 156, 173, 178, 180−1,
  224, 226−7, 233n19, 242

Savinkin, N. I. 64−5
science and technology
  57nn16−17, 77, 79, 88n35,
  103, 111, 119, 120−1, 123,
  127−8, 191−2, 200, 208,
  213n27, 216, 222−4,
  226−7, 231, 233nn10−11
Shalaev, S. A. 56n4
Shauro, V. F. 65
Shcherbina, B. E. 24
Shcherbitskii, V. V. 15, 22, 24,
  26−7, 36, 68
Shelepin, A. N. 83
Shevardnadze, E. A. 15, 22,
  24, 26, 28, 32−5, 68,
  89n51, 238
Siberia 69, 117
Silaev, I. S. 24, 67
Skliarov, Iu. A. 65, 85n11
Sliun'kov, N. N. 15, 24, 37n9,
  89n45, 242
sluzhashchie see white-collar
  workers
social mobility 61, 77,
  87nn26−7, 98−9,
  108nn24−5, 138
social structure 140−1, 151,
  226
socialism, 'developed', 'real'
  42−3, 46, 49−50, 57n10,
  151, 216, 228−9, 231

socialist commonwealth
community 53–4, 228
Sokolov, S. I. 15, 24, 203–4
Solomentsev, M. S. 15, 22, 26,
32, 65, 226
Solov'ev, Iu. F. 15, 36, 37n9,
69, 86n20
specialists, specialist training
62–3, 66–7, 79, 100–1,
117, 123
Stalin, J. V., Stalinism 7, 25,
27–8, 33–4, 37n8, 44, 72,
79, 98–9, 109, 118, 124,
130, 142, 145, 148–50,
161, 202, 216, 237, 241,
244
State Agro-Industrial
Committee USSR
(*Gosagroprom SSSR*) 78,
84n2, 126, 134n33, 178–9
State Defence Council 24,
31–2
State Planning Committee
(Gosplan) 15, 28, 69, 82,
85–6n16, 143–4, 149
Stavropol' (city and province)
36, 69, 178, 243
Suslov, M. A. 67
Sverdlovsk (city and province)
36, 66, 69, 82, 96

Tadzhikistan, Tadzhik 94, 104
Talyzin, N. V. 15, 62, 64, 67,
86n19, 178
Tikhonov, N. A. 26, 64, 78,
178, 243
Tomsk (city and province) 36,
82
trade unions 14, 56n4, 67, 77
Turkmenistan, Turkmen 94,
104–5, 173

Ukraine, Ukrainian 27, 36, 68,
74, 78, 86n21, 87n29,
88n37, 93–4, 104
United States of America
(USA) 80, 163, 167, 169,
183n4, 191–4, 196–7,
199–201, 205–11 *passim*,
213n27, 215, 238
Ustinov, D. F. 62, 189, 203–4
Uzbekistan, Uzbek 86n21, 94,
104–5

Vietnam 201, 223, 238
Voronin, L. A. 24, 67, 89n45
178
Voronov, Iu. P. 65, 83, 89n50
Vorotnikov, V. I. 15, 24, 26,
32–3, 83

Warsaw Treaty Organisation
(WTO) 214, 226, 232n1
white-collar workers 92–3,
98–9, 101, 103, 108n22,
108n31
women 51, 67, 74, 77, 87n28,
95–7, 103
workers 74–5, 77, 92–3, 98–9,
101, 108n22, 108n24, 116,
121–2, 137–8, 143–4,
150–1, 220, 226

Yugoslavia 54, 87n30, 238

Zaikov, L. N. 15, 22, 28, 36,
62, 67, 69, 85n11, 86n20
Zamiatin, L. M. 65, 84n10
Zaslavskaia, T. I. 112, 129,
132n4, 146
Zhivkov, T. 220, 225, 232n9
Zhukov, G. D. 202–5
Zimianin, M. V. 24, 85n11, 242